NTOA 13

Jerome Murphy-O'Connor, O.P.

The École Biblique and the New Testament:
A Century of Scholarship (1890-1990)

NOVUM TESTAMENTUM ET ORBIS ANTIQUUS (NTOA)

Im Auftrag des Biblischen Instituts
der Universität Freiburg Schweiz
herausgegeben von Max Küchler
in Zusammenarbeit mit Gerd Theissen

Zum Autor:

Jerome Murphy-O'Connor, geb. 1935, seit 1952 Mitglied des Dominikaner-Ordens, studierte Philosophie und Theologie in Cork, Dublin, Freiburg/Schweiz, Rom, Heidelberg, Tübingen und Jerusalem, Promotion 1962 in Freiburg/Schweiz. Seit 1967 Professor an der Ecole Biblique et Archéologique Française in Jerusalem, mit weltweiter Vortragstätigkeit.

Buchveröffentlichungen: Paul on Preaching 1964; Paul and Qumran (Ed.) 1968; L'existence chrétienne selon saint Paul 1974; Becoming Human Together: The Pastoral Anthropology of St. Paul 1982; The First Epistle to the Corinthians 1979; Saint Paul's Corinth 1983; The Holy Land. An Archaeological Guide from Earliest Times to 1700, 1980/1986 (dt.: 1981); The Theology of Second Corinthians 1990.

NOVUM TESTAMENTUM ET ORBIS ANTIQUUS   13

Jerome Murphy-O'Connor, O.P.

The École Biblique and the New Testament: A Century of Scholarship (1890-1990)

With a Contribution by Justin Taylor, S.M.

UNIVERSITÄTSVERLAG FREIBURG SCHWEIZ
VANDENHOECK & RUPRECHT GÖTTINGEN
1990

CIP-Titelaufnahme der Deutschen Bibliothek

Murphy-O'Connor, Jerome:
The École Biblique and the New Testament:
a Century of Scholarship (1890-1990)/
Jerome Murphy-O'Connor. With a Contribution by Justin Taylor. – Freiburg
[Schweiz]: Univ.-Verl.; Göttingen: Vandenhoeck u. Ruprecht, 1990
  (Novum testamentum et orbis antiquus; 13)
  ISBN 3-7278-0682-6 (Univ.-Verl.)
  ISBN 3-525-53914-2 (Vandenhoeck u. Ruprecht)
NE: GT

Veröffentlicht mit Unterstützung des Hochschulrates
der Universität Freiburg Schweiz

Die Druckvorlagen der Textseiten
wurden vom Autor ab Datenträger
als reprofertige Vorlage zur Verfügung gestellt

© 1990 by Universitätsverlag Freiburg Schweiz
Paulusdruckerei Freiburg Schweiz
ISBN 3-7278-0682-6 (Universitätsverlag)
ISBN 3-525-53914-2 (Vandenhoeck und Ruprecht)

TABLE OF CONTENTS

INTRODUCTION

"Of making many books there is no end!" (Eccl 12:12). This may not be the meaning of what Qoheleth said, but the sentiment is so true that it is unlikely that the phrase will pass from the English language. So many books are written because there are so many reasons for writing a book -- to entertain, to instruct, to make a name, to secure a position, to exorcise a personal demon, to remember; the list is endless. This book is written to celebrate a school and a discipline.

The first Catholic school specializing exclusively in biblical studies was founded exactly a century ago. It was also the first modern academic institution to be established in Jerusalem. It is now known as the École Biblique et Archeologique Francaise. When it was opened on 15 November 1890 it was called the École Pratique d'Études Bibliques.

The qualification "Practical School" highlighted what made it different from the great universities of Europe and the Americas. It was situated in the Land in which the Bible was written, and thus it could offer more than good libraries and well-qualified teachers. Climate and geography had not changed since biblical times. Many place-names remained the same. The terrain was strewn with ruins which could be identified. The student hardly needed to reflect in order to absorb the most important lessons concerning the environment of the Bible. What elsewhere took a tremendous imaginative effort, in the Holy Land came as naturally as breathing. One was part of the same scene. One could shop where Abraham traded, and make the observations on which Jesus based his parables.

The tide of history runs more strongly in the Middle East than elsewhere, and the École Biblique has not escaped the vicissitudes of its privileged location in Jerusalem. Its century has been neatly quartered by four very different regimes. At first part of the Ottoman empire, it passed into the hands of the British when the Turks shared the defeat of Germany in the First World War. Fought over by Jews and Arabs in 1948 when Britain surrendered its mandate to govern Palestine, it was first the prize of the Jordanians, and then of the Israelis, after another war in 1967. The professors of the École Biblique have been expelled and imprisoned. They have been explorers, intelligence officers, diplomats, and royal tutors.

The changing circumstances and the differing roles the professors had to play never disturbed the basic consistency of their lives, which flowed from their committment as Dominicans to the church and scholarship. They were dedicated students who wrote incessantly. The published research of the École Biblique covers the whole spectrum of biblical studies and its ancillary disciplines. It can look back on a century of notable achievements which deserve to be celebrated by being recorded. In order to produce volumes of managable size, it was decided to treat the École's record in the major areas of Old Testament, New Testament, and archaeology/topography separately

The New Testament volume was entrusted to Jerome Murphy-O'Connor, O.P., who has been at the École Biblique for a quarter of its history. In depicting the careers of his preccecessors and colleagues, he has not only drawn attention to the extraordinary productivity of a tiny department, but he has illuminated the most important period in the development of critical NT exegesis in the Catholic Church. Most of the men of whom he writes made crucial contributions at key moments. These studies are analysed in terms of their context and their impact. Since Father Murphy-O'Connor is part of the history with which he is dealing, his own contribution has been studied by a younger colleague, Justin Taylor, S.M., who joined the faculty of the École Biblique only last year.

The École Biblique is more than an academic faculty. It is also a religious community whose members' committment to each other is multi-faceted and lifelong. They share a vision of scholarship as service to church and society, which has been refined and strengthened by a century of common endeavour. Although team projects are rare, no one works in isolation. Challenge, support, advice and criticism are integral to a way of life dedicated to the beauty of truth. From it is born a sustaining solidarity which explains the strength of a tradition combining faith and reason.

                                          Jean-Luc Vesco, O.P.
                                          Director
                                          École Biblique de Jérusalem

Chapter 1

THE BEGINNINGS OF A TRADITION

The École Pratique d'Études Bibliques came into being on 15 November 1890. The inaugural speech of the founder, Father Marie-Joseph Lagrange, was solemn. But it was pronounced in a refurbished slaughterhouse, whose walls still held the rings to which animals were once tied, and which was lit only by an open door. The small audience noticed the poverty of the equipment, a table, a blackboard, a map of Palestine, and a few books bought cheap from a missionary.[1]

The quality of the faculty was scarcely better. Only Lagrange himself had received any professional formation in biblical studies. Father Paul Séjourné had been trained as a priest of the diocese of Seez, but transferred to the Dominican order after a pilgrimage to the Holy Land in order to live and work in Jerusalem. Father Doumeth was a Maronite priest who had recently joined the Dominicans, and whose assignment to Jerusalem was based exclusively on his knowledge of Arabic. Abbe Heydet of the Latin Patriarchate knew the country and the local customs very well, but had no scientific training.[2] Under such circumstances, the simplest solution, as Lagrange notes, "would have been for Paul Séjourné and me to consider ourselves on permanent mission to study the country, excavate sites, and to play host to scholars visiting the Holy Land."[3] It is perfectly clear that both would have liked nothing better. Students, however, had to be taught. That there should be students at all is in itself surprising. Their presence, and in particular their numbers -- 3 in 1890, 14 in 1891, 32 to 34 in 1892[4] -- were explained by new military conscription laws in France.

All young men were obliged to three years military service. Exemption was accorded to those who were outside France on their nineteenth birthday, and who stayed abroad for ten years. Since young religious spent that time in formation, and were not involved in pastoral work, it was relatively easy

---

1   M.- J. Lagrange, "Après vingt-cinq ans," RB 12 (1915) 248. L.-H. Vincent, "Le Père Lagrange," RB 47 (1938) 334; id. "Père Lagrange," Blackfriars 19 (1938) 397-411, 474-486

2   Père Lagrange. Personal Reflections and Memoires. Translated by H. Wansbrough. Foreword and Notes by P. Benoit. New York/Mahwah, Paulist Press, 1985, 21-22.

3   Père Lagrange, Personal Reflections,22.

4   Père Lagrange, Personal Reflections, 22; RB 1 (1892) 130-131; 2 (1893) 145.

for religious orders to make arrangements for their students to be trained outside France. The French Dominican provinces sent their novices and students to Jerusalem. A similar measure was adopted by the Augustinians of the Assumption, whose students took classes at the École Biblique. All these young men were being formed, not as biblical scholars, but as priests, who merely had to know enough of the Bible for them to be able to preach adequately. It is surprising, therefore, to discover that at this period the New Testament was manifestly the least important subject at the École Biblique.

Theoretically it was the responsibility of Paul Séjourné,[5] but his real interest was the topography of the Holy Land. The New Testament may have figured on the program of 1890-91, but it appears in that of 1891-92 only as a second-year course, and was not taught at all in 1892-93. Lagrange taught both Genesis and Galatians in 1895-96, but two hours were devoted to the former and only one to the latter. This was increased to two hours the following year (1896-97) when Lagrange taught Romans. For the next three academic years, however, no exegesis course in NT is listed. The explanation must be that Lagrange was fully absorbed by the OT and in dealing with the political fallout from his article on the sources of the Pentateuch in the 1898 Revue Biblique.[6] Nonetheless he was on the lookout for a professor of NT. The program for 1900-01 contains the entry, "NT Exegesis. The Gospel of John. Wednesday and Friday at 3.15 pm. Father N.N.," which suggests that the negotiations had not been completed when the Revue Biblique went to press.

The individual in view was almost certainly Father Thomas Calmes of Rouen, who in fact taught a course on the gospel and apocalypse of John in 1901-02. He was already a contributor to the Revue Biblique,[7] in addition to publishing a book on inspiration, Qu'est-ce que l'Écriture Sainte? (Paris: Bloud et Barral, 1899). His course resulted in a long study of the Johannine prologue,[8] which grew into the first commentary on John in the Études Bibliques (1904). Calmes was just the type of scholar that Lagrange wished to attract to the École Biblique. The fact that he was not a Dominican perhaps explains why he stayed only one or two years. While willing to help out the struggling École Biblique, his superiors in the Picpus Fathers would not have wanted to cede such a competent scholar and teacher on a perma-

---

5   Père Lagrange, Personal Reflections, 21. All that follows concerning classes and professors is based on the academic programs published each year in the Revue Biblique.

6   For details see Père Lagrange, Personal Reflections, 53-83.

7   Two long reviews of Zahn's Introduction to the New Testament (RB 7 [1898] 77-89; 8 [1899] 428-443), and an article "La prologue du quatrième évangile et la doctrine de l'incarnation," (RB 8 [1899] 232-248.

8   "Étude sur le prologue du quatrième évangile," RB 9 (1900) 5-29, 378-399; 10 (1901) 512-521.

nent basis. He did not in fact remain in scholarship, preferring the life of a missionary in South America.[9]

His place at the École Biblique was taken by Pierre Magnien, OP, who was professor of NT exegesis from 1902 to 1907. He focused exclusively on the Pauline letters, and the fact that he produced only one article [10] may be explained by the fact that he was also burdened with courses in scholastic philosophy which changed each year. This happened to others as well, but not to the same degree.[11] Such courses formed part of the seminary curriculum, and were taught for the last time in the academic year 1911-12. The French military conscription law had changed, and seminarians no longer had to do their philosophical and theological studies abroad. In consequence, the number of students at the École Biblique dropped dramatically. There had always been a sprinkling of trained graduates, but these now became the only students. The easing of the class burden facilitated research, and the competence of the students gave the professors the opportunity of dealing with new material without worrying about the demands of a fixed curriculum.

Lagrange assumed responsibility for the NT in 1907, but before dealing with his contribution, another aspect of NT studies at the École Biblique deserves mention. In calling his foundation "The Practical School of Biblical Studies" Lagrange wanted to draw attention to its characteristic methodology, the combination of textual and archaeological evidence.[12] At the beginning there may not have been adequate stress on the documents of the NT, but this cannot be said of the monuments. "Archaeology of the New Testament" is one of the courses listed in the very first program. Though no course with this title is ever listed subsequently, there can be little doubt that the implicit promise was fulfilled by the classes of Raphael Savignac (21 July 1874 - 27 November 1951) and Felix-Marie Abel (28 December 1878 - 24 March 1953).

Savignac came to Jerusalem as a Dominican novice in 1894, and Abel followed him in the same capacity in 1900. Both were to spend all their lives at the École Biblique, and acquired international reputations in their respective fields. Savignac specialized in semitic epigraphy. In quest of material he ventured into many dangerous places and in the process amassed an extraordinary knowledge of Palestine and its neighbours. The results of his researches appeared in a stream of scientific articles. Abel's vast erudition and keen critical sense resulted in an unrivalled mastery of the Greek

---

9   M.-J. Lagrange, Évangile selon saint Jean (EB), Paris: Gabalda, 1925, i.

10 "La résurrection des morts d'après la 1re épître aux Thessaloniciens. Étude exégètique sur 1 Th 4:13-5:2," RB 16 (1907) 349-382.

11 Those who know the specialities of R. Savignac and F.-M. Abel (see below) will be amused to find the former listed for Ius Canonicum and De Ecclesia, and the latter for De Ecclesia and De Religione!

12 Père Lagrange, Personal Reflections, 23.

sources (texts and inscriptions) concerning the history and geography of Palestine. In addition to 125 articles, he contributed the historical sections to the massive studies of Jerusalem, Bethlehem, and Emmaus, on which he collaborated with the archaeologist of the École Biblique, L.-H. Vincent (31 August 1872 - 30 December 1960). Of particular importance for NT studies was Abel's Grammaire du Grec biblique, suivi d'un choix de Papyrus (EB; Paris: Gabalda, 1927) which dealt with over 3500 NT passages. To understand the NT, however, one needs much more than Greek grammar. A clear grasp of the physical environment and the cultural framework is indispensable. Abel met these needs by his Géographie de la Palestine (EB; Paris: Gabalda, I. 1933; II. 1938) and his Histoire de la Palestine depuis la conquête d'Aléxandre jusqu'à l'invasion arabe (EB; Paris: Gabalda, 1952). Both books were widely aclaimed for their prodigious documentation and sureness of judgment, qualities which make them indispensable even today.

After taking over the course on "The Topography of Jerusalem" from Vincent in 1906, Abel shifted the emphasis from the architectural to the historical, and every second year made the NT the primary focus of the course. This rhythm he maintained until the end of his career in 1953, regularly incorporating all the new data brought to light by the archaeologists.[13] His skill as a guide is nowhere better illustrated than in the extraordinary distillation of history and archaeology, which he wrote as a guidebook to Palestine in the famous Guide Bleu series.[14] His occasional courses on NT introduction (1922-23, 1933-34, 1947-49) were strongly historical in orientation, focusing essentially on the Hellenistic and Roman periods. He once taught the Pauline letters, presumably from a philological perspective.

Savignac was one of the stop-gap professors of NT in 1903-05. Thereafter he concentrated exclusively on epigraphy until 1924, when he inaugurated a course entitled "Historical Introduction to the New Testament", which he taught until 1933. In it he dealt with the political, social, economic and cultural factors which made up the world of the first Christians.

The tradition of this type of course, so valuable as background to the NT, was revived only in the 1970s. From 1971 to 1976 Dr. Bentley Layton, a recent graduate of Harvard University and a specialist in Coptic and Gnosticism, offered course on such topics as: Early Christian Literature, Gnosticism, Christian Gnostic Texts and their 2nd Century Literary and Doctrinal Background, and The Diatribe. This study of the prolongation of NT themes into the following century proved to be a most valuable hermeneutical tool. The first layman (and a Protestant to boot) to be a faculty member of the École Biblique, Layton could not afford to work indefinitely for the

---

[13] In order to give opportunities to younger colleagues just beginning their careers as archaeologists at the École Biblique, Abel handed over the topography course to G. A. Barrois in 1929-33, and to A.-M. Steve in 1948-49.

[14] Syrie-Palestine-Iraq-Transjordanie, Paris: Hachette, 1932, 504-625.

pittance which the École could afford, and he is now Professor of Ancient Christian History at Yale University, New Haven, Connecticut.

From 1972-80 H. D. Saffrey, O.P., a research director at the Centre National de la Recherche Scientifique in Paris, came each year to Jerusalem to offer a course. Three were devoted to the history of doctrine, the rest to the milieu of the NT. These latter treated such subjects as: The Political, Religious, and Cultic Life of Ephesus at the Beginning of the Christian Era according to the Inscriptions, Emperor Worship at Ephesus, Civic and Religious Life at Ephesus in the NT Period according to the Inscription of Vibius Salutaris, The Jews at Ephesus, Ephesian Inscriptions from the Reigns of Claudius and Nero, and The Political, Religious, and Cultic Life of Thessalonica at the Beginning of the Christian Era according to the Inscriptions. This type of course on the historical context of the NT is now taught by Justin Taylor, SM (see chapter 7).

Chapter 2

MARIE-JOSEPH LAGRANGE, O.P.

Lagrange's career is too well known for there to be any need to rehearse the details yet again.[1] Certain points, however, must be recalled, if his approach and contribution to NT studies are to be understood correctly.

Born on 7 March 1855, he had done his military service, acquired a doctorate in law, and tested his vocation at the Sulpician seminary at Issy near Paris, before entering the Toulouse province of the Dominican order in 1879. During his theological studies at Salamanca (1880-86) his talent for biblical studies was recognized by his superiors, but it was only in 1888 that he was sent to the University of Vienna. He himself explained what he did there and what he hoped to achieve. "I did not follow any course of theology, only languages. I had done some studies of my own of Syriac and Arabic, and started Assyrian. Prof. David-Heinrich Müller was my teacher for Arabic and Assyrian, Prof. Reinisch for Egyptian, both hieroglyphic and hieratic, and I studied Arabic under M. Wahrmund at the Commercial School. M. Müller was kind enough to give me instruction on some particular aspects of rabbinical exegesis and the Mishnah. He gave me the impression of being a very good Jew, and it was at his home that I met Prof. Euting who taught me how to take impressions of inscriptions. I was not intending to make myself expert in all these fields, but to form later on in Toulouse a body of biblical teachers."[2]

As things turned out, it was in Jerusalem that he had to form professors. This, however, is less important than the orientation implied by what he says, which shows how aware he was of the conditions of his age. The cutting edge of biblical studies in the late 19th century was the Old Testament. This was the arena in which the traditionalists, who in the past had unthinkingly taken the Bible at face value and now defended its literal truth, confronted the critical scholars, whose discoveries called accepted interpretations into question. For example, the recognition that legal codes abounded in the ancient Near East made it impossible to maintain that the legal institutions of Israel had come directly from heaven, as the OT claimed. According to the Bible, Moses laid down in minute detail the arrangement of the Israe-

---

1   Père Lagrange. Personal Reflections and Memoirs. Translated by H. Wansbrough. Foreword and notes by P. Benoit, New York/Mahwah, 1985. F.-M. Braun, O.P., L'oeuvre du Père Lagrange. Étude et bibliographie, Fribourg: Éditions Saint-Paul, 1943. H.-L. Vincent, "Le Père Lagrange," RB 47 (1938) 321-354.

2   Père Lagrange, Personal Reflections, 17-18.

lite cult, but this was contradicted by the overwhelming evidence for gradual development in all other known cults. For many within the church acceptance of such views endangered the faith. For Lagrange and a minority of Catholic scholars refusal to accept the implications of modern discoveries endangered the credibility of the Catholic Church, with disastrous consequences for those who trusted its judgment. Scientific curiosity and pastoral concern, therefore, conspired to direct him to this critical field of research. There was also the intangible element of his own character. Though the language is a little grandiose there is more than a grain of truth in what J. Chaine said, "Where the battle is hardest is the place of greatest danger and of greatest service."[3]

The Inspiration of Sacred Scripture

Underlying specific questions was the fundamental problem of the authority of the Bible. This forced Lagrange to take a position on the inspiration and inerrancy of Sacred Scripture. When he began teaching, the dominant theory maintained that God was responsible for the content of Scripture but not for its wording. The revival of Thomism in the mid-19th century called into question the theology of grace on which this theory was based. Gradually an alternative solution developed, which invoked St Thomas Aquinas' notion of instrumental causality in order to explain how God and the human author were both entirely responsible for the whole work, but each in his own way. Lagrange first articulated his support for this new hypothesis in a comment on an article by a fellow Dominican from Toulouse, Thomas Pègues.[4]

At this stage, however, "he simply played the Dominican theologian, following Zigliara and Pègues into an attack on the Jesuit ideology of grace and inspiration." This acute observation by J. Burtchaell serves to highlight what he considers to be the more important second and third phases in the development of Lagrange's thought on this issue.[5]

Two critical reactions forced Lagrange to explain his position more adequately, which meant that he had to face the problem of inerrancy. He wrote, "We have the traditional principle of exegesis: God teaches infallibly only what the sacred writer teaches. We have the principle of common sense: the sacred writer teaches only what he wants to teach. We have the principle of literary criticism: the intention of the author is revealed by the literary form he has chosen. All that remains is to look at these principles in

---

3   "The Old Testament" in Père Lagrange and the Scriptures, translated by R. T. Murphy, Milwaukee: Bruce, 1946, 18.

4   "Une pensée de saint Thomas sur l'inspiration Scripturaire," RB 4 (1895) 563-571.

5   Catholic Theories of Biblical Inspiration since 1810. A Review and Critique, Cambridge: University Press, 1969, 139.

the light of an equally elementary principle of logic: a word is neither true nor false; an idea is neither true nor false; there is error or truth only when there is a judgement, i.e. a categorical affirmation or negation, and there is a categorical judgement only when an author decides to make one."[6] The crucial importance here given to literary forms is manifest. Each had its own appropriate way of articulating truth, and by careful investigation of the multiple possibilities of meaning the critical scholar could determine exactly what the sacred author intended to say. In this way, Lagrange was sure, all conflict between the Bible and modern discoveries could be avoided.

Lagrange's third phase is represented by the lectures on "The Historical Method with Special Reference to the Old Testament," which he delivered at the Institut Catholique de Toulouse in November 1902, and which were published the following year.[7] This book outlined a vast program of authentically critical Catholic scholarship, and one whose continuing relevance was underlined by its reprinting in 1966, with an introduction by Roland de Vaux, OP.[8] In the chapter devoted to inspiration, however, he went back on his previous position regarding the link between inerrancy and a judgment which the sacred author intended to inculcate. Arguing from the imperfection of the OT when compared with the NT he wrote, "Inspiration leads to writing; and the aim of writing is to fix and record previously-acquired knowledge, so that the grace of inspiration has as its primary object not to teach, but to preserve the memory of revealed truths, and of the historical facts which enable the order and sequence of revelation to be understood, and that, although the aim of the sacred writer himself be to teach."[9]

This extraordinarily liberal insight should have really set the cat among the conservative pigeons, but it attracted little or no attention.[10] One reason may be that Lagrange himself immediately began to back away from it. He was not prepared to apply it to the NT, or even to OT history. In order to explain difficulties in the latter he proposed a theory of "apparent history."[11] For this he was venemously attacked by A. Delattre, SJ.[12] The atmosphere deteriorated so quickly that his superiors did not permit Lagrange to publish

---

[6]   "L'inspiration et les exigences de la critique," RB 5 (1896) 507.

[7]   An English version appeared very quickly. Historical Criticism of the Old Testament, translated by E. Myers, London, CTS, 1906.

[8]   La méthode historique, surtout à propos de l'Ancien Testament, Paris: Cerf, 1966.

[9]   Historical Criticism of the Old Testament, 100.

[10]   As far as I am aware the only attempt to work out its implications is that of F. Schroeder, SSJ, "Père Lagrange: Record and Teaching in Inspiration," CBQ 20 (1958) 206-217.

[11]   Historical Criticism of the Old Testament, 112-116.

[12]   Autour de la question biblique: Une nouvelle exégèse et les autorités qu'elle invoque, Liège/Paris: Dessain, 1904.

Marie-Joseph Lagrange, O.P.

a reply.[13] This prohibition was very soon extended to other subjects , and he wrote no more on inspiration. J. Burtchaell has noted perceptively that "At the peak of his career, Lagrange was struggling to work out a theory [of inspiration] that would be both critical and systematic. His ideas still lacked resolution and consistency."[14] Lagrange made verbal inspiration the dominant theory among Catholics, but the premature termination of scientific dialogue certainly deprived the church of insights which would have enriched its life had he been permitted to struggle with his ideas.

The Great Commentaries

By 1907 the intellectual climate had become so poisoned that authorities both in the church and in the order felt it would be inopportune for Lagrange to publish a commentary on Genesis on which he had been working for ten years.[15] Lagrange's acceptance of this cross did nothing to allay the suspicions of which he was the object. And so "in order to render them ineffective, I entirely abandoned the study of the Old Testament except in function of the New, and since my superiors would not permit me to say goodbye to scripture studies, I dedicated myself to the study of the Gospel."[16] According to L.-H. Vincent, it was the Master General of the Dominicans, Hyacinthe-M. Cormier, who suggested the NT as a compromise.[17] Such a radical change of direction must have appeared incomprehensible at the time, but with the advantage of hindsight it is possible to discern the hand of Providence in this decision, of which Patrick W. Skehan has said, "Whatever the needs in the Old Testament field may have been, the absence of his [Lagrange's] Gospel studies would have left an unquestionably greater void."[18]

Thus in the program of the École Biblique for 1907-08 Lagrange was listed for a course on the theology of the synoptic gospels. The next year he taught an exegesis course for the first time since the academic year 1896-97. The subject was the Gospel of Mark, on which he published a massive commentary in 1911; it was the only time he taught it! He had commented on Romans three times (1896-97, 1910-11, 1913-14) before writing his commentary, which was finished in 1914, though published only in 1916.

13　Père Lagrange. Personal Reflections, 111-119.

14　Catholic Theories of Inspiration, 145.

15　Père Lagrange. Personal Reflections, 67, 124, 130-131.

16　Père Lagrange. Personal Reflections, 133.

17　"Le Père Lagrange," RB 47 (1938) 347.

18　"Père Lagrange and History in the Bible," in Lagrange Lectures 1963, Dubuque: Aquinas Institute, 1963, 26.

Exiled from Palestine by the Turks in 1915,[19] it was natural for him to use his leisure moments in Paris for the composition of a commentary on Galatians (1918).

This diversion into Paul requires an explanation because Lagrange had been working on a commentary on Luke since 1912,[20] and had lectured on it twice (1911-12 and 1914-15). He had also been scheduled to teach it during "the terrible year", when he was abruptly ordered from Jerusalem on 4 September 1912 by Father Cormier and was permitted to return to the École Biblique only the following July.[21] What he did that summer provides the basis for an answer. "I returned to Jerusalem at vacation time. I used the vacation to write a little life of St. Justin. There was a theory to be found among our opponents that a lack of theology spoiled my learning. It was therefore with some satisfaction that I heard it said of me by the Master General that the examiner had been 'delighted not only by the facts but by the competence in philosophy and theology which you show.'"[22] Here we catch a glimpse of the shrewd political skill which was just as much part of Lagrange's character as his sanctity. A commentary on Romans gave him a further opportunity to demonstrate how well founded he was in scholastic theology. Among the commentators he gave pride of place to St Thomas Aquinas, and underlined that one of the contributions of his own interpretation was "to show that independent scholarship was moving towards the Catholic position over the ruins of Lutheran exegesis." [23]

Once Lagrange had made his point, he turned back to his real concern, the gospels. When the École Biblique reopened after World War I, the first course he taught was on Luke (1919-20), and his commentary appeared the following year. He may have taught Matthew in 1920-21. He certainly did so during the next academic year in preparation for his commentary on the First Gospel, completed in 1922 and published the year after. Only the Fourth Gospel now remained, and it is not surprising that his classes for 1922-24 were devoted to John. Finished in 1924, his commentary was issued in 1925. Thereafter, he was to teach only a single NT course, "Comparative Exegesis of the Gospels" (1925-26), obviously in preparation for his Synopsis Evangelica Graeca (1926), from which flowed his one popular book, L'Évangile de Jésus-Christ (1928), which was translated into

---

[19] An event which occasioned the stirring words, "It was up to us apparently to insist on the international character of our Ecole [in order to keep it open]. We replied that, if we indeed received numbers of foreigners and with an open heart, it was because that heart was French.... The Practical School of Biblical Studies was closed because it was French; it will be reborn French." ("Après vingt-cinq ans," RB 12 [1915] 261).

[20] Père Lagrange. Personal Reflections, 247 note 62.

[21] Père Lagrange. Personal Reflections, 155-165. L.-H. Vincent, "Le Père Lagrange," RB 47 (1938) 349.

[22] Père Lagrange. Personal Reflections, 166.

[23] Saint Paul. Épître aux Romains (EB), Paris: Gabalda, 1916, iv.

many languages, and which at one stage was in the library of virtually every Catholic priest.[24]

The year in which he finished this series of six massive commentaries was Lagrange's 70th birthday. Not long afterwards in an unusual moment of self-pity he described himself as "a useless cog."[25] In their own disciplines his disciples had equalled his stature. His chosen successor in NT, Raphael Tonneau, O.P., who had been a student at the École Biblique since 1922,[26] was ready to begin teaching, and so with the future assured he could legitimately say his *Nunc Dimittis*. Tonneau, however, was to last only four years (1926-30). Abel was roped in to fill the gap in 1930-31, and the following year a young Dominican, Augustin Carrié, lectured on Mark. Lagrange had hopes of him as a possible successor, but after a year he decided that he was not suited to the austere intellectual life of the École, and he returned to France.

Despite Lagrange's age -- he was now 77 -- it is understandable that he should have felt impelled to resume the burden of classes. It is unlikely, however, that a sense of duty was his sole motive, because out of those classes (1932-35) came the first two volumes of his massive introduction to the study of the New Testament, one focusing on the canon of the NT (1933) and the other on the principles of textual criticism (1935). The third volume should logically have been that on literary criticism, which he taught 1934-35, but in fact it was devoted to historical criticism (1937), written in France after he had been obliged to leave Jerusalem for reasons of health in 1935. This time he did not return. He died on 10 March 1938, and it was only in May 1967 that his bones were brought back to Jerusalem for burial in the Basilica of St. Stephen.

This survey of the correlation between Lagrange's teaching and his major NT publications has made no effort to take into account the numerous articles written during this period. Surprisingly the number of studies flowing from preparatory work for his commentaries is very small.[27] The vast majority cover virtually every aspect of all topics which might be relevant to the NT or the history of early Christianity. They exhibit an extraordinary erudition brought into tight focus by an incisive mind and a facile pen. He worked with incredible speed and concentration.

---

[24] The English version is entitled <u>The Gospel of Jesus Christ</u>, London: Burns Oates and Washbourne, 1938.

[25] <u>Père Lagrange. Personal Reflections</u>, 166.

[26] R. Tonneau, "Le sacrifice de Josué sur le mont Ébal," RB 35 (1926) 108

[27] One (1910) for Mark; four (1911, 1914, 1915) for Romans; one (1917) for Galatians; two (1911, 1914) for Luke; and two (1923, 1924) for John.

From accounts written by students who lived at the École Biblique when Lagrange was in full vigor it is possible to reconstruct his working day.[28] An early riser he had said his mass, made a long thanksgiving, cleaned his room, and had a bite of breakfast before settling down to work at 7 am. From then until 11.45 am he would brook no interruptions. To a student who came to wish him a happy New Year on January 1, he replied, "We'll exchange greetings after lunch. This is not the moment. I am working!" If he left his room, it was to go to the library to check a reference. He wrote at a large wooden table with books piled at either end. He could organise his material so well in his mind that he rarely had to rewrite a phrase. The large white pages quickly filled with his sloping clear handwriting. He broke off only when the bell rang for the divine office, which he never missed. Lunch at noon was followed by recreation, during which he always took a childlike joy in opening the parcels of new books. Those that interested him he took to a shaded seat in the garden in fine weather or to his room in winter, and read until afternoon tea at 4.30 pm. He then sometimes took a walk. If not, it was back to his room to read proofs or write his book reviews. During the recreation after supper he would play a game of chess before going to choir for Compline, and then early to bed.

His extraordinary productivity demanded such discipline, but only the sensible variety which he worked into his daily routine explains how he was able to maintain this rhythm for so long. In addition, he visited friends in Jerusalem, went to scientific conferences, and took a holiday in France with his family every second year. In conversation he could be extremely witty. On one occasion someone commented that his École had been imitated in Jerusalem by the English, the Americans, the Germans, the Franciscans and the Jesuits. "If I had taken out a patent," he replied, "I'd have made a mint!" His light-heartedness is delightfully illustrated by a clever and funny article which does full justice to its title, "Julian the Apostate Preacher of Priestly Retreats."[29]

The Intellectual Climate

Any attempt to evaluate Lagrange's contribution to NT studies must take into account the circumstances in which he wrote. Despite the submission to the authorities of the church, manifested by his abandonment of the Genesis commentary and his switch to a completely different field, suspicion still clouded the minds of his enemies, whose reports inevitably affected the attitude of Rome, which just at that stage was struggling to deal with the Modernist crisis. Whatever he published was minutely scrutinized, but no for-

---

[28] J. Chaine, "Journée et menu propos du Père Lagrange," in Mémorial Lagrange, Paris: Gabalda, 1940, 355-360. F.-M. Braun, L'oeuvre du Père Lagrange. Étude et bibliographie, Fribourg: Editions Saint-Paul, 1943, 175-176.

[29] "Julien l'Apostat prédicateur de retraites sacerdotales," VSpirSup 17 (1928) 242-248.

mal charge was ever levelled against him. Pope Pius X put his finger on the problem in saying, "Now there is nothing, but it is the past."[30] Even then there had been only doubts and criticism of his work in OT, never condemnation or even censure. Yet he was tainted with unorthodoxy. Those who distrusted him, and who were not prepared to read his works with the attention they deserved, tended to lump him together with Renan and Loisy.

Ernest Renan wrote his Vie de Jésus in 1863. In it he dressed stolid German scholarship in the robes of the mysterious Orient and made it seductive. By the time Lagrange came to deal with this book formally, the main edition had been reprinted 52 times and the cheap edition 120 times.[31] Such popularity only intensified the revulsion of the church at the portrait of Jesus it presented. Renan analysed the relations of the four gospels in such a way as to permit him to accept as historical only the basic narrative outline of John. On this slender framework he then projected his fantasies. Jesus was not even a sage or a prophet, but a charmer, whose essential work was to draw to himself the unreserved admiration of a group to whom he communicated the seed of his doctrine. Their naive interpretation of the serene gaity which he spread about him in Galilee generated the feeling that he had inaugurated a paradisical state. Hence he must be the Messiah, a title which he accepted with some embarassment, knowing full well that he was not. This minor deception was excused by a desire to please but, according to Renan, it led to Jesus faking miracles because he needed to succeed. Obviously no Catholic could accept this vision of Jesus Christ.

If Renan was still a force at the beginning of the 20th century, Alfred Loisy had the advantage of actuality. His books represented the summit of critical biblical studies in France, and Lagrange reviewed them as they appeared. He was a brilliant exegete, whose observations of detail retain much of their value even today. His notes on any text are still worth reading. The problem was with the way in which he put the pieces together. He did not believe in a personal God and, in consequence, denied any authority to the church. Its dogmas were a decrepit obstacle to freedom of research. Since he knew that a frontal assault on such a massive institution could only mean defeat, he made it his objective to undermine it by subtlely altering the meaning of its teachings.[32]

Who was the historical Jesus for Loisy? "A village artisan, naive and enthusiastic, who believed in the imminent end of the world, in the inaugura-

---

[30] Père Lagrange. Personal Reflections, 139.

[31] "La vie de Jésus d'après Renan," RB 27 (1918) 432-506.

[32] "For twenty years I have been aware of the decrepitude of this system, whose signification I have endeavoured to enlarge little by little, being convinced, on the one hand, that as such it is an obstacle to all liberty of thought and all scientific progress, and on the other hand, that it contains a soul of moral truth whose excellence will be manifest only when it is freed from its venerable sheath." Quelque Lettres sur des questions actuelles et sur des événements récents, Ceffonds: Chez l'auteur, 1908, 68-69.

tion of a reign of justice, in the advent of God on earth; who, on the basis of this primary illusion, gave himself the principal role in the organisation of the unrealizable city; who began to prophesy, inviting all his contemporaries to repent of their sins in order to conciliate the supreme judge whose imminent arrival would be as unexpected as that of a thief; who recruited a small number of illiterate followers, the only type he could attract, and provoked an insignificant movement among the lower classes; who should have been arrested by the proper authorities, and was; who could not escape a violent death, which found him."[33] Paul was the first to give this death a redemptive value, and from this all other elements in the gospel tradition flowed. There developed an interest in the life of Jesus, and so episodes and teaching had to be invented. Miracles became necessary to illustrate his relationship with God. Theological speculations when placed on the lips of Jesus became claims revelatory of his self-understanding.[34]

Both Renan and Loisy maintained that their conclusions flowed from their critical study of the NT. Such conclusions were unacceptable to even the most liberal elements in the church, and suspicion inevitably attached to those who claimed that their approach to the gospels was modern and critical. It was thought that this was but a prelude to a portrait of Jesus similar to those developed by Loisy and Renan. Lagrange, however, saw that the conclusions were related, not to the historical method in itself, but to the bias of certain of its practitioners.[35] He was not so naive, however, as to believe that this statement of principle would satisfy his detractors. He correctly read the extreme hostility of the intellectual climate within the church, and realized that he was not fee to say all that he thought, and that what he did say had to be very carefully formulated. If his motives had been distorted, his words could certainly be twisted. Nor was he at liberty to determine his own agenda. To have refused to deal with Loisy's opinions would have been interpreted as tacit agreement.

Consequently he was forced into an apologetic attitude. He had to defend the traditional positions of the church on the authorship and dates of the NT books. These were given an official character by successive decrees of the Pontifical Biblical Commission on John (1907), Matthew (1911), and Mark and Luke (1912). Hence, he had to walk a very fine line. On the one hand, he had to do justice to the solidly based conclusions of the historical method, but on the other hand, he had to demonstrate his respect for the tradition. His personality was well adapted to this challenge, because Lagrange

---

33 Les Évangiles Synoptiques, Ceffonds: Chez l'auteur, 1907, I, 252.

34 Loisy synthesized his gospel studies in Jésus et la tradition évangelique, Paris: Nourry, 1910, which was reviwed by Lagrange in RB 20 (1911) 294-299; see also his Monsieur Loisy et le Modernism. A propos des "Mémoires" d'A. Loisy, Paris: Cerf, 1932.

35 See "Jesus and the Criticism of the Gospels," originally an open letter to Pierre Batiffol, which was published as an appendix to the second edition of Lagrange's Historical Criticism of the Old Testament.

was fundamentally conservative, and adopted liberal positions only when forced to do so by the evidence.

The Gospel of Mark

In the precritical stage of the church's attitude towards the Bible the historicity of the gospels was taken for granted. It was assumed that they were verbatim accounts of things that really happened. What people knew about the gospels were the broad outlines of the stories plus significant details. No significance was attached to the fact that in some cases the various gospels diverged seriously in their versions of the same episode.

Such discrepancies became a problem only with the advent of critical scholarship. Thus when Mark said that the grass was green in the Feeding of the Five Thousand (6:39) and Matthew did not (14:19) critical scholars concluded that Matthew had judged a detail in Mark's account to be insignificant and had decided to omit it. The immediate implication of this type of conclusion was that Matthew depended on Mark. To Catholic conservatives this meant only one thing, a reduction of the number of assumed eye-witnesses to the ministry of Jesus. In consequence the synoptic problem (the relationship of each gospel to the others) became a battleground.

By the time of Lagrange, however, a number of eminent Catholic scholars had publicly accepted the Two-Source Theory, which postulated that in the triple tradition Matthew and Luke depended on Mark, whereas in the double tradition Matthew and Luke depended on Q. This shifted the battleground to the Second Gospel, because it now appeared that the historicity of the entire gospel tradition hinged on the historicity of Mark.

There were two burning issues, the originality and unity of Mark. Starting with the assumption that Matthew and Luke would have used every available scrip of knowledge about the ministry of Jesus, and linking this with the observation that Matthew and Luke do not contain the whole of Mark, some critics deduced that Mathew and Luke depended on a more primitive form of Mark's gospel (Ur-Markus). After they had used it, new elements were added to create the present form of the Second Gospel. Other scholars insisted that Mark also drew on Q. Mark in its final form, therefore, was rather far removed from the events it recounted, and critics pointed out that its historicity could not be taken for granted.

If scholars without any particular axe to grind could arrive at such conclusions, what could be expected of those whose intention was to attack the church? Once literary criticism had been accepted as legitimate, Loisy exploited its unavoidably subjective element to accomodate his personal vision of Christian origins. Thus in Mark he distinguished four documents. Document A was "a rather material sketch of the life of Jesus of Nazareth who, after having recruited a few followers in his native Galilee and preached the imminent arrival of the kingdom of God, was crucified in Jerusalem on the orders of Pontius Pilate because he claimed to be king of the

Jews. Document B was a series of complements inserted into Document A, notably miracle stories and predictions of Jesus relative to facts in Document A. Document C was another series of complements designed to fill out the biography of Christ by giving an idea of his teaching. Finally D was the general perspective of the compilation as it emerged from the additions and retouches made by the last editor."[36]

It should now be clear that in writing his first commentary on Mark Lagrange was taking the bull by the horns. Even though he was moving into a new field, he gave himself no running-in period, but went straight to the heart of the contemporary debate. In his introduction Lagrange emphasized his concern to meet the radical critics on their own ground, but at the same time he pointed out that his approach was not the same. "The difference in method is basically this: M. Loisy treats the texts as defendants, whereas I look on them as witnesses." [37] In the French legal system the accused could be put through a pretty rough time in an attempt to verify the working hypothesis of the examining magistrate. Lagrange prefered the British system in which the veracity of a witness is taken for granted until evidence to the contrary is produced.

On the question of the unity of Mark, Lagrange could not confront Loisy directly, because the latter did not condescend to specify exactly which verses were to be assigned to each of his four "documents". Thus, he took as his opponent E. Wendling, who maintained that Mark acquired its present form through the successive efforts of an historian, a poet, and a theologian.[38] Drawing heavily on the work of Swete and Hawkings, moderate Anglicans whose concerns coincided with his own, Lagrange argued that typically Markan vocabulary, syntax, and style were found in all three levels postulated by Wendling. Here there is little that is original, and the procedure is flawed by the illegitimate transfer of statistics based on a text, which may be composite, to a single author. Lagrange is more personal in his analysis of Mark's narrative technique. He succeeded in demonstrating the unity, but he pressed the evidence too far in claiming to recognize the style of an uncultured eyewitness.[39] . One can detect here an apologetic concern to confirm the traditional view (Papias, Justin, Irenaeus) that Mark was the companion of Peter and recorded his preaching. The assumption that Peter was uncultured just because he was a fisherman is both unnecessary and unprovable. To underline that in Mark's gospel we have to do with the testimony of an eyewitness is sufficient, and this insistence on the part of La-

---

[36] Jésus et la tradition évangelique, 31.

[37] Évangile selon Saint Marc (EB), Pris: Gabalda, 1911, iii.

[38] Die Entstehung des Markus-Evangeliums. Philologische Untersuchungen, Tübingen: Mohr (Siebeck), 1908.

[39] Évangile selon Saint Marc, lxxv.

grange has stood the test of time.[40] The most original part of Lagrange's introduction is his treatment of the semitic substratum of Mark, for which his OT training had admirably prepared him. His conclusion that Mark is not a translation from an Aramaic original, but that its language is strongly colored by semitic usage has only been confirmed by subsequent studies.[41] To his credit this is not used as a further indication of a Petrine tradition.

While refuting the partition theories of Wendling and others, Lagrange did not intend to deny that Mark used sources. But he insisted that the evangelist was an author and not merely an editor.[42] By this he meant that Mark freely composed the oral material which came to him, but nuanced it by admitting that on occasion Mark acted more like an editor. He was very hesitant regarding Mark's relationship to Q. After balancing the arguments very carefully, he eventually concluded that Mark knew Q but did not use it. Such conclusions were very prudent, but given the temper of the time, just to speak as he did was highly adventurous. To certain pastors of the Catholic church it seem that he opened doors which should not have been even noticed still less unlocked.

The courage of Lagrange is highlighted by the fact that the devoted a whole chapter to the question of the historicity of the Second Gospel. He began by asking a question which has not yet received a satisfactory answer: what is a gospel?[43] He was the first to put the question in terms of literary form,[44] an obvious application of his earlier attempts to discern the truth of the OT in terms of the modalities of its literary expression. The quest for parallels which would clarify the genre was not pushed very far, and he decided that the best analogy to Mark was the Elijah narrative.[45] He then asked if Mark was controlled by any bias in his selection and use of traditional material, and answered in the negative on the basis of those passages which militate against the evangelist's thesis that Jesus was the Son of God, e.g. the relatives of Jesus think that he is out of his mind (Mk 3:21). If Mark reported such facts, it was because fidelity to his sources dominated any personal preference.[46]

---

[40] See for example, V. Taylor, The Gospel according to Mark, London: Macmillan, 1963, 148-149.

[41] Taylor gives an excellent synthesis (Mark, 55-66).

[42] Évangile selon Saint Marc, cx. The full truth of this insight became apparent only with the advent of Redaction Criticism after the Second World War.

[43] See the discussion in D. E. Aune, The New Testament in its Literary Environment (Library of Early Christianity, 8), Philadelphia: Westminster, 1987, ch. 1 "The Genre of the Gospels."

[44] Évangile selon Saint Marc, cxiii.

[45] Évangile selon Saint Marc, cxiv.

[46] Évangile selon Saint Marc, cxvii.

Thus far Lagrange gets full marks for sound methodology, but once he entered the domain of the verisimilitude of the facts in themselves, mere possibility is consistently confused with probability. [47] Things could have happened as Mark says, but this not quite the same as proof that they did. In principle there is nothing wrong with Lagrange's approach but the detailed knowledge of the psychology and personalities of the actors and of the contemporary historical forces, which is required to make it work, is lacking in the case of Mark.

A more nuanced appreciation of Lagrange's treatment of history can be derived from the way in which he dealt with a number of critical points. Time and time again he repudiated the liberals' apriori exclusion of anything supernatural in the gospels, but he evidently had problems with the Voice and the Spirit at the Baptism of Jesus (Mk 1:10-11). In the large print of the comment he wrote of "the objective character" of "this very material theophany" and excluded the idea that it could have been a purely internal phenomenon.[48] But in the small print of the technical notes he said, "It is question of a physical apparition, but a supernatural physical apparition may be seen by only one specially favored person.... The two phenomena [Voice and Spirit] could have been perceived by all or by merely one person."[49] It is difficult to say what Lagrange really believed, and this was undoubtedly deliberate. It was his form of protest against the intellectual terrorism of the time.

A different type of hedging appears in his treatment of "hearing this those with him went out to seize him, for they said 'he is out of his mind'" (Mk 3:21). Lagrange refused the easy option of identifying "those with him" as friends or disciples, and maintained that the reference was to the family of Jesus, his immediate relatives. But he then went on to explain "He is out of his mind" as an expression of their concern that Jesus was not getting regular meals! At the same time he approvingly quoted Loisy to the effect that "They do not say that Jesus was mad ... but they believed him to be in a state of mystical exaltation in which he lost his sense of reality as regards life and his own situation."[50] . The last words suggest that the family of Jesus felt that he had developed pretentions beyond his station. In which case "he is out of his mind" would amount to an expression of disbelief in his mission. This, of course, Lagrange could not say, because Mary was certainly included among the immediate relatives of Jesus, but he had given a pointer to the discerning reader.

In dealing with the list of women at the foot of the cross (Mk 15:40-41), in which Mary the mother of Jesus is not mentioned, Lagrange ignored the

---

47   Évangile selon Saint Marc, cxviii.

48   Évangile selon Saint Marc, 13.

49   Évangile selon Saint Marc, 9.

50   Évangile selon Saint Marc, 63-64.

contradiction with Jn 19:25. On other occasions he could turn such contradictions to his own advantage. He offered an explanation of the call of the first disciples (Mk 1:16-20) which would have delighted the heart of any conservative, "The whose episode is unintelligible unless one supposes that Jesus could move wills," which gives the impression that he disposed of some miraculous power to draw disciples to him instantaneously. But Lagrange then slips in the short sentence, "Things are better explained in John."[51] which indicates precisely the opposite, because in Jn 1:35ff. it is John the Baptist who directs the same disciples to Jesus, and after having gotten to know him, they recruit others. This version of the vocation of the first disciples is much more probable. By not giving a precise reference to the Fourth Gospel Lagrange gambled that the average reader would not check the point, and he had the rare satisfaction of saying the expected and at the same time articulating his own interpretation.

Such subterfuges will appear as lack of intellectual integrity only to the naive. Integrity is related to manifest truth and, whatever the strength of his convictions, Lagrange had the humility to recognize that his interpretations were merely opinions which might be disproved on the morrow by new evidence. It is also a well-founded scientific attitude.[52] Furthermore, he was a religious in whom a strong sense of community responsibility had been inculcated from his young manhood. He did not feel that he could take risks which would endanger the École Biblique, the institution which made the researches of his disciples possible.[53] Nor was he prepared to trouble needlessly the thinking of believers at a time when much more fundamental issues were being questioned. The ethos of the period, and particularly among those formed in French piety, demanded that such practical and commonsense reasons for keeping one's head down should be expressed in an elevated theological submission to the all-embracing authority of the church.[54]

There cannot be the slightest doubt of Lagrange's sincerity in making such professions. He would willingly have accepted an obedience imposed upon him. But he was not naive, and he did not for a moment imagine that

---

51 Évangile selon Saint Marc, 19.

52 "Most knowledge and all explanations are only working hypotheses, whose constant refinement is the very stuff of intellectual endeavor and whose major criterion of value is not so much their possible truth as the degree to which they can serve to direct further studies, even if the latter end up by abandoning them." (O. Grabar, The Formation of Islamic Art, New Haven-London: Yale University Press, 1973, xviii).

53 Père Lagrange. Personal Reflections, 159.

54 E.g. the last paragraph of Lagrange's introduction to his Mark commentary, "In trying to understand what Mark wrote, the echo of what Peter, the witness of Jesus, said, I have had no other intention than to hear the words of life. Without any reserve I submit what I have written to the judgment of the infallible successor of Peter, who is as he was the Vicar of Jesus Christ." (p. v).

the attention which he was receiving was motivated exclusively by a profound concern for the pastoral mission of the church. He was fully aware that various political games were being played, and as the stakes got higher the tactics of his enemies became more vicious.[55] Thus Lagrange would have been a fool had he not expressed himself very carefully, and less than human had he not attempted to get away with what he could.

I have dealt with the Mark commentary at length because it was Lagrange's pioneering NT work. It illustrates the intellectual climate in which he wrote, the pressures to which he was subject, and the results that he achieved. It is typical of his other gospel commentaries in both structure and approach. Its significance has been well formulated by F.-M. Braun, "The Gospel according to Saint Mark marked a date in the history of Catholic exegesis of the New Testament. Prior to it there was not a single scientific French commentary on the gospels."[56] In other words, its importance was political not scientific. In terms of his formation at the University of Vienna and the resources of contemporary scholarship available to him, the Mark commentary was a very creditable achievement in which a responsible scholar took a well-argued position on controverted issues. Had he been an Anglican divine writing from an Oxford or Cambridge college, Lagrange's commentary would have been welcomed internationally as a valuable addition to the literature on the Second Gospel, but not one which opened new perspectives. It met the standard for serious work, but it did not invigorate the discipline of gospel studies.

Lagrange's Mark was epoch-making only to Catholics and only because it was Catholic. When one recalls the numbers of Catholics throughout the world this was no mean achievement. It was also of tremendous political significance that he was permitted to publish commentaries on the other three gospels, because such acceptance by church authorities made his work the reference point for scholars who followed him. Between the two World Wars Lagrange reigned supreme as the authority. Catholic scholars felt that they could be as liberal as he, but not more critical. Subsequent efforts to push back the frontiers in Catholic circles were few and timid. There was no serious participation by Catholics in the ongoing NT debate.

---

55 E.g. the Mark commentary was condemned by an Italian Jesuit for deliberate doctrinal disobedience on the basis of a decree of the Pontifical Biblical Commission which only appeared after the publication of the commentary! See Lagrange's reply, "A propos d'une critique par le R. P. Rinieri du Commentaire de Saint Marc," RB 21 (1912) 633-637. The decree is reproduced on pp. 605-607 of the same issue of the RB.

56 L'oeuvre du Père Lagrange, 117.

Form Criticism

To what extent was Lagrange responsible? It is a curious paradox, but this question is but an acknowledgement of his authority among Catholics. The most significant development in NT studies after World War I was the appearance of Form Criticism. Lagrange's commentary on Luke was submitted to the printers in 1919, the year in which the pioneering form-critical studies of M. Dibelius and K. L. Schmidt were published. It was too late to take them into consideration. By the time he came to write the introduction to his commentary on Matthew (1922), these had made their mark, and their impact was augmented by R. Bultmann's Die Geschichte der synoptischen Tradition (1921). Ever alert to new developments Lagrange accepted the challenge, but in a way which deprived his disciples of authentic guidance.

In the Matthew commentary he took a positive approach.[57] He listed a number of the forms proposed by Schmidt, Dibelius and Bultmann, found analogies in contemporary Jewish and Greek literature, and then integrated them into his own vision of the origins of the gospel tradition in such a way as to reduce the distinctions between the various forms to irrelevance. In his review of Bultmann, however, Lagrange took a completely negative stand,[58] whose essence is reproduced in the revised edition of his Mark commentary.[59] He ruthlessly exposed the underlying assumptions, highlighted the arbitrary character of a number of Bultmann's exegetical decisions, and poured scorn on the idea that a community could be creative. The violence of Lagrange's reaction, which was maintained in subsequent reviews of books which used form criticism,[60] was the measure of his fear of a scepticism which reduced the verifiable facts about Jesus to his existence, his preaching of the kingdom of God in Galilee, and his death in Jerusalem.

Such fear was contagious and it was to be at least ten years before Catholic scholars discussed the method as such.[61] Even then their positive appreciation was limited to applause for the attention directed to the oral

---

57 Évangile selon Saint Matthieu (EB), Paris: Gabalda, 1923, cxxiv-cxxxii.

58 RB 31 (1922) 286-292.

59 Évangile selon Saint Marc (EB), 4ème édition corrigée et augmentée, Paris: Gabalda, 1929, lv-lviii.

60 See RB 32 (1923) 442-445 on G. Bertram; RB 33 (1924) 280-282 on K. L. Schmidt; RB 39 (1930) 623-625 on K. Kundsin.

61 L. Cerfaux, "'L'histoire de la tradition synoptique' d'après Rudolf Bultmann," RHE 28 (1932) 582-594; F.-M. Braun, "Formgeschichte (École de la)," DBS 3 (1936) 312-317; E. Florit, "La 'storia delle forme' nei vangeli in rapporto alla dottrina cattolica," Biblica 14 (1933) 212-248; S. E. Donlon, "Form-Critics, the Gospels and St. Paul," CBQ 4 (1944) 306-325.

tradition which must have preceded the written gospels. In the end, Lagrange showed himself the most liberal. Reviewing Vincent Taylor's The
Formation of the Gospel Tradition, he wrote, "I do not think that the problem of the genesis of the tradition has been completely resolved. But to
have drawn attention to the fact that the gospels contain hints as to the way
in which they were composed is an element from which we can profit with
all the prudence required by such a delicate subject. One can show the radi-
cals, who begin by destroying everything and then have the effrontery to
write entirely subjective history, a much more critical use of their vaunted
method."[62] He was here on the point of separating the critical tool from the
philosophical system in which he had been presented, and of recognizing
that the assumptions of its liberal practitioners were not integral to its use.
Had he written his planned volume on literary criticism, it seems likely that
he would have made this separation, and saved Catholic exegesis twenty
years of struggle.

Johannine Studies

When Lagrange wrote his commentary on John in 1925 critical opinion
considered the Fourth Gospel to be a mid-second century AD Greek compilation completely devoid of historical value.[63] Lagrange would have rejected the entirely arbitrary judgments invoked to sustain this fantasy, even if
he had not felt bound by the authority of the Pontifical Biblical Commission, which in 1907 had decreed that the author of the Fourth Gospel was
John the Apostle, and that the words and deeds of Jesus contained therein
were not literary creations.[64]

Lagrange believed that the question of authorship was intrinsically related to the unity of the Fourth Gospel. Thus the year before the commentary
appeared he devoted an article to a review of the various dissection theories.[65] He analysed the hypothesis of successive additions (Wellhausen,
Loisy), and that of the compilation of different sources (Spitta, Soltau,
Faure), but in a way that failed to do justice to the seriousness of the issue.
By highlighting flaws in internal logic, and by drawing attention to the
contradictions between the various proposals, he knew that he was arguing
merely ad hominem.[66] He used the variety of inconsistent hypotheses as
evidence of failure. Their very multiplicity demonstrated the unity of John.

---

[62] RB 43 (1934) 303.

[63] For an excellent survey see R. E. Brown, "Père Lagrange and the Fourth Gospel," in
      Lagrange Lectures 1963, Dubuque: Aquinas Institute, 1963.

[64] Évangile selon Saint Jean (EB), Paris: Gabalda, 1925, ii, cxcix.

[65] "Où en est la dissection littéraire du quatrième évangile?" RB 33 (1924) 321-342.

[66] Évangile selon Saint Jean, xvii.

In reality, however, the multiplication of hypotheses is the clearest proof that a problem has not been satisfactorily solved.

Lagrange's refusal to invest in serious literary criticism forced him into blatant self-contradiction. Within the same year (1924) he could write, "We only note that so many observations of detail have proved that the Fourth Gospel does not have the unity of a perfect work of art... it is a work conceived in the semitic way, which was not written at a single sitting, and which, like all ancient literary works, was retouched by copyists, who fancied themselves as revisors."[67] Shortly afterwards he could state, without any indication that he was changing his opinion, that the question of the unity of authorship of the Fourth Gospel "could not have been dealt with before the investigation of the style and vocabulary, and it is answered by their perfect unity, which excludes both a multiplicity of sources and a series of additions. The gospel was written at one sitting, and contains no foreign element.... John of course, as other documents, suffered from copyists' mistakes, revisors' manipulations, author's retouches, or even negligence in its composition."[68]

Was the gospel written "at one sitting" or not? Was the text "revised" or merely accidentally disturbed? Was its unity "perfect" or not? Lagrange's literary sense was too refined and his power of observation too developed for him to miss the differences in Greek style, the inconsistencies in sequence, and the divergent repetions in the discourses. In the commentary he dealt with them on an individual basis by a multitude of partial hypotheses, but something held him back from developing an adequate general hypothesis. Perhaps it was the awareness that he would have to devise a much more sophisticated concept of apostolic authorship. The Fourth Gospel is not a literary unity, and modern scholars concur with Lagrange's opponents by assigning to it three (R. Schnackenburg), four (Boismard and Lamouille), or even five literary levels (R. E. Brown).

The importance that the author of the Fourth Gospel had for Lagrange is underlined by the extraordinary phrase, "Were it proven that the Second Gospel was written by Silas and not by Mark, it would loose hardly anything of its authority. The Fourth Gospel would loose its authority if it was not the work of an eyewitness."[69] The gospel contains a number of pointers to its author and, if we excuse a number of lapses into rather mawkish psychologizing,[70] Lagrange's analysis of the data to obtain the conclusion that

---

[67] "Où en est la dissection littéraire," 341.

[68] Évangile selon Saint Jean, cxix-cxx.

[69] Évangile selon Saint Jean, xi.

[70] Lagrange repeatedly returns to the author's silence regarding himself and all members of his family (pp. xiv, xvii, xviii, xx) and finds in this "the imprint of a very delicate soul, as self-effacing as it is generous; a way somewhat subtle but exquisite of resolving the problem of witness without a disagreeable insistance on 'I'." (p. xviii; cf. p. xvi).

the author was John the son of Zebedee has stood up rather well. R. E. Brown, for example, has written, "When all is said and done, the combination of external and internal evidence associating the Fourth Gospel with John the son of Zebedee makes this the strongest hypothesis, if one is prepared to give credence to the Gospel's claim of an eyewitness source."[71] Others argue for John Mark,[72] or for Lazarus.[73] This difference, however, is less important than the consensus that the Fourth Gospel is based on the testimony of an eyewitness. C. K. Barrett, has written most judiciously, "The most the evidence that has now been surveyed can prove is that here and there behind the Johannine narrative there lies eye-witness material. It is certainly not proved, and is perhaps not provable, that the gospel as a whole is the work of an eye-witness.[74] Lagrange might have agreed, and done better justice to the data, had he had the opportunity to revise his introduction after the force of the decrees of the Pontifical Biblical Commission on technical matters had been severely attenuated in 1954.[75]

One aspect that Lagrange would not have to change is his insistence that Johannine thought is rooted in a solidly Jewish milieu. It was common then and subsequently to assert that the development of Johannine theology owed much to Gnostic or Philonic Hellenism. Although virtually no mention is made of either in his John commentary, Lagrange had written widely on many different aspects of Greco-Roman culture and his silence was certainly not the result of ignorance.[76] His arguments drawn from the OT can now be supplemented by numerous parallels in the Dead Sea Scrolls. As R. E. Brown has stressed, "The critical import of the parallels between the Scrolls and John is that one can no longer insist that the abstract language spoken by Jesus in the Fourth Gospel must have been composed in the Greek world of the early second century A.D. What Jesus says in John would have been quite intelligible in the sectarian background of first-century Palestine."[77]

---

71 The Gospel according to John (I-XII) (AB 29), Garden City: Doubleday, 1966, xcviii.

72 P. Parker, "John and John Mark," JBL 79 (1960) 97-110; id. "John the Son of Zebedee and the Fourth Gospel," NTS 9 (1962-63) 75-85.

73 F. V. Filson, "Who was the Beloved Disciple?" JBL 68 (1949) 83-88.

74 The Gospel according to St. John. An Introduction with Commentary and Notes on the Greek Text, London: SPCK, 1962, 104.

75 See E. F. Siegman, "The Decrees of the Pontifical Biblical Commission. A Clarification," CBQ 18 (1956) 23-29.

76 See the surveys by G. Bardy, "The Hellenistic Milieu," and E. Magnin, "The Comparative History of Religions and Revealed Religion," in Père Lagrange and the Scriptures, translated by R. T. Murphy, Milwaukee: Bruce, 1946.

77 "The Dead Sea Scrolls and the New Testament," in John and Qumran, ed. J. H. Charlesworth, London: Chapman, 1972, 8. For more detail, see R. E. Brown, "The Qumran Scrolls and the Johannine Gospel and Epistles," CBQ 17 (1955) 403-419, 559-574. F.-

In the last month before he left Jerusalem definitively Lagrange had the satisfaction of finding indisputable proof that the very late date assigned to the Fourth Gospel by the radical critics could not be correct. In 1935 H. I. Bell and T. C. Skeat published Papyrus Egerton 2.[78] The document was dated palaeographically to about A.D. 150. The editors recognized that parts of the text reflected the Fourth Gospel, but maintained that John depended on the papyrus or, less probably, that both shared a common source. On the basis of his own analysis, Lagrange on the contrary insisted that the papyrus quoted John in its final form, and concluded, "Providence has furnished incontestable proof that the Gospel of Saint John existed in its present form at the beginning of the second century and on the same level as the Synoptics."[79] This interpretation of Papyrus Egerton 2 and this date for the Fourth Gospel are those that have prevailed.[80]

Introduction to the New Testament

At an age when most men would be comfortably retired, and when anyone with Lagrange's prodigious publishing record might be content to look back with some complacency on what had been achieved, he turned to a new task. With a view to providing a solid base for a new generation of scholars he committed himself to the publication of an Introduction to the New Testament. The plan was as simple as the issues were fundamental. What books belonged to the NT? How could one be sure of their original text? How should those texts be studied from a literary point of view? What external elements needed to be taken into account in their interpretation?

Lagrange's study of the formation of the canon of the NT appeared in 1933, and was a thorough and erudite discussion of all the available data.[81] It was also concerned to argue a particular thesis. The basic question that any discussion of the canon must confront is: how were the various books first recognized? Theologians unanimously answered that an individual special divine revelation identified each document. Such a speculative response, unsupported by any evidence, could not but be unpalatable to an historian. So Lagrange went against the consensus, and argued that apostolicity had been the criterion. Any book thought to have been composed by an

---

M. Braun, "L'arrière-fond judaique du quatrième évangile et la Communauté de l'Alliance," RB 62 (1955) 5-44.

[78] Fragments of an Unknown Gospel and other Early Christian Papyri, London: British Museum, 1935.

[79] "Deux nouveaux textes relatifs à l'Évangile," RB 44 (1935) 343.

[80] See F.-M. Braun, Jean le Théologien et son évangile dans l'église ancienne (EB), Paris: Gabalda, 1959, 87-94.

[81] Histoire ancienne du Canon du Nouveau Testament (EB; Introduction à l'étude du NT, 1), Paris: Gabalda, 1933.

apostle was accepted by the first Christians as authoritative. From an historical point of view this is certainly the most probable hypothesis. Lagrange, however, went on to envelope it in a purely theoretical discussion of the relations between apostolicity, inspiration, and canonicity. This was the only aspect on which Catholic reviewers focused, and with manifest disapproval.[82] From this others got the impression that the book was but another scholastic manual, and it had little influence. Its basic thesis, however, is widely accepted today, though as the result of the work of other scholars.

Lagrange's second volume, on textual criticism,[83] was immediately recognized as "an extraordinary contribution" by specialists of the caliber of Kirsop and Silva Lake. The title they gave their review -- "From Westcott and Hort to Father Lagrange and Beyond" -- underlined the book's seminal significance.[84] The basic work of Westcott and Hort was published in 1881 and that of von Soden in 1907-10. But a completely new text type appeared in 1913, the Caesarean, when MS Koridethi was edited for the first time. Subsequently the data base was enriched by numerous papyri discoveries. There was an urgent need, therefore, for an overview which would classify the acquisitions of fifty years of research and highlight the problems that remained to be solved.

Lagrange had the courage to undertake this formidable task, because he was not an expert; he simply wanted to clarify the situation for beginners.[85] This was not false modesty. An expert, for Lagrange, was one who devoted his or her whole life to a subject and who took nothing for granted.[86] Nonetheless his synthetic grasp was so sure and his critical sense so fine-tuned that his book enabled specialist text-critics to recover from the myopia engendered by exclusive focus on specific problems.[87] His contribution could not have come at a better time. The book was almost finished when Sir Frederic Kenyon published the fragments of a codex containing the four gospels and the Acts of the Apostles, which antedated all previously known manuscripts by a century.[88] This give the field an entirely new dimension which could be clearly perceived because the state of the question had been so precisely established by Lagrange.[89]

---

[82] E.g. F. Ogara, Gregorianum 15 (1934) 451-466; L. Cerfaux, ETL 11 (1934) 635-637.

[83] Critique textuelle. II. La critique rationelle (EB; Introduction à l'étude du NT, 2), Paris: Gabalda, 1935.

[84] "De Westcott et Hort au Père Lagrange et au-delà," RB 48 (1939) 497-505.

[85] Critique textuelle, viii.

[86] Critique textuelle, viii.

[87] See in particular the remarks in this sense by A. Merk, SJ, who had produced his critical edition of the NT in 1933, in Biblica 20 (1939) 458-459.

[88] The Chester Beatty Biblical Papyri, London: Emery Walker, 1933.

[89] See K. and S. Lake, RB 48 (1939) 502.

He worked on these texts as soon as they appeared, and the results of his analysis were published in three long articles in the Revue Biblique for 1934, but he was not given the time to appreciate fully their significance, which became apparent only when their complex implications had been worked out. Thus in one respect a major work was out of date as soon as it appeared, but Lagrange would have been the first to agree with the Lakes that "knowledge is a quest not a conclusion."[90] His goal had been to carry his share of the burden of scholarship and to produce something useful, not to create a monument for future generations to admire. No scientific conclusions were for him definitive. They were but working hypotheses, integral parts in an ongoing process, generous participation in which represented true success.

Instead of treating literary criticism, as his program demanded, Lagrange devoted the next volume of his Introduction to historical criticism. He offered no explanation for the change of plan, but it is not difficult to work out what motivated him. All his life he had chosen to work on problems of burning actuality and he was not about to change in his old age. The principles of literary criticism were widely accepted, and his exegesis shows that Lagrange had no original contribution to make in this domain. He would have dealt with it only for the sake of completeness. The mystery religions, however, were quite a different matter. The history of religions approach to the NT, which had begun in Göttingen in the last decade of the 19th century, had become an increasingly powerful force in German theological faculties, through which it exercised an international influence. A long series of articles and reviews starting in 1910 attests the attentiveness with which Lagrange followed developments in this field.

Orphism in particular attracted his attention. On the one hand, there were those who maintained that Paul drew on Orphism for his key theological ideas, while on the other hand, there was no unanimity among specialists as to the exact nature of Orphism. Lagrange saw that in one and the same study he could make a contribution to a particularly difficult field of study, and at the same time highlight the transcendance of Christianity. The economy of such a project certainly appealed to one whose time was running out; he was 80 when he began! L'Orphisme (1937), which appeared the year before he died, proved to be a fitting climax to an extraordinary career.

His analysis of the diffuse, ambiguous, and disparate Orphic material was remarkable, not only for its precision and the care to set each piece of evidence in its cultural context, but for the manifest sympathy with which Lagrange approached his subject. The methodology is exemplary. The dating of the different documents was respected, and he consistently refused to make combinations which were not attested historically. He thus avoided the unrealistic (in the literal sense) syntheses which are the bane of much work in the history of religions. Such critical rigor made manifest the ten-

---

90 RB 48 (1939) 497.

dentious character of the generalisations which served as the basis of the claim that Paul depended on Orphism. In this book Lagrange inaugurated a genuinely critical approach to comparative studies in religion. The conclusions to which he came have been fully confirmed by the recent exhaustive study by Alan Wedderburn.[91]

*   *   *

German scholarship paid little or no attention to Lagrange's work in New Testament. This was not a judgment, but simply another manifestation of its refusal to take seriously works that did not originate in Germany. Moreover radical German critics rarely if ever visited the Holy Land, where they could have made personal contact with Lagrange; contact with reality apparently was not considered to be either useful or necessary. The rest of the scholarly world accorded him the eminence merited by the number, range and quality of his publications. His relations with his colleagues has never been more felicitously described than by the Lakes, "He was a man with whom discussion was an education, a difference of opinion a discipline, and agreement an inspiration."[92]

For Catholics Lagrange played a much more important role. He restored pride and identify to Catholic biblical scholarship by giving it a program, a method, and a sense of purpose, thereby moving the church into the scientific age. His greatest contribution, however, was on a much more fundamental level, as Jean Guitton perceptively noted, "First of all, it is eminently appropriate to thank P. Lagrange for the great service he has rendered to many Christian university people, who had been (or who could have been) led astray from the faith by biblical criticism. Thanks to him, sincere belief could become (or remain) a 'reasonable service,' when everything conspired against it."[93]

---

[91] Baptism and Resurrection. Studies in Pauline Theology against Its Graeco-Roman Background, Tübingen: Mohr (Siebeck), 1988.

[92] RB 48 (1939) 505.

[93] "The Influence of Père Lagrange," in Père Lagrange and the Scriptures, translated by R. T. Murphy, Milwaukee: Bruce, 1946, 170.

Chapter 3

PIERRE BENOIT, O.P.

From the fact that Lagrange acquired a successor in New Testament only in his extreme old age, it might appear natural to infer that throughout his career he had jealously excluded all competiton in this field at the École Biblique. Not only would such an attitude have been alien to his character, but it is demonstrably false. Lagrange's writings on NT represent only about 15% of his published work. Nothing could demonstrate more clearly that the NT was not his primary interest. He accepted it out of a sense of duty, but personally he was more attracted by other areas of research in which he felt that he could make more substantive contributions.

Thus from the end of the First World War, when the dust of the Modernist crisis had settled, he eagerly sought a replacement. He must have been bitterly disappointed when the two Dominicans who actually accepted posts at the École Biblique -- Raphael Tonneau (1926-30) and Augustin Carrié (1931-32) -- failed to stay the course. As to why this was we can only speculate. Lagrange's eminence would have made any potential successor think twice; the standard against which he would be measured was impossibly high.

Moreover, NT studies still carried a certain degree of risk for the independent minded. Even though the Modernist crisis was past the Pontifical Biblical Commission still considered itself a watchdog of the faith, and the atmosphere it generated can be gauged from the facts that on 1 July 1933 it issued a decree on the meaning of Mt 16:26//Lk 9:25, and on 30 April 1934 it insisted that all liturgical translations of the OT and NT should be based on the Latin Vulgate. In consequence, those ambitious to make their mark in the scientific world tended towards linguistics and/or archaeology, fields of study in which originality was not considered dangerous. It is not without significance that Tonneau's literary output consisted of three articles on biblical topography,[1] two on epigraphy,[2] and one on the history of the city of Ephesus.[3] He published nothing on an exegetical or theological problem.

It was only at the last moment that Lagrange found a candidate who was prepared to confront these difficulties. Highly idealistic and amply endowed with the stubbornness of his native Lorraine, Pierre Benoit responded ea-

---

1 RB 35 (1926) 98-109; 35 (1926) 583-604; 38 (1929) 421-431.
2 RB 36 (1927) 93-98; 40 (1931) 544-564.
3 RB 38 (1929) 5-24, 321-363.

gerly to what he saw was a simple call of duty. He accompanied Lagrange to Jerusalem in the late summer of 1932, and thereafter devoted his whole life to the École Biblique.

The son of Auguste Benoit and Elizabeth Geny, Maurice Benoit was born in Nancy, France, on 3 August 1906, and was educated at the College Saint Sigisbert in the same city. After his Baccalaurate (Science and Philosophy) he did a year of specialized study in mathematics. But instead of sitting the competetive exam for one of the Grandes Écoles, he decided to become a Dominican.

In 1924 he entered the noviciate of the Paris province in Amiens where he received the religious name of Pierre in honor of Peter of Verona, the first Dominican martyr. The following year he began his philosophical and theological studies in Belgium. Even though the French anti-religious laws were no longer applied rigorously because of the heroic service that so many religious had given to France during the First World War, the house of studies of the Paris province was at Kain near Tournai. The numerous willows (in French, saule) that grew in the vicinity explains why the monastery became known as Le Saulchoir. There he was ordained priest on 25 July 1930, and two years later a thesis on "La satisfaction du Christ chez saint Thomas d'Aquin" won for him the Lectorate in Sacred Theology, which was then the equivalent of a doctorate. This meant that his future lay in academic work rather than in pastoral ministry. His orientation towards biblical studies was due to the influence of P. Synave, his professor of Sacred Scripture at the Saulchoir. At the end of his first academic year in Jerusalem (1932-33), Benoit passed the Licentiate in Sacred Scripture before the Pontifical Biblical Commission in Rome.

The Early Years

Lagrange then asked for him to be formally assigned to the École Biblique, where he began to teach immediately. In the next seven years (1933-1940) he literally taught himself into his subject. Each year he taught special introduction and never repeated a course, covering the Gospels, the Pastoral Letters, the Catholic Epistles, the Synoptic Problem, the Hellenistic Cultural Milieu, and the Mystery Religions. Each year he also taught an exegesis course, and his selection of subjects indicate what became lifelong interests; he explained Romans (twice), the Captivity Epistles (twice), the Acts of the Apostles, Mark, and the Passion and Resurrection in the Synoptic Gospels. From his second year he added a course for advanced students on different problems posed by the Greek of the NT. The intention to immerse himself systematically in all aspects of NT studies is manifest, and is typical of his disciplined approach.

But this was not all. From 1934 he was responsible for the field trips of the École, which involved guiding students on a monthly one-day excursion within Palestine, and three times a year on much longer trips (one to three weeks) to the surrounding countries, Jordan, Egypt, Syria, and Lebanon. As if this were not enough to tax the energies of a young professor, for whom each course demanded a new preparation, he did a survey of Ain Qades in 1937 with Savignac,[4] and prospected the region around es-Salt with de Vaux in 1938.[5] Nonetheless in the period 1937-40 he managed to publish five articles, all being the outgrowth of his exegesis courses

The stamina displayed in these overlapping activities makes it difficult to believe that Benoit had been declared unfit for military service. But it explains why he was recalled to France when the French army was mobilized in September 1939. When the first diagnosis of a slight heart murmur was confirmed, he was free to return to Jerusalem. He made the voyage in early 1940 before the Second World War disrupted traffic in the Mediterranean, and travelled from Cairo to Jerusalem by train.

He found the École Biblique unchanged. The mobilisation was much less disruptive than that of 1914, because all the senior professors were too old to serve, and Fathers Bernard Couroyer and Roland de Vaux were mobilized into the service of the French Consulate General in Jerusalem, where they finished work at 1.30 pm each day. Students, of course, could not come to the École, but that was all to the good because it meant more time for research. What they could not do was publish.

Caught in France at the outbreak of hostilities Father Vincent was forced to spend the rest of the war in Paris. Despite enormous difficulties he and the publisher, Gabalda, managed to bring out the first two fascicles of the Revue Biblique for 1940 before the Nazis interfered. This, however, did not exhaust the articles and book reviews which he had accepted for publication, and he was firmly determined that he would not do less than Lagrange, who single-handed had kept the Revue Biblique alive during the First World War (1914-18).[6]

This time, however, the Germans occupied Paris, and Vincent was forced to take the RB underground. At the end of the war he explained what happened. "The German regulations imposed on the press during the period of occupation contained conditions which quickly made it clear that the Revue Biblique could not continue to appear in its normal form. However, publications which did not appear regularly could get permission, provided that they were passed by the Censor. It was decided to accept this solution

---

4   RB 47 (1938) 89-100.

5   RB 47 (1938) 398-425.

6   One cannot but admire Lagrange's laconic understatement at the time, "Hopefully our subscribers will excuse the delay of this issue. At the beginning of August the professors of the École Biblique de Jérusalem left for the service of France. The Director, all alone, could not correspond with Europe. Finally the École was officially closed by the Turkish authorities. Fortunately this measure does not affect the Revue Biblique, which will continue to appear. Subscriptions therefore will be received as in the past." (RB 23 (1914) 626).

provisionally, but we had to find a harmless label which would disguise the fact that the contents were those of the <u>Revue Biblique</u>. The title <u>Vivre et Penser</u> was chosen precisely because it meant nothing. The sub-title "Researches in Exegesis and History" was added as a discrete hint of what we were trying to keep alive."[7] The stratagem worked. The first series, containing the material Vincent had brought from Jerusalem, appeared in July 1941. Thereafter he had to rely on contributions from scholars based in France, as Lagrange had done in 1914-18. Nonetheless, the second series was published in July 1942, and the third at the beginning of June 1945.

The lead article in the restored <u>Revue Biblique</u> in 1946 was a study by Benoit on Seneca and St Paul. He had used the war years to extend his knowledge of the world of early Christianity, of which another fruit was an article on Porphyry (1947). He had also devoted considerable time to mastering modern Hebrew and to the study of rabbinism. From this there flowed an article on Rabbi Akiba (1947), and in the years following the war he several times offered a course on Rabbinic History and Literature.

Students returned to the École Biblique for the academic year 1946-47, but it soon became clear that full-scale war between Jews and Arabs would break out when the British withdrew from Palestine on 15 May 1948. In anticipation, not only of danger but of severe shortages, students were advised to leave Palestine in the early spring of 1948. Thus the program announced for 1948-49 was never carried out.

In fact the only lectures held at the École Biblique in 1948 were a series on the four great sieges of Jerusalem, which were delivered by Abel and de Vaux to the group of United Nations military observers billeted at the École. They had asked for something to distract them from the heavy gunfire, whose noise enveloped the École Biblique every evening. The most intense fighting in November 1948 took place along Nablus Road; it eventually determined the armistice line which was to divide Jerusalem until 1967.

The outlook for the academic year 1949-50 was so uncertain that no program was printed in the <u>Revue Biblique.</u> In the course of 1949, however, conditions improved dramatically once it became clear that the armistice was going to hold, and classes in fact resumed early in 1950.

The Jerusalem Bible

During this difficult period Benoit managed to produce the annotated translations of the Captivity Epistles (1949) and the Gospel of Matthew (1950) for the <u>Bible de Jérusalem.</u> With the exception of the epigrapher, R. Savignac, and the archaeologist, A.-M. Steve, all the professors of the École Biblique were involved in this extraordinary project. The principles it em-

---

7   RB 53 (1946) 5-6.

bodied -- translations from the original texts each done by a specialist in that book, detailed introductions and notes reflecting the best in modern research, literary revision -- have now become standard practice. Then they were revolutionary. The qualities of its editors and contributors made the Bible de Jérusalem the dawn of a new age in Catholic biblical studies, and it got its name, first as a nickname and then officially, because it was produced under the auspices of the École Biblique de Jérusalem.

Benoit was one of the two representatives of the École on the twelve member steering committee. Thus he played a key role in the selection of the NT contributors, and was responsible in the name of the École for deciding as to the suitability of their work for publication. In addition he acted as exegetical consultant for Mark, Luke, Acts, Hebrews, and the Catholic Epistles. The first fascicles appeared in 1948 and the last in 1954.

Then the task was to combine the fascicles in order to produce a one-volume Bible. As a member of the new committee charged with this responsibility, Benoit played his part in the final revision of the translations. His most significant contribution, however, came at another level. With the exception of the Johannine material, he wrote the introductions to all the NT documents. Drawing on the data which had appeared in the fascicles he rewrote all the explanatory footnotes, deciding what should be omitted, modified, or added. Among these footnotes there appeared a new phenomenon, mini syntheses in which numerous references grouped into a highly condensed text outlined all the aspects of theologically significant themes, e.g. Son of God, Son of Man, Miracles, Kingdom of God, Holy Spirit. The system of exegetical and literary revision had already somewhat diluted the individuality of the authors of the various fascicles. In the preparation of the one-volume edition uniformity was raised to the level of a principle. Benoit had no obligation to preserve the particular vision of any contributor. On the contrary, his brief was to reduce, if not eliminate, any diversities. Inevitably, therefore, the NT exegesis and biblical theology of the highly influential one-volume Bible de Jérusalem was that of Benoit and reflected his priorities. Essentially these were an insistence on a very high Christology, and a concern not to disturb the faithful by any divergence from classical Catholic theology.[8]

The appearance of the one-volume edition in 1956 did not put an end to work on the Bible de Jérusalem. New editions of the fascicles continued to appear and Benoit played an ever increasing role in the revision of the gospels of Mark, Luke and John. The first translations, while not in any way

---

[8]   As a precedent he could have cited the principle behind St. Augustine's refusal to accept St. Jerome's more accurate translation of Jonah 4:6, "I do not wish your translation of the Hebrew to be read in the churches, for fear of upsetting the flock of Christ with great scandal, by publishing something new, something seemingly contrary to the authority of the Septuagint, which version their ears and hearts are accustomed to hear." (Ep. 82, 35; CSEL 34, 386).

inaccurate, used a range of vocabulary which enhanced their literary quality but made a comparative study of the gospels impossible. In response to this need, Editions du Cerf commissioned Benoit to compose a synopsis of the gospels based on the Bible de Jérusalem translations, and this affected revisions of the gospels which appeared after the publication of the synopsis in 1965.

Such updating reached a climax in 1973 when a new one-volume edition of the Bible de Jérusalem "completely revised and enlarged" was published. In it Benoit played the same major role with respect to introductions and notes as he had in its predecessor. In his review (JBL 95 [1976] 640-41) J. A. Fitzmyer praised the extensive revision or expansion of many of the notes, and illustrated this development by two examples. In the 1956 edition the note to Lk 1:34 implied that Mary may have made a decision not to marry. Such a romantic interpretation has no basis in the text, and the 1973 edition said so; "Nothing in the text suggests a vow of virginity." The 1956 edition translated *porneia* in the exceptive clause in Mt 19:9 by "fornication" and the rather confused explanation managed to find in it a reference to separation without the right of remarriage. In the 1973 edition it is rendered by "prostitution", which is correctly explained as a technical term for marriages within the forbidden degrees of consanguinity (cf. Lev 18). Such unions were not true marriages and, in consequence, their dissolution was not divorce. This effort to integrate the acquired results of critical study deserved Fitzmyer's praise. The latter, however, cannot have checked the introductions very carefully, because he could not have said the same of them. With one exception the introductions reproduced word for word those of the first edition. He abandoned his original solution to the synoptic problem in favour of that proposed by his colleague Marie-Emile Boismard.[9]

This was not sufficient to preserve the reputation of the Bible de Jérusalem as representative of the best of biblical scholarship. The problem became acute in 1979, when Benoit was asked by the publishers of the English version, the Jerusalem Bible (1966), to authorize a revision in the light of the 1973 French version. He was only too willing, because he had been seriously disappointed in the first English version. He was determined that the same mistakes should not be repeated.[10] He selected Dom Henry Wansbrough, OSB, an ex-student of the École Biblique and a monk of Ampleforth Abbey, as the one responsible for the new edition, and maintained very close contact with him. This was the beginning of a five year dialogue during which Benoit was persuaded to permit the NT notes and introduc-

---

[9]   The details will be given later. At this point it is sufficient to compare BdeJ, 1956, 1283-4 with BdeJ, 1973, 1407-8, and note Benoit's remarks in his preface to Synopse II (see below), which appeared a year before the second edition of the BdeJ.

[10] For one account of how the JB came into being, see Anthony Kenny, A Path from Rome, An Autobiography, London: Sidgwick & Jackson, 1985, 113-123.

tions to reflect more accurately the transformation that Catholic biblical scholarship had undergone since 1956.

The extent of this transformation is illustrated by a selection of the differences between the 1973 Bible de Jérusalem and the 1985 Jerusalem Bible. The figures in brackets are page numbers and 'a' and 'b' indicate left and right columns respectively:

1973 Bible de Jérusalem

• The traditional ascription of the synoptic gospels is confirmed by internal evidence. (1407a)

• Apologetic treatment of the authority of gospels which differ. (1410b)

• The historical value of Acts is guaranteed by the intrinsic probability of the events. Lk's respect for his sources and the authenticity of the speeches. (1568b)

• Paul's conversion is dated AD 36. (1615a).

• A radical partition theory about 2Cor is judged as "fort possible". (1618b)

• The partition of Phil into a number of letters is said to be conjectural. (1621a)

• Phil 2:6 is rendered "Lui, de condition divine" and interpreted as a reference to the divine preexistence of Christ. (1696)

• Defends the authenticity of Col and Eph. (1621b)

1985 Jerusalem Bible

• "These traditions are not in any way definitive." Levi the tax collector did not write Mt; the tradition radically oversimplifies the relation of Mk to Peter's preaching. (1599)

• Simple statement of the fact of inspiration. (1604)

• Lk was less concerned with material exactitude than with the theological meaning of events, and created the speeches to suit his purpose. (1795)

• Paul's conversion is dated AD 34. (1849)

• The same theory is presented as a certitude. (1855)

• A detailed division of Phil into three letters is presented as a most satisfactory hypothesis. (1859)

• The hymn "has been understood of Christ's *kenosis* in emptying himself of his divine glory. ... More probably Jesus is here contrasted as the second with the first Adam." The divine *kenosis* interpretation "is not only less scriptural but also anachronistic." (1941b)

• Highlights the weight of the arguments against authenticity and concludes "the genuine Pauline authorship of these two letters is the strongest but not the only possible hypothesis". (1860)

• The differences between the Pastorals and the Great Epistles is accounted for, as in Eph, by the hypothesis of a secretary to whom Paul gave greater freedom. (1623b).

• The arguments against authenticity are given in detail; "the best explanation may be that the Pastoral Epistles are letters written by a follower of Paul," between AD80-90. (1863)

It is not to be supposed that Wansbrough succeeded in changing Benoit's mind on all these points. In 1980 Benoit was 74, an age at which one does not easily abandon the convictions of a lifetime, but he was open to persuasion that his views were no longer representative of the mainstream of Catholic scholarship. Even though he continued to believe that his opinions were correct, he accepted the modifications proposed by Wansbrough, because he did not think that the Jerusalem Bible should be a vehicle for options which were not part of the general consensus.

The Topography of Jerusalem

Thirty years earlier, however, Benoit had been in the forefront of Catholic scholarship, and it is to 1950 that we must return to take up the thread of his career. Once the École settled down to regular classes after the turmoil associated with the establishment of the state of Israel, a definite pattern began to develop in his teaching. At the beginning he regularly taught three courses, NT introduction, NT exegesis, and Greek. He dropped the last mentioned in 1957, and no longer offered a course on NT introduction after 1968. He maintained an exegesis course until 1980; the two subjects which predominate are the Infancy Gospels and the Captivity Epistles. His focus on the former is explained by the fact that it was a subject of controversy, and his concentration on the latter was due to his promise to Lagrange to write the commentary for the Études Bibliques.

With visible regret he surrendered the direction of the field trips to François-Louis Lemoine, O.P., in 1952. He attached great importance to the intimate involvement with archaeology which only teaching responsibility provided. Nontheless room had to be made for young professors, and other responsibilities had begun to accumulate. Another opportunity for involvement in archaeology occured in 1959, and Benoit grasped it eagerly. This was the course on the topography of Jerusalem which had been taught by M. du Buit, O.P., since the death of F.-M. Abel in 1953.

Benoit taught this course for twenty-five years (1959-84) and made it a legendary experience. When ex-students congregate each one has a Benoit story. The class on Tuesday morning and the visit to a section of the city in the afternoon drew, not only the students of the École Biblique, but a wide selection of the international and diplomatic community. Since Benoit firmly believed that everything historical which existed should be seen, and that things which no longer existed should be described in detail, it was often after dark when ambassadors, consuls general, eminent professors, and students trudged up Nablus Road. Those with the interest to pay close attention, and the stamina to keep up with him, knew that they were privileged to get an unrivalled introduction to the history and archaeology of the city. Benoit knew the texts, the monuments, and the excavations in a detail that is unlikely ever to be surpassed. He did not focus specifically on the OT or NT, as some of his predecessors had done, but treated all periods from the earliest vestiges of settlement to the Ottoman occupation. He did, however, manifest a special concern for sites associated with the NT.

In terms of his publications on topography, one site virtually monopolized his attention, the Praetorium in which Pontius Pilate condemned Jesus to death. Benoit's arrival in Jerusalem coincided with the first excavations at the Ecce Homo Convent in the Muslim Quarter of the Old City.[11] Vincent identified the great pavement as the courtyard of the Antonia fortress, which he insisted was the place of Jesus' condemnation, the Praetorium (Jn 18:28; 19:13).[12] The two issues were not the same.

There was no doute about the location of the Antonia at the north-west corner of the Temple, which is the immediate vicinity of the Ecce Homo. F.-M. Abel, however, had shown that in terms of first century documentary evidence the Praetorium must be located at the Palace of Herod near the present Jaffa Gate.[13] To this Vincent could only offer the weak reply that, during the Passover when Jesus was judged, Pilate must have been at the Antonia. Much later he attempted to improve his position by insisting on "the concrete and, so to say, spontaneous adaptation of all the details of the trial of Jesus to what is thus far known of the architectual arrangement of the Antonia."[14] He concluded this article with an explicit invitation to debate the issue, an invitation which he personally addressed to Benoit, whom he knew to be of Abel's persuasion. Nothing better illustrates the freedom of opinion which reigns among the professors of the École Biblique. At a later stage in the debate Benoit was to manifest the same generosity of spirit.

In his reply Benoit accepted Vincent's archaeological reconstruction of the Antonia, but refused its relevance to the trial of Jesus.[15] He raised the hypothesis supported by Abel (among others) to a level of probability amounting to historical certitude by demonstrating (a) that "praetorium" in first-century usage meant an official residence, and did not have a mobile juridical sense; (b) and that "Gabbatha" would most naturally have been ap-

---

11 Soeur Marie Aline de Sion, La forteresse Antonia à Jérusalem et la question du Prétoire, Jérusalem: Sion, 1955, 39-43.

12 "L'Antonia et le Prétoire," RB 42 (1933) 83-113.

13 Jérusalem Nouvelle, Paris: Gabalda, 1914, 562-571.

14 "Le lithostrotos évangélique," RB 59 (1952) 530.

15 "Prétoire, Lithostroton, et Gabbatha," RB 59 (1952) 531-550.

plied to the highest point within the walled city of the period, namely the site of the Palace in the Upper City.

This double argument was challenged by Soeur Marie Aline de Sion, but her arguments amounted to no more than a restatement of the possibility that the Antonia could have been the Praetorium.[16] Vincent also found Benoit's literary arguments unconvincing, but instead of a direct critique he merely insinuated that the Antonia might have been recognized as a palace because of its luxury and size![17] It is natural, though perhaps uncharitable, to interpret this as a Machiavellian attempt to muddy the documentary waters so that in future the debate would be conducted on a purely archaeological level.

Benoit accepted the challenge, and thereafter scrutinized all new archaeological discoveries in Jerusalem for anything that might throw light on the problem. He gradually accumulated enough data to show (a) that the great pavement of the Ecce Homo Convent (interpreted by Vincent as the courtyard of the Antonia) was not unique, and so could not have been known as "The Pavement"; (b) that the pavement must be dated to the time of Hadrian in the early second-century A.D., and so could not have belonged to the Antonia which was destroyed by the Romans in A.D. 70; and (c) that the Antonia could not have been as big as Vincent's reconstruction supposed. The pavement, therefore, must have been a forum of Aelia Capitolina with a triumphal arch. The only problem for which Benoit did not have a satisfactory answer was the eccentric position of the arch.[18]

Some years later Benoit encouragd one of his students, Yves Blomme, to attempt to solve this latter difficulty in the context of a wider study of Aelia Capitolina. Blomme did so in a fashion that no one could have anticipated. He proved that it was not a triumphal arch of the second century, but a city gate of the first century A.D.[19] This destroyed one of Benoit's key archaeological arguments in support of point (b) above, which was based on the architectural unity of arch and pavement. It was Benoit, however, who forced the timid Blomme to publish, because the latter's demonstration had convinced him and he was happy to have his argument corrected in public.

Of course, he also saw it as an important new element in the interminable discussion concerning the Third Wall, on which he had published what is certainly the most objective and balanced study.[20] The arch can only

---

16   La forteresse Antonia, 201-237.

17   "L'Antonia, palais primitif d'Hérode," RB 61 (1964) 87-107.

18   "L'Antonia d'Hérode le Grand et le forum oriental d'Aelia Capitolina," HTR 64 (1971) 135-167. See also "The Archaeological Reconstruction of the Antonia Fortress," AJBA 1/6 (1973) 16-22.

19   "Faut-il revenir sur la datation de l'arc de l'"Ecce Homo'?" RB 86 (1979) 244-271.

20   "Où en est la question du 'Troisième mur'?" in Studia Hierosolymitana in onore P. Bellarmino Bagatti, Jérusalem: Franciscan Press, 1976, I, 111-126.

be the eastern gate by which this wall of Herod Agrippa I was anchored to the Antonia and the Temple.

It is unfortunate that Benoit never took the opportunity to explore the implications of this discovery. At this stage, however, the promised commentary on the Captivity Epistles weighed heavily upon him, and his publications were directed to that end. There were only two exceptions. He wrote a response to B. Pixner's attempt to locate the trial of Jesus in the old Hasmonaean palace on the slope of the Tyropoeon Valley.[21] His justification can only have been his committment to Lagrange's method of text and monument; the issue concerned the NT. His last article was the one that he was uniquely qualified to write, the history of the archaeological discoveries made by the École Biblique in pursuit of Lagrange's ideal.[22]

The Inspiration of Sacred Scripture

Concomitant with the absorbing interest in the artifacts of history there went an equally intense concern with the speculative problem of inspiration and inerrancy. His writings on this subject were to make his name a household word in ecclesiastical circles. His first contribution was not dictated by the needs of controversy. Since the contribution of Lagrange at the beginning of the century there had been no original work on the topic.[23] It was an act of pietas towards the man who had oriented him to biblical studies. Paul Synave, OP, had died in 1937 leaving unfinished his annotated translation of St Thomas Aquinas' treatise on prophecy (Summa Theologica, II-II, qq. 171-178). The hiatus in his teaching and publishing schedule caused by the Second World War gave Benoit not only the opportunity to complete this work, but to write a long (well over half the book) synthetic presentation of Thomistic thought on prophecy and inspiration.[24]

When published in 1947 this study had an immediate impact and became "the classic theory of the years immediately after 'Divino Afflante Spiritu'".[25] The interest it aroused as the first creative contribution for half a century led to an invitation to write the section on inspiration for Initiation Biblique which became a very influential teaching manual. As he engaged

---

[21] "Le Prétoire de Pilate à l'époque byzantine," RB 91 (1984) 161-177.

[22] "Activités archéologiques de l'École Biblique et Archéologique Française à Jérusalem depuis 1890," RB 94 (1987) 397-424.

[23] See J. Burtchaell, Catholic Theories of Biblical Inspiration since 1810. A Review and Critique, Cambridge: CUP, 1969, 234-237.

[24] Traité de la Prophétie, Paris: Revue des Jeunes, 1947. The American version published in 1961 is not a simple translation, but incorporates Benoit's changes and additions, Prophecy and Inspiration. A Commentary on the Summa Theologica II-II, Questions 171-178, translated by M. Sheridan and A. Dulles, New York: Desclee, 1961, 13.

[25] J. Burtchaell, Catholic Theories, 245.

in published dialogue with those who commented on his theory Benoit's thought developed, but he never wrote the definitive book which he had promised as one of the series of supplementary volumes to the Bible de Jérusalem.[26] This was unfortunate because as one surveys his writings on inspiration it becomes clear that two Benoits are struggling for expression, and that the one who is dominant at the beginning is not the one who speaks loudest at the end. Failure to resolve this tension, when combined with the realization of the complexity of the problem in a new context, would explain why the promised synthesis never appeared.

The *first* Benoit is the Thomistic theologian. To a certain extent this attitude was imposed on him by the nature of his first publication on the subject in 1947, but it was also very congenial to his personality. He thought of himself as a theologian, and his formation in this field had been purely scholastic. Not surprisingly, therefore, his analysis of the interplay of the speculative and practical judgments and of the working of divine grace was characterized by a masterful use of fine distinctions in order to lay bare what happens in the psychology of the sacred writer. Under the pressure of objections the distinctions became more and more rarified.

His focus on the act of judgment was related to the problem of inerrancy. The guarantee of truth, he insisted, could not be established speculatively, as if it were intrinsically related to a certain category of subjects, but only empirically by a careful assessment of the writer's intention. Three aspects must be kept in mind when making this calculation: the formal object of the judgment (i.e. the point of view from which the subject is treated), the degree of affirmation (i.e. the weight the writer attaches to a statement), and the quality of his committment to communication (i.e. the degree to which he is concerned to get an idea across).[27] The natural inference is that it is here that he is most original, but it is then disconcerting to find that no one highlights what is truely distinctive in his contribution. This hint that the assessment of Benoit as primarily a speculative theoretician might not be correct is confirmed by Benoit himself. On this level he claimed to have done no more than clarify, correct, complement the much older studies of Calmes, Merkelbach, and Pesch.[28] It is the other Benoit who was the creative thinker, and the seminal nature of his contribution has not been given the prominence it deserves.

---

[26] See his Prophecy and Inspiration, 13.

[27] Prophecy and Inspiration, 134-135, and RB 63 (1956) 420. – Discussions of Benoit's work on inspiration have tended to focus exclusively on these aspects. See the surveys of J. Burtchaell, Catholic Theories, 239-247, and of B. Vawter, Biblical Inspiration, Philadelphia: Westminster/ London: Hutchinson, 1972, 102-104.

[28] Aspects of Biblical Inspiration, Chicago: Priory Press, 1965, 124 note 115.

Pierre Benoît, O.P.

The *second* Benoit is the exegete wedded to the historical-critical method. Both Burtchaell [29] and Vawter [30] give the credit to R. A. F. MacKen-
zie, SJ, for being the first to question the validity of the concept of 'author',
which is assumed by scholastic treatments of inspiration.[31] Eleven years
earlier, however, Benoit had written, "The old idea of a single author personally composing and writing the entire work which bears his name has gradually had to give way to less simple but more realistic conceptions. Many
of the prophetic books today appear to be collections -- sometimes rather
disorderly collections -- of oracles and speeches compiled by later disciples.
Some of these are perhaps not even the work of the principal prophet to
whom they were ascribed." [32] For Benoit such a multiplicity of authors posed no problem. All who contributed anything to the final product, be it
even a copyist who made a significant alteration, enjoyed the charism of inspiration.

Here we find in embryo the social understanding of inspiration, which is
associated with the name of J. L. McKenzie.[33] This scholar, however, explicitly proclaimed his indebtedness to Benoit for "the most constructive
addition to the theory of inspiration in the last fifty years," namely, "the social character of inspiration."[34] In 1954 Benoit had analogously extended
inspiration to the people of God as readers of Sacred Scripture,[35] and in
1959 he stressed that the inspired text is the outcome of a long history directed throughout by the Holy Spirit, "who was not satisfied merely to move a
number of authors to write, but rather began by bringing heroes to life and
inspiring prophets and apostles to speak, who, in brief, directed the whole
history of salvation before committing it to the books which he transmitted
to the church."[36] The society which existentially proclaimed God's revelation by obedience to his will was inspired.

This line of thought made it impossible for Benoit to deny inspiration to
the church, whose history is directed by the Holy Spirit.[37] In this sense inspiration is an ecclesial charism. This insight had already been proposed by
K. Rahner, but in a slightly different sense and limited to the apostolic
age.[38] For Benoit it was a permanent possession of the church, but he never

---

[29] Catholic Theories, 248.

[30] Biblical Inspiration, 104.

[31] "Some Problems in the Field of Inspiration," CBQ 20 (1958) 1-8.

[32] Prophecy and Inspiration, 123.

[33] "The Social Character of Inspiration," CBQ 24 (1962) 115-124.

[34] "Social Character," 118-119.

[35] Initiation Biblique, éd. A. Robert et A. Tricot, Paris: Desclee, 1954, 30-31.

[36] Aspects of Biblical Inspiration, 31.

[37] Aspects of Biblical Inspiration, 32.

[38] Inspiration in the Bible (QD 1), New York: Herder, 1960.

explored the potentially explosive implications of this idea. The extension
that Benoit gives to inspiration necessarily implies that he understood it
analogically. Only hinted at in his first study,[39] this element progressively
occupies an ever greater place in his thought,[40] and explains the breadth of
vision he brought to what had been a sterile problematic.[41]

The tension between Benoit the theologian and Benoit the exegete is
easy to detect in what has already been said. It becomes blatant when they
deal with inerrancy. The former writes, "Truth is the *adaequatio rei et intellectus.'* It exists only in the judgment ... the formal act by which the in-
tellect *(intellectus)* affirms its conformity *(adaequatio)* to the object of
knowledge *(res),*" [42] and he is concerned to limit the number of instances in
which such a judgment is found, because only in them is the truth of the Bible at stake. Burtchaell gives the impression that such reductionism is all
there is to Benoit's understanding of biblical truth.[43]

Benoit the exegete, however, condemns this vision of truth as a Greco-
Roman concept heavily conditioned by rationalism and positivism. He
stigmatizes it as a totally inappropriate category with which to approach the
Bible, whose concept of truth is practical rather than speculative, since its
authors were Semites. He insists, "It is as Semites that we must open this
book [the Bible] in order to there encounter God as he offers himself to us:
a God who acts, who enters our history, who speaks to our heart, who
'reveals' himself, certainly to our minds, but by a lived-out process which
calls forth in response a type of knowledge which is made up of love,
obedience, and total committment. This approach is totally foreign to our
western formation, but it is imperative that we absorb it if we are to read the
Bible as it wishes to be read."[44]

The liberation latent in this approach to the truth of the Bible, which
dates from 1954, was made explicit two years later when he maintained that
inspired truth is to be found, not in any particular text, but in the Bible as a
whole. "Just as the teaching of each verse, of each chapter, is perceived only
by seeing that verse, that chapter in the framework of the book as a whole,
so the teaching of each biblical book merits our response of faith only according to the place it occupies in the Bible as a whole."[45]

---

[39] Prophecy and Inspiration, 120, 145.

[40] Initiation Biblique, 23, and especially "Analogies of Inspiration" in Aspects of Biblical
Inspiration, 13-35.

[41] J. T. Forestell, CSB, has acutely observed that "the core of Benoit's thought lies in
what he describes as the analogous nature of inspiration" ("The Limitation of Inerrancy," CBQ 20 [1959] 9).

[42] Prophecy and Inspiration, 134.

[43] Catholic Theories, 243.

[44] Initiation Biblique, 43.

[45] "Note complémentaire sur l'inspiration," RB 62 (1956) 421.

This radical insight, which transforms the whole problematic of inerrancy, was given extraordinary precision ten years later, "God does not commit his whole truth to each phrase of the Bible: to take literally an expression that he will later correct is to do violence to his Word. I have said 'correct,' because the divine pedagogy has not developed only by means of complements and refinements; there have also been corrections, and indeed suppressions."[46] In order that there be no ambiguity he continued, "God took two thousand years to write a huge book, whose chapters are so many distinct volumes composed by a great variety of authors. In the course of this long process he expressed his truth by successive touches. In order to attain this truth, one has to accept the whole work, from the first stammerings to the fulness of revelation in Christ. There only, when God has said his last word, can humanity claim to grasp the inerrancy of his revelation; in brief it is in the whole work."[47] This is Benoit at his theological best -- the Thomist is nowhere in sight -- drawing on a profound insight into the complementarity of all the components of the Bible. It was from insights such as this that canonical criticism eventually developed.

Given Benoit's recognition of the crucial importance of the canon, and his extension of inspiration to all who made any contribution to the final text of the Bible, it was perhaps inevitable that he shoud have argued in favor of the inspiration of the Septuagint, the Greek translation of the OT.[48] This proposal generated considerable discussion, which was by and large unsympathetic to Benoit's point of view.[49]

---

[46] "La vérité dans la sainte Écriture," in his collected essays Exégèse et Théologie, Paris: Cerf, 1968, III, 153.

[47] "La vérité dans la sainte Écriture," 154. It is very difficult to see any difference between Benoit's position here and that of Burtchaell, who gives the impression of making an original contribution by writing three years later, "In sum the Church does find inerrancy in the Bible, if we can agree to take that term in its dynamic sense, and not a static one. Inerrancy must be the ability, not to avoid all mistakes, but to cope with them, remedy them, survive them, and eventually even profit from them." (Catholic Theories, 303). Burtchaell had been somewhat supercilious in his discussion of Benoit's work, and it must have been with a secret smile that his old professor gave him a little pat on the head for this belated discovery; see his review in RB 91 (1974) 121-124, here 124.

[48] "La Septante est-elle inspirée?" in Vom Wort des Lebens. FS Max Meinertz, ed. N. Adler, Munster: Aschendorf, 1951, 41-49; "L'inspiration des Septante d'après les Pères," in L'homme devant Dieu. FS Henri de Lubac, Paris: Aubier, 1963, I, 169-187.

[49] E.g. P. A. Auvray, "Comment se pose le problème de l'inspiration des Septante?" RB 59 (1952) 321-336. F. Dreyfus, "L'inspiration de la Septante. Quelques difficultés a surmonter," RSPT 49 (1965) 210-220.

The Gospels

If Benoit is recognized as having revived the debate about inspiration and inerrancy, he also deserves credit for having reintroduced Form Criticism to Catholic scholars. His 1946 article "Reflexions sur la 'Formgeschichtliche Methode'" was one of the major liberating factors in the development of critical Catholic scholarship after the Second World War. In terms of content there was very little that was new in his presentation. Most if not all of his observations had been anticipated by Lagrange (see pp. 16-17 above), but this in no way diminishes Benoit's contribution. Lagrange's attitude toward Form Criticism had been so negative that Catholic scholars between the two World Wars had avoided the subject, and in consequence had put themselves outside the mainstream of NT studies. Benoit's return to the topic was a conscious test of the freedom granted Catholic scholars by the encyclical "Divino Afflante Spiritu" (1943). It was a couragous gesture, because the encyclical explicitly recognized the presence of obscurantist elements within the church by warning them that "they must avoid that somewhat indiscreet zeal which considers everything new to be for that very reason a fit object for attack or suspicion" [50]

There was no reaction to Benoit's article in either official or scholarly circles. This is more likely to have been due to the amount of intellectual energy deflected into the reconstruction of post-war Europe than to general agreement.[51] Almost by default, therefore, it became a standard to which scholars could appeal. Thus the timing of the article was of prime importance. The second factor contributing to its impact was the pedagogic clarity of its systematic analysis. Without any distortion Benoit simplified the method to the point were anybody could see what Form Criticism was all about, and could appreciate the difference between its factual observations and its philosophical presuppositions. Moreover, he did so with manifest sympathy, and highlighted the positive aspects of the method in such a way as to encourage Catholics to adopt it.[52] It did in fact become part of the normal equipment of serious Catholic exegetes, but it was only in 1964 that the method received the approval of the Pontifical Biblical Commission in a paragraph which is an excellent summary of Benoit's article. [53]

---

[50] CTS translation, London, 1953, para. 49.

[51] The smoldering opposition to "Divino Afflante Spiritu" burst into flames only at the beginning of the 1960s. See J. A. Fitzmyer, "A Recent Roman Scriptural Controversy," TS 22 (1961) 426-444.

[52] Note in particular the conclusion, RB 53 (1946) 512.

[53] Instruction concerning the Historical Truth of the Gospels, para. 5. See J. A. Fitzmyer, "The Biblical Commission's Instruction on the Historical truth of the Gospels," TS 25 (1964) 390-391, 403.

The article on Form Criticism was followed not long afterwards by an equally important study of the Ascension.[54] This was the fruit of a seed sown much earlier. In 1938 Victorien Larranaga, SJ, published a doctoral thesis of almost 700 pages in which he argued for the literal historicity of the Ascension, which took place exactly forty days after the Resurrection.[55] Benoit gave it an unusually brief review for a work of this type and the words of praise were decidedly perfunctory.[56] Experienced book reviewers will immediately recognize this phenomenon as an indication that Larranaga's volume had given Benoit an idea which he intended to develop later. Virtually everything in the article which he eventually wrote is found somewhere in Larranaga's exhaustive compilation. Benoit's originality lies in the way he set up the problem. Whereas Larranaga had dealt with the issue as a defense of the traditional understanding of the Ascension against rationalist criticism, Benoit considered it in terms of diversity within the New Testament.

Today this would pass without remark; in fact the reverse would draw criticism. Things were not the same forty years ago. Despite the recognition of the individuality of NT writers found in major commentaries, e.g. those of Lagrange, the vast majority of scholars and believers operated on the unquestioned and unspoken assumption that all NT documents said the same thing theologically. Works were being presented as biblical theology, whose framework was derived from the Summa Theologica of St Thomas Aquinas, and in which NT data were ruthlessly harmonized to provide answers to scholastic questions.[57] In this intellectual climate there was a definite risk in forcing people to recognize that NT authors exhibited radically different attitudes to Jesus' transition from earth to heaven. Some sacred writers do not mention it at all. Others treat it in purely theological terms as the invisible exaltation of Christ to the right hand of God. Just one author, Luke, presents it as an historical fact, a visible physical ascension. Moreover, Luke's own dating of the event is not only inconsistent, but the version of Acts (40 days later) is contradicted by the second group. They see it as the continuation of the upward movement of the Resurrection and so assign it to the same day.

How did Benoit reconcile such diverse opinions? Despite their inspired character he could not give equal importance to all, and his refusal to do so was another breakthrough. "It is clear that the invisible, transcendant accession of the risen Christ to the divine world is the essential element of the mystery, that which is supremely important for the faith. His visible departure from this earth is only a secondary aspect, which in itself is not neces-

---

54 "L'Ascension," RB 56 (1949) 161-203.

55 L'Ascension de Notre-Seigneur dans le Nouveau Testament, Rome: PBI, 1938.

56 RB 48 (1939) 130-131.

57 E.g. F. Ceuppens, Theologia Biblica, I-IV, Rome:Marietti, 1938-1950.

sary." [58] He then diluted the historicity implicit in this latter phrase by insisting, "Both are equally 'historical' in the sense that both belong equally to the web of human events."[59] His next step was to evoke Luke's intention and to stress his need for a dramatic finale to the post-resurrection appearances in order to prepare the way for the descent of the Holy Spirit at Pentecost. The highly nuanced way in which Benoit made these points is a model of discrete indirect persuasion.

The intelligent reader who had been picking up the carefully placed clues should by now have concluded that the physical ascension was merely a literary device created by Luke to move Jesus definitively from the historical scene. This was undoubtedly Benoit's intention, but he could not say so explicitly. The sophisticated reader of the period would have been aware that he had to contend with censors notorious for the sollicitude with which they catered to the unspoken sensitivities of the most conservative element in the Vatican. Thus at the very end Benoit was careful to speak of the Ascension as "a visible manifestation" of the mysterious exaltation which took place on Easter Sunday, and to describe it in language typical of the theological rhetoric of the time as "an indulgent concession made to our weakness as beings with senses."[60]

"Divino Afflante Spiritu" would have remained a dead letter were it not for the type of prudent pioneering exemplified by Benoit's studies of Form Criticism and the Ascension. They extended the limits of acceptability, but in such a way as to avoid the dangers of a backlash which might have set Catholic biblical studies back a generation. Dissimulation cannot have been pleasant, but it was necessary. The *sacrificium intellectus* was for the good of the church, and Benoit had a perfect role model in Lagrange who had not always felt free to say exactly what he thought.

The few years (1932-35) which he spent with Lagrange made an indelible impression on Benoit. Lagrange became for him the model of the scholar-religious dedicated to science and totally committed to the church. Throughout his life Benoit consciously strove to meet the personal and professional standards set by the one whom he revered above all. Under this stimulus he reached heights which he might not have achieved otherwise. There was, however, another side. Lagrange was a genius and his literary productivity is without parallel -- 29 massive books, 248 lengthy scientific articles on a wide variety of subjects, and over 1500 book reviews. This was the standard against which Benoit unrealistically measured himself. The volume of scholarship increased exponentially throughout his career, and it took much more time and energy just to keep up to date. But Benoit would never permit this to function as an excuse, and he lived with the nagging sense of somehow having failed Lagrange.

---

[58] "L'Ascension," 195.

[59] "L'Ascension," 196.

[60] "L'Ascension," 408 and 402.

Benoit's approach to the gospels was certainly influenced by that of Lagrange, but he was anything but a servile disciple content to parrot the opinions of his master. Though discretion was still imperative, there was a significant improvement in the intellectual climate in the 1950s, which enabled Benoit to ask questions which would not have been tolerated in the time of Lagrange.

The latter, for example, in his treatment of the death of Judas did not even hint at the discrepancies between Mt 27:3-10 and Acts 1:16-20.[61] Thirty years later Benoit was able to introduce a detailed discussion of these texts by insisting that the fundamental problem was to determine "the rather odd literary form of these stories and the degree of historical precision that one has the right to expect of it."[62] He concluded that they were popular legends, which contained an element of truth, and which in the case of Matthew had been elaborated by "a very subtle midrashic interpretation of various prophetic texts, which supposes the intervention of Christian scribes versed in the Scriptures."[63] This study manifested Benoit's mastery of the literary critical method and consolidated his position as a prominent member of the small group of exegetes who brought Catholic scholarship into the mainstream of international NT studies.

Despite his talent for gospel criticism, Benoit's papers in this field do not reflect any systematic program of research. The article on the death of Judas was written to honour A. Wikenhauser, and virtually all his major gospel articles were composed in response to invitations to contribute to special volumes, notably the Silver Jubilee issue of the CBQ (1963; "'Et toi-meme, un glaive te transpercera l'âme' [Lc 2,35]"), and Festschriften for Joachim Jeremias (1960; "Marie-Madeleine et les disciples au tombeau selon Jn 20,1-8"), Oscar Cullmann (1962; "Les outrages à Jésus prophète [Mc 14,65 et par.]"), and Fathers Donato Baldi and Paulin Lemaire, OFM (1962; "Les épis arrachés [Mt 12,1-8 et par.]").

Uniformly these articles are characterized by exactitude in observation, precision in analysis, and mastery of the secondary literature, in addition to the more important qualities of insight and originality. Both history and theology are each given their due place. The article in the Baldi-Lemaire volume, however, had a different objective. It was a frontal attack on the one real dogma of NT studies, the Two Source Theory, and Benoit did not mince his words, "This simplistic confidence is regretable, because it blinds the exegete to facts which contradict the theory and prohibits observations which would advance biblical research."[64] He had little difficulty in

---

61 L'Évangile selon Saint Matthieu (EB), Paris: Gabalda, 1923, 514.

62 "La mort de Judas," in Synoptische Studien. FS Alfred Wikenhauser, München: Zink, 1954, 1.

63 "La mort de Judas," 19.

64 Liber Annuus 13 (1962-63) 76.

showing that in certain respects Mt 12:1-8 is more primitive than Mk 2:23-28. It was by studies such as this that Catholic NT scholarship came of age. It followed the line dictated by the evidence, without concern for a sterile apologetic or an obsequious acceptance of the majority view.

The one aspect of gospel studies on which Benoit wrote spontaneously, and on which he regularly taught a class, was the Infancy Narratives in the opening chapters of the gospels of Matthew and Luke. Curiously, it is precisely in this area that he failed to follow consistently the path indicated by the evidence. His position is an unusual blend of creative new insights and conservative inhibitions.[65]

He took seriously the discrepancies between the accounts of Matthew and Luke, and refused the traditional harmonisation, which makes the Lukan narrative the basis of the Christmas story. He recognized that Matthew provided the more plausible historical framework, and so accepted that Joseph was a native of Bethlehem who only went to Nazareth at a later stage. But then instead of investigating why Luke's account should be so different, he proposed a new reconstruction of what actually happened.

Joseph went from Bethlehem to Nazareth to complete the formalities of an arranged marriage with Mary whose home was there. She had had an ineffable experience of God during which she had become pregnant. Nonetheless Joseph married her, and intended to stay in Nazareth until the birth. Then came the census which explains, not only why he had to register in Bethlehem (it was his permanent domicile), but why he brought his pregnant wife with him. By law she was not obliged to accompany him, but if she had not done so now, he would have had to make a second trip to escort her to her new home in the south. In Bethlehem they were visited by the Magi after the birth of Jesus. A subsequent persecution prompted the flight to Egypt. Herod's death offered the hope of return, but the character of his successor, Archelaus, made it imprudent to return to Bethlehem, and so Joseph chose the alternative of a new life in Nazareth, the village of his wife.

Benoit himself saw one objection to this reconstruction. Joseph would not have needed to look for an inn in his home town of Bethlehem (Lk 2:7). In reply he argued that *katalyma* need mean only a large room, which he assumed was the living room of Joseph's parental home.[66]

This wickedly clever reconstruction makes very adroit use of the known regulations concerning censuses in the Roman empire at the time of Christ.

---

[65] An overview of his position is given in "Les récits évangéliques de l'enfance de Jésus," in Exégèse et Théologie, Paris: Cerf, 1982, IV, 63-94. He also commented briefly on Mt 1-2 and Lk 1-2 in Benoit-Boismard, Synopse des quatre évangiles en français, Paris: Cerf, 1972, II, 61-66.

[66] "'Non erat locus in diversorio' (Lc 2,7)," in Mélanges bibliques en hommage au R. P. Béda Rigaux, Gembloux: Duculot, 1970, 173-186.

Its weakness is that it simply sets aside Luke's understanding of the events surrounding the birth of Jesus. Benoit's response was that we should not expect fiddling accuracy of mundane detail in a document concerning the Saviour's entrance into the world.

Yet when a specific detail was questioned, he moved heaven and earth to maintain Luke's veracity. I refer to his treatment of the census of Quirinius (Lk 2:2).[67] While admitting that a mistake on the part of Luke was the obvious and simple solution,[68] he personally preferred a more tortuous hypothesis. "The census of A.D. 6 by Quirinius was the final step in an incorporation of Judaea into the Empire which had been prepared since the end of the reign of Herod by measures such as the census of which Luke speaks. This explains, or if you wish excuses, the anticipation of the evangelist."[69] To say the least, the formulation is disingenuous, because the evidence for anything like a census in the last years of Herod is decidedly unimpressive.[70] Moreover, there is no evidence for the series of administrative measures culminating in the census of Quirinius, which Benoit's solution demands.

Such defensiveness is difficult to explain. There was a deeply conservative streak in Benoit's personality, but only here did he attempt to defend the indefensible. A much truer apologetic is to be found in his immensely detailed linguistic analysis of Lk 1. This refuted the widespread view that Luke drew his information about the infancy of John the Baptist from a Johannite document, which then served as the framework on which the evangelist constructed his narrative of the infancy of Jesus.[71]

The Dead Sea Scrolls

A gospel at Qumran! This sensational news astounded the scientific world in 1972, when José O'Callaghan, SJ, claimed to have identified parts of Mark, Acts, Romans, 1 Timothy, James, and 2 Peter in the Greek Fragments from cave 7 at Qumran. [72]

---

67   "Quirinius (Recensement de)," DBS 9 (1978) 693-720.

68   "Quirinius," 713.

69   "Quirinius," 715-716.

70   When Benoit's extremely erudite discussion is boiled down to its essentials only two points remain: (1) the emperor Augustus had a policy of regular censuses; (2) the loyalty oath imposed by Herod c. 7 B.C. (Josephus, AJ, 17:42), whose historicity is not accepted by all, must have been accompanied by a census ("Quirinius," 697-698).

71   "L'enfance de Jean-Baptiste selon Luc 1," NTS 3 (1956-57) 169-194.

72   "Papiros neotestamentarios en la cueva 7 de Qumran?" Biblica 53 (1972) 91-104; " 1 Tim 3,16; 4,1.3 en 7Q?" Biblica 53 (1972) 362-367; "Tres probables papiros neotestamentarios en la cueva 7 de Qumran," Studia Papyriologica 11 (1972) 83-89.

Given the intimate involvement of the École Biblique in all aspects of the Qumran problem (buying of manuscripts, excavation, publication), it would have been impossible for any staff member to have held aloof from the contagious excitement of continuous new discoveries. Benoit participated actively in the intense discussions generated by each new text, and visited the excavations at every opportunity. His expertise in first-century Greek made him the ideal person to publish the non-biblical Greek documents found in the Wadi Murabba'at, a task which he accomplished with exemplary care and speed in the second volume of "Discoveries in the Judaean Desert" (1961). Naturally he had been consulted by M. Baillet in the latter's publication of the Greek texts from Cave 7.[73]

Benoit, therefore, had a certain propriatory interest in O'Callaghan's revelations. Had he missed something very important during the pre-publication discussions concerning those texts? After all, he not Baillet was the NT expert! If O'Callaghan was right, the implications and dangers were clear. There would have to be a radical revision downwards of the dating of most NT books, which in turn could give rise to sensationalized fundamentalism.

Benoit also had an official responsibility, because in 1971 he had succeeded Roland de Vaux, OP, as the chairman of the international group charged with the official publication of the Qumran manuscripts. This gave him access to the originals conserved in the Rockefeller Museum, Jerusalem, and he made it his business to verify the readings on which O'Callaghan's reconstructions depended. He found that a significant number were either extremely dubious or without foundation.[74] This proved to be a more effective answer than those of scholars who accepted O'Callaghan's readings and then strove to propose alternative identifications based on the Septuagint.

Once the authenticity and date of the Dead Sea Scrolls had been determined, scholars realized that they belonged to a unique category as regards NT studies. They were documents which revealed the inner life of a Palestinian Jewish community contemporary with Jesus and the early church, and which presented none of the dating problems which bedevilled the critical use of rabbinic materials. Once literary contacts were perceived and doctrinal analogies recognized, there began a trickle of comparative studies, which in the 1950s assumed the porportions of a flood. There were so many publications that control became virtually impossible. The academic scene came to resemble a new gold field where claim and counter-claim compounded confusion.

---

73 M. Baillet, J. T. Milik, R. de Vaux, Les 'Petites Grottes' de Qumrân (DJD 3), Oxford: Clarendon, 1962, 144-145.

74 "Note sur les fragments grecs de la grotte 7 de Qumrân," RB 79 (1972) 321-324; "Nouvelle note sur les fragments grecs de la grotte 7 de Qumrân," RB 80 (1973) 5-12.

The situation disturbed Benoit as it did many others. When a selection of the various comparative studies were discussed at the meeting of the Society for New Testament Studies at the University of Aarhus in 1960, his colleagues realized that Benoit was the best qualified to draw up a methodological statement which would bring some sanity and order into the debate. The professional compliment was very flattering, but he was expected to have the paper ready for the closing session. Much midnight oil was burnt, and the result was a memorable lecture, which became the very influential article "Qumran and the New Testament."[75]

Benoit insisted that NT dependency on Essene documents became an issue only when there was no possibility that both depended on a common source such as the OT. Once this condition had been met, the date of Essene influence should be determined, followed by a specification of the quality of the contribution. Within the framework of these methodological principles, Benoit claimed that Essene influence could in fact be detected in the NT, but only in the second Christian generation (Paul, John), and in secondary matters. At the time many who agreed with the principles would have found the prudence of the conclusions excessive. Subsequent assessments, however, have served only to confirm the accuracy of his judgments.[76]

Early Christianity

The literary skils which Benoit developed in his gospel studies were also applied to the Acts of the Apostles. He only wrote two articles in this field, both inspired by invitations to contribute to Festschriften, but the finesse of his observations and the clarity of his argumentation makes one regret that he did not give the history of the early church a greater share of his attention.

The three major summaries of Acts (2:42-47; 4:32-35; 5:12-16) had long been recognized as complex, but there was no unanimity as to the identity of the interpolations and the intention of the editor. In a tribute to M. Goguel Benoit convincingly argued that 2:42,46-47; 4:32,34-35; and 5:15-16 represented the original form of these summaries.[77] This made it clear that the editor's insertions occur near the beginning of each summary, pre-

---

[75] Published in NTS 7 (1960-61) 276-296, it antedated S. Sandmel's, "Parallelomania," JBL 81 (1962) 1-13, and H. Braun's magisterial study Qumran und das Neue Testament, Tübingen: Mohr (Siebeck), 1966; the articles on which this latter volume is based appeared in 1963.

[76] See J. A. Fitzmyer, "The Qumran Scrolls and the New Testament after Forty Years," RevQ 13 (1988) [= Memorial Jean Carmignac] 609-620. J. Murphy-O'Connor, "Qumran and the New Testament," in The New Testament and its Modern Interpreters, ed. Eldon Jay Epp and George WQ. MacRea, Atlanta: Scholars Press, 1989, 55-71.

[77] "Remarques sur les 'Sommaires' des Actes II, IV, et V," in Aux sources de la Tradition chrétienne. FS M. Goguel, Neuchâtel-Paris: Delachaux et Niestlé, 1950, 1-10.

sumably in order not to break the links between the summaries and the associated narratives. The basic framework of the first part of Acts, therefore, already existed. The style of the interpolations, in Benoit's estimation, excluded Luke. This led him to suggest that there may have been more than one edition of Acts, an hypothesis which was to be worked out in detail by his colleague M.-E. Boismard forty years later.

Benoit made a much more significant contribution in a volume celebrating the Golden Jubilee of the Pontifical Biblical Institute in 1959. There was general agreement that Gal 2:1-10 and Acts 15 contained different versions of the same crucial conference in Jerusalem between those who favored the mission to the gentiles and those who opposed it. The problem was that Paul specified that it was only his second visit to Jerusalem (Gal 1:18; 2:1), whereas according to Acts it was his fourth (9:26; 11:29-30; 12:25; 15:1-2). Many efforts had been made to solve this problem by postulating overlapping sources; when they were combined, two versions of the same visit could have appeared as separate visits. A very common opinion attributed Acts 11:27-30 + 12:25 + 15:1-33 to the same source, which was parallel to Gal 2:1-10. Benoit refined this hypothesis, and avoided the difficulty of placing the conference before the first missionary journey (Acts 13-14), by showing that Acts 15:1-2 was a redactional suture created by Luke to link 11:30 and 15:3, which meant of course that 12:25 was also redactional.[78]

This should have indicated to Benoit that Paul was a better guide than Luke as regards the chronology of his own ministry, but he was not prepared to accept the consequences for the historical value of Acts of the consistent application of such a methodological principle.[79] Thus he failed to realize that Acts 18:22 is also a reference to Paul's second visit to Jerusalem, and the outline of Paul's life, which he gave in the Bible de Jérusalem (1973 = Jerusalem Bible, 1985), is vitiated by his failure to give the data of the authentic letters priority over the information of Acts.[80]

---

[78] "La deuxième visite de saint Paul à Jérusalem," Biblica 40 (1959) 778-792 = Studia Biblica et Orientalia II (AnBib 11), Rome: PBI, 1959, 210-224. In considering the opening of Acts 15 to be redactional Benoit anticipated a key element in G. Lüdemann's fundamental study, Paul: Apostle to the Gentiles. Studies in Chronology, Philadelphia: Fortress, 1984, 149-150.

[79] See his review in RB 59 (1952) 126-127 of J. Knox, Chapters in a Life of Paul, New York-Nashville: Abingdon-Cokesbury, 1950.

[80] It must be emphasized, however, that Benoit is far from alone in this option. In the most recent study of Paul's life, J. A. Fitzmyer explicitly admits that "in the reconstruction of Paul's life preference must be given to what Paul has told us about himself," but nonetheless follows Acts (contrary to Paul) in dating the second missionary journey after the Jérusalem conference, which has serious consequences for the dating of the epistles (Paul and His Theology: A Brief Sketch, 2nd. ed., Englewood Cliffs: Prentice Hall, 1988, 3-5 and 14-17 = NJBC 79:5-6 and 31-38).

The Pauline Letters

This, however, was of little importance for Benoit's personal work on Paul, because what counted for his purposes was the relative order of the epistles. 1 and 2 Thessalonians were written early during Paul's first visit to Corinth in the course of his second missionary voyage. Ephesus became Paul's center during his third voyage. 1 Corinthians was dated early in his stay there, and Philippians towards the end. 2 Corinthians was composed in Macedonia shortly after his departure from Ephesus. Galatians was written before he reached Corinth from which he sent Romans. Accepting the authenticity of Colossians and Ephesians (see below), Benoit assigned them to the last period of Paul's life. Philemon and Colossians were written towards the end of Paul's Roman imprisonment, and Ephesians shortly afterwards.

In the 1973 edition of the <u>Bible de Jérusalem</u> (p. 1623) Benoit maintained that the Pastorals were written four or five years after Ephesians and during the lifetime of Paul, who would have given greater than usual freedom to a secretary. In 1977, however, he modified this position. "Although nothing, in my opinion, prohibits placing them in the last years of the Apostle, their style, language and doctrinal concerns clash too violently with the earlier letters for me to accord them more than indirect Pauline paternity."[81] What precisely he meant by this is far from clear (unauthorized letters, which Paul did not repudiate? authorized letters whose content Paul was not aware of?), but he eventually accepted the common view that the Pastorals reflect the ethos of the post-Pauline generation (<u>Jerusalem Bible</u>, 1985, p. 1863).

In all his summaries of the Apostle's thought Benoit explicitly recognized the centrality of Jesus Christ. It was only late in his career, however, that he formally articulated the understanding of Christ which informed his view of Paul's theology.[82]

He insisted on three series of texts. The first depicted the advent of Jesus on the stage of history as a change of condition (2 Cor 5:22; 8:9; Gal 4:4). The second gave the historical Jesus in his preexistent state a role in the creation of the universe (1 Cor 8:6; Col 1:15-16). The third spoke of a passage from heavenly preexistence to earthly existence (Gal 4:4; Phil 2:6-11; Rom 10:6; Eph 4:9-10). To Benoit this combination suggested "that Jesus, the concrete historical personage whom one met on earth, had not waited for the moment of the incarnation to come into being; he already existed although in a situation other than his earthly situation."[83]

---

[81] "L'évolution du langage apocalyptique dans le corpus paulinien," in <u>Apocalypses et Théologie de l'Espérance</u> (LD 95), Paris: Cerf, 1977, 302.

[82] "Préexistence et incarnation," RB 77 (1970) 5-29.

[83] "Préexistence," 19.

In order to explain this phenomenon Benoit postulated that the first act of creation was to bring into being a human nature to be united with the Second Person of the Trinity.[84] As a creature this God-Man could not belong to divine eternity. Nor can he have existed humanly before his conception in Mary's womb. Therefore, according to Benoit, he must have existed in an intermediate form of duration, the 'time' of salvation-history. He entered normal time and history only at the incarnation, and after the resurrection he returned to his previous mode of being.[85]

Benoit was deeply disappointed when the only reaction produced by this hypothesis was a shocked silence. His experience at the Second Vatican Council had brought home to him how rigid and insipid conventional theological categories had become. He wanted the church to experience the freedom and vitality of an authentic biblical theology. His intention was to open a dialogue between speculative theologians and exegetes by this attempt to reformulate in NT categories a central dogma, which hitherto had been articulated in essentially philosophical terms. When his challenge was not taken up, he consoled himself with the thought that the moment was not ripe for radical new ideas to be taken seriously. He was confirmed in his interpretation by the fact that his first draft had been turned down by the Roman censors.

The shock of his colleagues, however, was not due to what they perceived as unacceptable radicalism. With the exception of O. Cullmann, who was thinking along the same lines, they could not understand how a twentieth century exegete could even evoke such categories. What they had not realized is that there were two Benoits, whom we have already met in the discussion about his theories on inspiration. Apropos of preexistence and incarnation, it was Benoit the exegete who made the observations, which Benoit the scholastic then theorized about. While his instincts were right about the truth of the Bible, they were flawed in this case by an unjustified assumption. He presumed that Paul was aware of the divinity of Christ in the same way as John, and saw allusions to prexistence where in fact there were none.[86] His speculative logic then inflated the initial error into an hypothesis which only intensified the obscurity of the mystery of the person of Jesus and made an unnecessary demand on an overburdened faith.

Benoit's detailed knowledge of the text of the epistles is manifest in his outline of Paul's theology which he summarized in six points. (1) The believer is united with Christ, (2) delivered from sin and reconciled with God, (3) and justified by faith. (4) Since the Law is no longer necessary, salvation is universal, (5) and touches our corporeal existence. (6) Through union

---

[84] "L'évolution du langage apocalyptique," 306.

[85] "Préexistence," 26-27.

[86] See J. D. G. Dunn, Christology in the Making. A New Testament Inquiry into the Origins of the Doctrine of the Incarnation, London: SCM, 1980.

with Christ the believer enters the eschatological age.[87] He also recognized that there was an evolution in Paul's thought. Points 1 and 2 are fundamental to the basic kerygma and appear in all the letters. Points 3, 4, and 5 are the elements which are really distinctive of the Apostle's theology. They are not given the same prominence in each letter and the modalities are developed in various ways to suit the situations of the different communities. It is not clear whether one should speak of auch adaptations as an evolution. Only in point 6 is a substantial evolution evident.[88]

This last observation derived from the contrast between the Great Epistles and the Captivity Epistles. Ephesians had been the subject of Benoit's first major article,[89] and it had led to an invitation from Lagrange to contribute the commentary on Colossians and Ephesians to the Études Bibliques. It was not a responsibility that Benoit could refuse, and it became the major project of his career. Understandably, therefore, the bulk of his Pauline writings were directly related to the various problems of these enigmatic epistles.

The Captivity Epistles

The authenticity of Colossians was not a problem for Benoit. In his view the critical doubts of the 19th century, which Bultmann and a few of his followers vainly sought to keep alive, had been laid to rest by the work of Dibelius, Lohmeyer and Percy, and subsequent scholarship only served to confirm Pauline authorship. Any differences in style between Colossians and earlier letters could be accounted for by a change of secretaries, and the evolution of Paul's thought (the plan of salvation as a 'mystery', the cosmic supremacy of Christ, who is 'head' of the Body which is the church) was made understandable by recognition of the type of heresy he had to face at Colossae.[90]

The standard scepticism of Catholic scholars regarding the existence of Gnosticism in the first century A.D. gave Benoit the freedom to appreciate the insight of J. B. Lightfoot, who claimed that the Colossian heresy resembled Essene teaching, and to develop this hypothesis in the light of the Dead Sea Scrolls. He was one of the rare scholars to recognize that the presence in Asia Minor of the doctrines of a zenophobic Palestinian Jewish sect posed a problem for anyone claiming to find Essene influence in the Colossian heresy. A plausible explanation had to be offered, otherwise the

---

87 "Genèse et évolution de la pensée paulinienne," in Paul de Tarse. Apôtre de notre temps, ed. L. De Lorenzi, Rome: Abbey de S. Paul, 1979, 81-84.

88 "Genèse et évolution," 86. The sixth point received extended treatment in "L'évolution du langage apocalyptique."

89 "L'horizon paulinien de l'épître aux Ephésiens," RB 46 (1937) 342-361, 506-525.

90 "Colossiens (Épître aux)," DBS 7 (1966) 157-170.

conclusion drawn from the similarities would be much less probable. Benoit postulated Alexandria as the middle term, because the Therapeutoi of Philo exhibited Essene traits. From there missionaries, such as Apollos (Acts 18:24-19:7) would have brought their teachings (in somewhat garbled form) to Ephesus, whence they would have penetrated into the Lycus valley.[91]

In the last decade of his life Benoit knew in his heart of hearts that he was never going to expand the brilliant notes of the Bible de Jérusalem fascicle (3rd ed. 1959) into the promised full-scale commentary. Invitations to honor old friends (Morton Smith, C. K. Barrett, and Bo Reicke) fortunately forced him to publish portions of his on-going research. They offer a tantalizing glimpse of what the commentary might have been.

To Bo Reicke he presented an extraordinarly lucid analysis of the eleven textual variants of Col 2:2, and argued persuasively -- against the consensus -- for *eis epignosin tou mysteriou tou theou, en ho*.[92]

If this contribution exhibited his skills in textual criticism, his ability as a lexicographer is nowhere better represented than in his effort, on behalf of Kingsley Barrett, to determine the meaning of *hagioi* in Col 1:12. After a survey of all the relevant Jewish literature, he concluded that this verse was influenced specifically by 1QS 11:7-8. The primary reference, therefore is to angels, but this can be extended to include the elect associated with them, as is the case elsewhere at Qumran.[93]

Benoit's mastery of the secondary literature and his finesse as an exegete are perfectly illustrated in his treatment of a whole pericope, which appeared in the Morton Smith Festschrift. The hymn in Col 1:15-20 has given rise to over 80 studies. These Benoit presented and criticized while working towards his own highly original solution. He found evidence which suggested that after completing Colossians the author (Paul plus an assistant) went back and inserted a hymn (1:15-17 minus v. 16c-e), whose structure served as the framework for his own ideas which he added in 1:18-20.[94]

Ephesians did not benefit by the swing to the Pauline authorship of Colossians in 20th century scholarship. Some independent exegetes would concede that at most it might contain traces of an authentic Pauline letter,

---

[91] This crucial methodological point is not even raised in E. W. Saunders important study, "The Colossian Heresy and Qumran Theology," in Studies in the History and Text of the NT in honor of K. W. Clark (SD 29), ed. B. L. Daniels and M. J. Suggs, Salt Lake City: University of Utah, 1967, 133-145.

[92] "Colossiens 2:2-3," in The New Testament Age, FS Bo Reicke, ed. W. C. Weinrich, Macon: Mercer University, 1984, I, 41-51.

[93] "*Hagioi* en Colossiens 1.12. Hommes ou Anges?" in Paul and Paulinism, FS C. K. Barrett, ed. M. D. Hooker and S. G. Wilson, London: SPCK, 1982, 83-99.

[94] "L'hymne christologique de Col. 1,15-20. Judgement critique sur l'etat des recherches," in Christianity, Judaism and other Greco-Roman Cults (SJLA 12), ed. J. Neusner, Leiden: Brill, 1975, I, 226-263.

which was expanded by an interpolator a generation after Paul's death.[95] Benoit's first Pauline study was a response to this latter hypothesis.[96] He had little difficulty in showing the arbitrary character of the suggested interpolations, and the main thrust of the article was to highlight what was really new in Ephesians,[97] and then to show how and why Paul's thought would have evolved to that point under the pressure of the Colossian crisis.

What might be psychologically possible varies from individual to individual, and even for those predisposed to agree with him Benoit's argument proved no more than that it was not impossible for Paul to have developed the ideas contained in Ephesians. The literary expression was another matter altogether. The stylistic differences might be put to the account of a secretary, but how were the numerous contacts with the other Pauline letters to be explained?

Leaving Colossians aside for the moment, Benoit pointed out that Ephesians had contacts, not only with Pauline letters, but also with other early Christian documents, notably 1 Peter. Taking up an insight of Selwyn, he suggested that they all reflected a baptismal catechesis common to many groups within the early church. This led him to a very important insight, namely, collective responsibility for NT letters. "Behind the personalities of individual authors, of which Paul is an eminent example, one senses a shared catechetical and liturgical tradition to which these authors, even a Paul, are bound."[98] The writers have their individual voices, but at the same time the community speaks through them.

Such a common source, however, is too vague to explain the precise verbal contacts between Colossians and Ephesians. In 1937 it is clear that Benoit thought that Paul in writing Ephesians not long after Colossians must have been inspired by phrases from the latter.[99] Twenty-five years later he undertook the detailed analysis that the problem deserved. On the basis of a selection of passages he wrote, "Ephesians offers clear evidence of meticulous editorial work based on Colossians and in which two complementary techniques are used. On one hand, two passages from Colossians serve as the basis for one in Ephesians.... On the other hand, a single passage of Colossians is used twice, either in the same complex passage of

---

95 E.g. M. Goguel, "Esquisse d'une solution nouvelle du problème de l'épître aux Éphésiens," RHR 111 (1934-35) 254-284; 112 (1935-36) 73-99.

96 "L'horizon paulinien de l'épître aux Ephésiens," RB 46 (1937) 342-361, 506-525.

97 "It has been possible to organize these new elements around two interrelated concepts. One accentuates the cosmological dimension of salvation, which extends to heaven and the spiritual powers which dwell there. The second considers the salvation of believers, less in the interior transformation of their individual souls, than in the global, collective, growth of the social group which they constitute and which mounts progressively towards the heavenly Christ." (L'horizon paulinien," 506).

98 "Ephesiens (Épître aux)," DBS 7 (1966) 207.

99 "L'horizon paulinien," 518-519

Ephesians,... or in various passages dealing with the same subject."[100] He
immediately drew the obvious conclusion, "One hesitates to attribute such
leisurely, detailed, literary mosaic work to Paul."[101]

Benoit thereby admitted precisely what had caused many scholars to
deny the authenticity of Ephesians, but saved himself by the secretary hypothesis. Having done his duty by replying to the Colossians, Paul would have
spoken of his new ecclesiological vision to a disciple, whom he then told to
get it down on paper, where necessary drawing on previous letters and especially Colossians.[102]

At the same time, however, Benoit had to take account of C. Masson's
revival of Hans Holzmann's theory that both Colossians and Ephesians were
dependent on each other.[103] He was prepared to admit only that in certain
cases it looked as if Colossians might be dependent on Ephesians, and displayed evident distaste for any venture into such a morass.[104] Nonetheless
he kept an open mind, and his analysis of Col 1:15-20 forced him to recognize the truth of Holzmann's insight.

As a result he described the relationship between the two letters as follows, "I think that the secretary who put together Colossians, or another
disciple, perhaps with Paul's consent, reworked certain passages of Colossians in order to take advantage of the developments worked out during the
composition of Ephesians. The two epistles, as I have said, are in my view
practically contemporaneous. The letter called 'to the Ephesians' is the letter
that Tychicus and Onesimus carried to the church of Laodicea (Col 4:16), at
the same time as they brought Colossians to the church of Colossae. Worked out together, these epistles influenced each other in a way which is reflected in their literary relations. Basically Ephesians is dependant on Colossians; it takes up and develops the cosmic vision of Colossians in an ecclesiological perspective. But in a number of instances the disciple-editor of
Ephesians -- or another disciple of the Pauline group -- judged it appropriate
to improve Colossians in the light of these new insights."[105] This hypothesis
gives the impression of complete artificiality, but the scenario is not impossible by any means, and those who reject it have not undertaken the minute
literary analysis on which Benoit's position is based.

The theme of the Body of Christ was a key element in Benoit's defense
of the doctrinal authenticity of the Captivity Epistles. In his earlier studies

100 "Rapports litteraires entre les épîtres aux Colossiens et aux Ephésiens," in Neutesta-
     mentliche Aufsätze. FS J. Schmid, ed. J. Blinzler et al., Regensburg: Pustet, 1963, 20.
101 "Rapports littéraires, 20.
102 "Rapports littéraires, 22.
103 L'Épître de saint Paul aux Colossiens (CNT 10), Neuchatel: Delachaux et Niestlé,
     1950, 83-159.
104 "Rapports littéraires," 21.
105 "L'hymne christologique," 253-254.

he somewhat exaggerated the problem, believing that the theme appeared for the first time in the Captivity Epistles. At that stage he considered the body references in 1 Corinthians and Romans to be nothing more than a metaphor to express the moral union of believers in Christ.[106] He returned to the problem in 1956, and in what became a very influential article argued that the Body of Christ did appear in 1 Corinthians and Romans.[107]

This was the result of a deeper appreciation of Paul's sacramental theology within the framework of two Jewish ideas, monistic anthropology and corporate personality. In consequence, Benoit now insisted on the realism of the believers' union with the physical body of the Risen Lord, which is the fruit of Baptism and Eucharist.[108] It was only as a result of this insight, Benoit maintained, that Paul drew on the current concept of the social body to express the unity of believers which flowed from their union with Christ. The idea was Christian, the image profane. The primary referent is the body of Jesus, but "this 'Body of Christ' does not remain limited to this historical individual. Henceforth it incorporates all those who unite themselves to him, by their very bodies in the rite of baptism, and become 'his members'."[109]

The same sacramental understanding of the Body of Christ is found in the Captivity Epistles, but in a developed and modified form. The new elements can be summarized thus, "On one hand, the Body of Christ appears to be more personified and better distinguished from the individual Christ. On the literary level this is evident in the combination of *Soma* with *Ekklesia* and *Kephale*. On the other hand, the Body of Christ is viewed in a more cosmic perspective on salvation. This is manifested by its association with Pleroma."[110]

Benoit insisted that Paul first thought of Christ as 'Head' when reacting against those Colossians who attenuated the role of Christ by giving too much importance to spiritual powers.[111] In response Paul emphasized the authority which Christ had over them by using *kephale* with its biblical

---

[106] See "L'horizon paulinien," and in particular his review in RB 48 (1938) 115-119 of A. Wikenhauser, Die Kirche als der mystische Leib nach dem Apostel Paulus.

[107] "Corps, tête et plérôme dans les épîtres de la captivité," RB 63 (1956) 5-44. The same ideas are expressed in a popular form more suited to the level of the audience in Populus Dei. Vol. 2. Ecclesia. FS Card. Alfredo Ottaviani, Roma: Communio, 1969, 971-1028.

[108] See also his "L'aspect physique et cosmique du salut dans les écrits pauliniens," in Bible et Christologie (Commission Biblique Pontificale), Paris: Cerf, 1984, 253-269.

[109] "Corps, tête et plérôme," 14.

[110] "Corps, tête et plérôme," 21.

[111] These spiritual beings are discussed in greater detail in his "Angélologie et Démonologie pauliniennes. Réflexions sur la nomenclature des Puissances célestes et sur l'origine du mal angélique chez saint Paul," in Foi et Culture à lumière de la Bible (Commission Biblique Pontificale), Torino: Ed. Elle Di Ci, 1981, 217-233.

connotation of 'chief'.[112] His thought then moved to the Hellenistic connotation of kephale, namely, 'source,' which is the link with Body. As its
Head, Christ is the vitalizing principle of the Body.

Having thus explained the genesis of the concept of Head, Benoit had to
do the same for *Pleroma*. In the great epistles Paul relates Christ only to
those who have formally believed. The need to assert the authority of Christ
over the spiritual powers, and by implication over the world they governed,
obliged Paul in Colossians to define the relationship of Christ to unre-
deemed humanity and its societal framework. This he did by adopting the
Stoic term *Pleroma*, which for Benoit is the plenitude of all being, created
and uncreated.[113]

This definition underwent a certain modification through being assumed
into Paul's new synthesis in Ephesians. Paul was now no longer interested in
the spiritual powers. The church filled his field of vision. "It is a vision filled with optimism. Eschatology is 'realized'. The defeat of adverse Powers,
which is still awaited in 1 Cor 15:24-26, is taken as having been achieved in
Eph 1:21f. The baptized, who have already died with Christ but whose resurrection has yet to come according to Rom 6:3-4, and then have risen in
Col 2:12, are by now already seated in heaven with Christ (Eph 2:6). The
incredulity of the Jews, which caused such anguish in chapters 9-11 of
Romans is now a thing of the past: Jews and pagans, reconciled by the cross
of Christ, march in step and in the same Spirit towards the Father (Eph
2:14-18)."[114] The divine plan of salvation is complete. All has been restored to its pristine order under the headship of Christ, and his Body has become coextensive with the whole matrix of being. Thus, "from 'the fulness
of being' which it was in Colossians it [pleroma] becomes the 'fulness of
grace'."[115]

This extremely schematic presentation of the essential points of Benoit's
understanding of the Captivity Epistles does scant justice to the power of a
doctrinal synthesis which remains the best defense of the substantial authenticity of Ephesians.

---

[112] "Corps, tête et plerôme," 25. This is the weakest point of Benoit's reconstruction. He
recognized that *kephale* did not have this connotation in profane Greek, but assumed
that in the LXX it translated *rosh* whose connotation of authority it acquired. *Kephale*, however, is never used to render *rosh* in this sense.

[113] "Corps, tête et plérôme," 32, 37. See also his "The 'plérôma' in the Epistles to the Colossians and the Ephesians," SEA 49 (1984) 136-158.

[114] "The 'plérôma'," 156. For further development of this theme, see his "L'unité de
l'Église selon L'Épître aux Ephésiens," in Studiorum Paulinorum Congressus Internationalis Catholicus 1961, Rome: PBI, 1963, I, 57-77.

[115] "The 'plérôma'," 157.

Salvation and the Jews

Although the Captivity Epistles were Benoit's primary concern, there was one other Pauline document to which he returned again and again, namely, Romans 9-11. The slaughter of six million Jews by the Nazis forced the world to face up to the implications of anti-semitism. It also obliged Christian theologians to reflect more seriously than ever before on the place of the Jews in the divine plan of salvation. Benoit wrote only one article on the subject, within the framework of the discussions of Vatican II on the relations of the church with non-christian religions,[116] but he played his part in the debate by a series of lengthy book reviews.[117]

The critical issue was the situation of contemporary Judaism. There were those who argued that the Jews are still a Chosen People, endowed with all the privileges of pre-Christian Israel, and for whom observance of the Law remained a valid means of salvation.[118] Benoit was severely critical of the caricatural presentation of Judaism which was a staple of Christian teaching,[119] and freely admitted the responsibility of Christians throughout the centuries for violent outbursts of anti-semitism, but he was not prepared to accept such a revision of the church's position. An understandable desire to make reparation for the Holocaust should not be permitted to distort what he understood as divine revelation.

Though individual Jews are not culpable and can be and are in fact saved as people of good will, the Jewish people as such bears the consequences of its refusal of the light. Benoit compared them to the children of a bankrupt, who inherited only ruin, a religion deprived of messianic fulfillment.[120] The plan of salvation will be fulfilled only by the conversion of the Jewish people, which Paul presents as a certitude of the future (Rom 11:25-26). Only then will it once again become a People of God.

---

[116] Published by the Dutch Council Documentation, 144-144a, it is reproduced as "La valeur spécifique d'Israël dans l'histoire du salut," in his collected essays Exégèse et Théologie, Paris: Cerf, 1968, III, 400-421. The same material is treated in "L'Église et Israël," III, 422-441.

[117] In particular the following should be noted RB 55 (1948) 310-312 (K. L. Schmidt); 56 (1949) 610-613 (J. Isaac); 61 (1954) 136-142 (P. Demann); 68 (1961) 458-462 (D. Judant); 71 (1964) 80-92 (G. Baum); 89 (1982) 588-595 (F. Mussner).

[118] A detailed exegetical justification of this view is to be found in F. Mussner, Traktat über die Juden, München: Kösel, 1979, ch. 1, but Benoit had already encountered it in the work of P. Demann and in the reaction of G. Baum.

[119] See RB 61 (1954) 137-138.

[120] See RB 56 (1949) 613. Elsewhere he calls it a religious system no longer conformed to God's plan. ("L'Église et Israël," in Exégèse et Théologie, III, 438)

Yet Benoit refused to place the Jewish people on the same level as other peoples who do not yet know Christ. On the basis of Rom 11:28 he regularly insisted that they are the objects of God's predilection. They were loved the first and, since God does not change, they continue to enjoy a special place in the divine heart.[121] This privilege implied a mission, which Benoit struggled to articulate. The Jewish people is "a permanent sign of religious disquiet."[122] "It remains among the nations a permanent witness to the fearsome demands of the divine choice."[123]

One of the most controversial proposals at Vatican II was a statement on the Jews. Pro-Sionists hoped for a tacit recognition of the state of Israel. Christians from Muslim countries feared an Arab backlash. Within the church the discord was no less bitter. Extreme conservatives maintained that the tradition of the church was being abandoned, while their liberal counterparts worked for a generous gesture of apology. In this malestorm it was inevitable that Benoit should have been solicited for an explanation of the NT perspective on the issue. This was the occasion of the above mentioned article published by the Dutch Council Information.

He provided a critique for French bishops of the second draft of the statement on the Jews on the very day it was presented to the Council (25 September 1964).[124] He found that it lacked balance, and suggested that, if the Council wanted an irenic gesture of reconciliation, it should adopt the literary form of an exhortation or a condemnation of anti-semitism. His personal preference, however, was: "If the matter is to be treated theologically, it has to be done completely and thoroughly, spelling out without fear the things that are pro and contra Israel. The history of salvation is valid only in its integrity, and the integral witness of the New Testament must be respected. Neither doctrinal truth nor pastoral utility is well served by emphasizing only those elements favorable to Israel, while passing over in silence those which are opposed."[125]

Two further revisions of the document did little to satisfy him. On 4 August 1965 he wrote of the second. "It is a good attempt to restore balance, but in my view it is still insufficient. The text as a whole stresses what is favorable to the Jews and avoids what is unfavorable.... This prejudice is particularly evident in the use made of texts of Saint Paul." He went on to

---

[121] See RB 68 (1961) 459; 71 (1964) 89; "Conclusion par mode de synthèse," in Die Israëlfrage nach Röm 9-11, ed. L. De Lorenzi, Rome: Abbey of St Paul, 1977, 233.

[122] RB 68 (1961) 460.

[123] "La valeur spécifique d'Israël," 421.

[124] See G. M.-M. Cottier, "L'historique de la Déclaration," in Les relations de l'Église avec les religions non chrétiennes (Unam Sanctam 61), ed. A.-M. Henry, Paris: Cerf, 1966, 37-78).

[125] From Benoit's private papers.

highlight the misuse of Rom 9:4-5; 11:18; and 11:28. Nonetheless this draft was approved by the Council on 15 October 1965.

The Second Vatican Council

It came as a surprise to find Benoit listed as a consultor of one of the commissions set up to prepare the agenda for the Council. At that stage scholars of his liberal persuasion were kept at a distance, if not actually blackballed. What happened is a curious little story.

Whoever recruited the consultors for the Commission on the Eastern Church -- presumably someone on the staff of the corresponding Roman Congregation -- invited representatives of the three theological institutes in Jerusalem, Basil Talatinian of the Francisan Seminary, Maurice Blondeel of the White Fathers Seminary, and Roland de Vaux of the École Biblique. The last mentioned refused a role in which he was neither competent nor interested. Benoit, however, who was part of the European theological scene, and who was fully aware of the importance that the Council would have in the life of the church, argued very strongly that the École Biblique should be represented. If the present offer was an insult, it could be a steppingstone to a more significant role, and he persuaded de Vaux to suggest his name as a replacement. The Vatican accepted, and during the autumn of 1961 Benoit took part in the deliberations of the commission in Rome.

In September he circulated a paper containing a series of theological reflections which he felt would be helpful in any discussion of the reunification of the Eastern and Western Churches. The key idea was that the unique church has two dimensions, one heavenly and invisible, the other terrestrial and visible. This theme became the leitmotif of the biblically based theological introduction which he wrote for the penultimate draft of the schema "The Unity of the Church" in December 1961. Portions were severely cut, but his wording and framework were preserved in the final version of the proposed schema.[126] It was discussed towards the end of the first session of the Council (27 November-1 December 1962), but it was returned to be fused with two other schemas on the same theme, one produced by the Theological Commission and the other by the Secretariate for Christian Unity.[127]

Such organisational confusion admirably reflected the poor quality of the schemas distributed during the first session of the Council (11 October-8 December 1962). The Council Fathers rejected their narrow traditionalism. They demanded that new schemas should be prepared. They were to be positive, pastoral, open, and ecumenical. A new spirit demanded a new team, and from 1962 the slighted liberal scholars were brought in as expert

---

[126] Pontificia Commissio de Ecclesiis Orientalibus Preparatoria Concilii Vaticani II, documents 155/1961 and 191-192/1961.

[127] See R. Rouquette, La fin d'une chrétienté. Chroniques (Unam Sanctam 69a), Paris: Cerf, 1968, I, 259-260.

consultants (periti). These were named by Pope Paul VI, and official lists were published regularly.[128] Benoit's association with one of the ill-fated preparatory commissions may have retarded his nomination, which did not take place until 1964. He came on the scene just in time to participate very actively in the formulation of two of the most important documents to come out of the Council.

"The Church in the Modern World" was unique, not only in the range of subjects treated, but in the fact that it was addressed to all humanity, and not to Catholics alone. It became anathema to the traditionalists because it was new, and drew opposition from theologians who had no methodology to handle it. Despite a difficult gestation period, it grew with the Council, and eventually came to symbolize its spirit. From the first rough draft in the early spring of 1963, its atmosphere, method and content gradually developed through wide consultation, intense discussion, and multiple revisions.

Benoit came into this process at the beginning of September 1964, when the central sub-committee in charge of drafting the schema assigned him to the theological working group.[129] His real contribution, however, came a year later. A new version of the schema had been circulated during the summer of 1965. The suggested changes filled almost 500 pages when the first debate in the Aula closed on 8 October 1965. Some questioned whether an acceptable revision was even feasible, because 14 September-8 December 1965 was to be the last session of the Council. The traditionalists used every delaying tactic in their power.

Both the church and the world, however, expected a document. In order to handle the tremendous workload the central drafting sub-committee divided itself into ten working groups. As a biblical specialist Benoit found himself in group 3, which was concerned with the section on "The Dignity of the Human Person", and whose members were Bishops Doumith, Granados, Menager, Parenta, Poma, and Wright. The other experts were Fathers Coffey, Congar, Danielou, Gagnebet, Kloppenburg, de Lubac, K. Rahner, and Semmelroth.[130]

Benoit had written a critique of the theological part of the version of the schema distributed on 28 May 1965 for a group of French bishops. As a result he was invited to prepare an improved draft of chapters 1-3 of the schema for the French Episcopal Conference. Subsequently he submitted this text to working group 3, to which he belonged, and eventually to the

128 See U. Betti, "Histoire chronologique de la Constitution," in L'Église de Vatican II. Études autour de la Constitution conciliaire sur l'Église (Unam Sanctam 51b), ed. Y. M.-J. Congar, Paris: Cerf, 1966, II, 62 note 4

129 See R. Tucci, "Introduction historique et doctrinale à la constitution pastorale," in L'Église dans le monde de ce temps. Constitution pastorale 'Gaudium et spes' (Unam Sanctam 65b), det. Y. M.-J. Congar et M. Peuchmaurd, Paris: Cerf, 1967, II, 73-75.

130 The list given by Tucci, ("Introduction historique," 107 note 103) is that of 22 September 1965. This one is taken from Benoit's papers and is dated 5 October 1965.

coordinating group. After discussion of the changes demanded by the Conciliar Fathers, Benoit was selected to rewrite chapter 1 of the schema. He slightly modified this draft in the light of discussions within the working group (15 October 1965), and it was sent to the coordinating group. The major differences between this document and the final version promulgated by the Copuncil on 7 December 1965 are the addition of the sections on Sin (n. 13) and on Atheism (nn. 20-21).

The same day the Council also promulgated "The Declaration on Religious Liberty." This schema had had an equally difficult passage. It was adamantly opposed by the conservatives, because it represented a genuine development of doctrine which sclerosed minds could not contemplate. The draft discussed in the Aula debate of 23-25 September 1964 was criticized for being too juridical and philosophical.[131] In the next revision a section on religious liberty in the light of revelation was added, and we are told by one of the drafters, "One can sense here that the authors of the schema have been inspired by two excellent pages of Father J. Leclerc's Histoire de la tolérance au siècle de la Reform."[132]

A vote should have been held on this revision on 19 November 1964, but amid great agitation it was postponed until the beginning of the next session (14 September-8 December 1965). The delay gave the opportunity for further revision, and the section on relevation was expanded;[133] this time, however, with the aid of two exegetes resident in Rome, Fathers Lyonnet and McCool of the Pontifical Biblical Institute.[134] The debate on this version (distributed 28 May 1965) took place on 15-22 September 1965. Although the schema as a whole received overwhelming approval, there were several criticisms of the scripture section.[135]

It was at this moment that Benoit's assistance was requested.[136] He reworked the biblical material completely in a series of drafts during the early part of October, and was in fact responsible for the organisation of the substance and for most of the wording of nn. 11-12 of the definitive version, which was distributed on 25 October and approved by a huge majority on 19 November 1965.

---

[131] See J. Hamer, "Histoire du texte de la Déclaration, " in La Liberté religieuse. Déclaration 'Dignitatis humanae personae' (Unam Sanctam 60), ed. J. Hamer et Y. Congar, Paris: Cerf,1967, 79.

[132] J. Hamer, "Histoire," 85.

[133] J. Hamer, "Histoire," 91-92.

[134] Y. Congar, "Avertissement," in La Liberté religieuse. Déclaration 'Dignitatis humanae personae' (Unam Sanctam 60), ed. J. Hamer et Y. Congar, Paris: Cerf, 1967, 11 note 1.

[135] J. Hamer, "Histoire," 93.

[136] Y. Congar, "Avertissement," 11 note 1.

Benoit, therefore, was admirably equipped to comment on "Religious Liberty in the Light of Revelation" in the comprehensive study of the document edited by J. Hamer and Y. Congar. In one footnote, however, we read, "A new draft in this sense was in fact proposed to the commission charged with drafting the conciliar document. While recognizing the interest, and even the importance, of this suggestion the commission did not feel able to present it for approval by the Fathers of the Council. The end of the debate was approaching, and it seemed inopportune, even imprudent, to put forward a new and subtle element."[137] This is pure Benoit. The allusion is to a distinction between the heavenly and earthly worlds, and the proposal must have come from Benoit himself. It was an idea which he had proposed to a preparatory commission of the Council in 1961! The wheel had come full circle, but in between what ground had been covered!

Service to Scholarship

Benoit's involvement in three of the most bitterly contested documents of Vatican II brought home to him the extent to which the right wing in the church was implacably opposed to change. The attacks on liberal biblical scholars which had preceded the opening of the Council,[138] could not be maintained in the face of the open, positive attitude of the vast majority of the Conciliar Fathers. But once they had dispersed, he feared that conservative forces in the Roman Curia would make a determined effort to regain what they had lost. In order to prevent any recrudescence of obscurantism, which would restrict the legitimate liberty of scholars and inhibit the dissemination of their research to the church at large, Benoit decided to publish Lagrange's account of the insidious campaign waged against him and the École Biblique from 1906 to its culmination in what he called "the terrible year" of 1912.

It appeared in 1967 as Le Père Lagrange au service de la Bible: Souvenirs personnels. Benoit's concern was not to attribute blame or to fan the embers of old disputes. In fact he first submitted the manuscript to the Jesuits of the Pontifical Biblical Institute, because Lagrange had done little to hide his conviction that one of the instigators of the malicious gossip which clouded his reputation and endangered the École Biblique had been Leopold Fonck, SJ, the first rector of the Pontifical Biblical Institute. Benoit's courtesy was met by generosity. The Jesuits, who had themselves suffered the same type of persecution in the period immediately prior to Vatican II, insisted that the full truth should be made public. They identified with Benoit's

---

137 "Liberté religieuse à la lumière de la Révélation," in La Liberté religieuse. Déclaration 'Dignitatis humanae personae' (Unam Sanctam 60), ed. J. Hamer et Y. Congar, Paris: Cerf, 1967, 210 note 5.

138 See J. A. Fitzmyer, "A Recent Roman Scriptural Controversy," TS 22 (1961) 426-424.

objective, namely, to demonstrate that the critical study of the Bible could go hand in hand with complete fidelity to the church and a profound faith that never wavered. The Council had taught all scholars that Lagrange's attitude towards the Scriptures was as important as his method. Unless scholarship becomes service it degenerates into sterile erudition.

Benoit did not believe in scholarship for its own sake. He studied the Word of God in order to communicate it, and never refused an invitation to write a popular article or to give a lecture to a group of non-specialists. He never condescended to an audience, but the rigor of his thought was made accessible by the simplicity of his language and the clarity with which he organised his material.[139] His passionate conviction of the importance of what he had to communicate always made a deep impression. He was even prepared to lecture in English, and did so with great success in the United States (1969), in Australia (1973), and in England (1980).

He also accepted the burden of administration as a form of service. He edited the Revue Biblique from 1953 to 1968, and directed the two monograph series -- Études Bibliques and Cahiers de la Revue Biblique -- until his retirement. He served as Director of the École Biblique from 1964 to 1972. Prior to his tenure the professors of the École were exclusively French (at least as regards language) and all authority was vested in the Director. Benoit's first significant act when he assumed office was to appoint an Irish Dominican, Jerome Murphy-O'Connor, to teach New Testament. This was such a novelty that it drew a low-level protest from the French Consul General in Jerusalem. Benoit was not dissuaded and even authorized him to teach in English. Although a quintessential Frenchman, Benoit rated ability above nationality, and it was also he who took the initiative in the recruitment of the first American professor, Benedict Viviano, O.P.

As Director he was also responsible for institutional changes. Even though by temperament an autocrat, he had been so imbued with the spirit of Vatican II that he willingly responded to a request of the younger professors for a radical change in the governmental structure of the École Biblique. During his last year in office he drafted the statutes which made the École a democracy with ultimate authority vested in the Academic Council.

The impact of Benoit's many and varied contributions to scholarship is highlighted by the honors he received. He was elected the first Catholic president of the Society for the Study of the New Testament in 1961-62. The Society of Biblical Literature (1963) and the Catholic Biblical Association of America (1964) granted him honorary life membership. The universities of Munich (1972) and Durham (1977) awarded him honorary doctorates. Popes Paul VI and John Paul II appointed him to the Pontifical Biblical

---

[139] These qualities are perfectly illustrated by his book, which in fact originated as a series of popular lectures, Passion et Résurrection du Seigneur (Lire la Bible 6), Paris: Cerf, 1966.

Commission (1972-87). The French Government made him first a Chevalier (1959) and then an Officier de la Légion d'Honneur (1974).

Yet he never wrote a major book. At his death the commentary on Colossians for the Études Bibliques, on which he had been working for many years, remained unfinished. His gifts of great erudition, theological insight, and historical judgment were to a great extent frustrated by a perfectionism which made a large-scale project impossible. There were always new books and articles to be evaluated. His respect for the insights of his colleagues and his own humility meant that he was never able to decide that a draft was final. The positive side of this character trait is most clearly evident in his article-reviews of especially significant books. His sympathy for the intention of the author raised criticism to the level of authentic dialogue.

Although he had ceased to teach exegesis in 1980, Benoit continued his course on the topography of Jerusalem until 1984. The first sign of his increasing frailty was a fall during a visit to new excavations, which resulted in a broken arm. The true cause of his weakness was diagnosed only subsequently. He was suffering from a form of lymphatic cancer (Hodgkin's Disease). After an operation at the Hadassah Hospital, Jerusalem, when a massive tumour was removed, he went to Paris for further treatment. He returned to the École Biblique in early 1985 with the good news that the cancer had been arrested. When it broke out again in early 1986, he preferred to be treated at the Hadassah Hospital for fear that he would die away from Jerusalem. At first at the École, and then in a convalescent home, he struggled on for another year, and on 23 April 1987 he died quietly at St. Joseph's Hospital, Jerusalem. He is buried among his brethren in the crypt of the École Biblique in the city he had loved for 55 years.

Chapter 4

MARIE-EMILE BOISMARD, O.P.

Mention has already been made of Pierre Benoit's role in the recruitment of the two non-French professors of New Testament. He was also responsible for the addition to the faculty of the one who was to become his best-known colleague.

Born on 14 December 1916 at Seiches-sur-le-Loir in Anjou, Claude Boismard was the fourth child (out of eight) of Armand Boismard, a businessman, and Marie Collière. He grew up in Angers and his schooling, first at the Lycée David d'Angers and then at the College Urbain Mongazon, was crowned by the Baccalaureate (Philosophy). His father having been a tertiary, Boismard was familiar with the Dominicans of the Lyon Province and admired their way of life.

In October 1933 he entered the novitiate of the Lyon Province in Angers, where he received the religious name of Marie-Emile. After his simple profession on 4 November 1934 he did two years of philosophy at the Dominican house of studies of Saint Alban-Leysse in Savoy. Compulsory military service was then in force in France, and there were no exceptions. Boismard was called up in November 1937, and he was assigned to the eighth technical regiment at Versailles.

He was trained as a radio operator and should have been demobilized in October 1939. But when war broke out he was assigned as a radio operator at the Corps headquarters of three light tank divisions in Belgium. The attacks and manoeuvres of this confused period are not our concern here. Suffice it to say that he was one of those fortunate enough to find a place in a boat leaving the beach at Dunkirk on 30 May 1940. After a week or so in southern England he, with the rest of the army corps, was shipped back to Cherbourg. They reequipped and reformed in the forest of Rambouillet, and held a position at Pacy-sur-Eure, south of the Seine, before being forced ever further south by German attacks.

They had reached Perigord when the Vichy government disbanded the army. In July 1940 Boismard returned to the monastery of Saint Alban-Leysse, where after three years of theology he was ordained priest in April 1943. Having noted his special interest in the gospels, and particularly Saint John, his superiors decided that he should be sent to specialize in New Testament. Their mistaken belief that a doctorate in theology was a necessary prerequisite to the Licentiate in Sacred Scripture led to him being assigned to the Saulchoir outside Paris, which was the only Dominican pontifical faculty in France. There in the last year of the war, despite hard times and harsh conditions, he was awarded the Lectorate in Theology (then equivalent to a doctorate) for a thesis on "*Doxa* in the Pauline Letters," which was directed by Ceslas Spicq, OP. The next step was the preparation of the Licentiate in Sacred Scripture, which Dominican students normally did at the École Biblique.

No regular sailing service was available on the Mediterranean in the winter of 1945, but Boismard managed to find a place in a troopship leaving Toulon on 31 December. He disembarked at Port Said on 4 January 1946. The next day he took an overnight train, with changes at Kantara and Lod, which got him to Jerusalem on 6 January, a day associated with the arrival of other wise men in the Holy City!

Once he had completed his LSS before the Pontifical Biblical Commission in Rome in November 1947, Boismard was destined to return to the House of Studies of the Lyon Province. Benoit, however, thought differently. Forseeing the need for greater specialization within the NT, and recognizing Boismard's extraordinary talents, he insisted that the latter should be assigned to the École Biblique. This met with strong opposition from the Provincial of Lyon, which was overcome only by an unequivocal directive from the Master General of the Dominican Order. In January 1948, therefore, Boismard joined L.-H. Vincent, the only other professor from his province, as a permanent member of the École Biblique.

Sowing the Seed

Benoit's struggle to retain Boismard in Jerusalem becomes fully intelligible in the light of a study which the latter wrote while still a student. Commentators had been divided on the authorship of Jn 21. Some considered it an afterthought of the author of the Fourth Gospel, while others maintained that it was an addition by a later editor. In order to decide between them Boismard analysed the vocabulary and style in a detail never attempted before.[1] A remarkable feature of this study was the sophistication of the hapaxlegomena argument; they were divided into four categories and studied in function of synonyms and cognates.[2] His conclusion was equally nuanced, "Chapter 21 of the Gospel of John was not written by John himself, but by an anonymous editor, certainly a disciple of John, who was influenced by Johannine narratives and style. The identity of this author remains a mystery despite certain curious similarities between his style and that of Luke."[3]

---

[1]   "Le chapitre xxi de saint Jean: Essai de critique littéraire," RB 54 (1947) 473-501.

[2]   Study of these pages (pp. 484-495) is an important complement to the methodological remarks of G. D. Fee regarding this type of argument ("II Corinthians vi.14-vii.1 and Food offered to Idols," NTS 23 [1977] 144).

[3]   "Le chapitre xxi de Jean," 501.

It was some years before Boismard again took up the problem posed by the similarities of style between John and Luke, and concluded, "Luke certainly took an active part in the redaction of the Fourth Gospel. It is probable that it was he who collected the different Johannine traditions in order to create a primitive gospel, which could be called Proto-John."[4]

The relationship between stylistic observations and literary attribution is anything but certain. The assessment belongs less to the sphere of factual judgment than to that of artistic comprehension, where a refined sensitivity, not always susceptible of rationalization, is the dominant factor. Hence, a literary judgment is always open to revision and Boismard's career manifests his committment to this principle. He never had any trouble changing his mind when he became convinced of the implications of new data.

When he viewed the Luke-John relationship in the wider perspective of the whole synoptic problem, he suggested that it could be explained by a Johannine editor's use of the first edition of Luke's gospel (Proto-Luke).[5] He had to deal with the problem again in the context of his analysis of the Fourth Gospel, Then he wrote, "now having a better knowledge of the literary problems posed by the Fourth Gospel, we situate the relations between John and Luke on two different levels. John II-A and Proto-Luke depend on the same source, whereas John II-B used the last edition of Luke's gospel.... Not having made this distinction in vol. II, we attributed all the agreements of Luke and John against Matthew and Mark to Proto-Luke."[6]

Some critics have considered such changes of opinion as evidence of haste and inconsistency. It witnesses rather to an idealistic committment to truth coupled with a realistic acceptance of how much the mind can assimilate at any given moment. Boismard's consistency has always been with regard to the evidence. If it indicated a modification, he made it. He never defended a position simply because he had once adopted it. Thus even into old age he manifested both in class and in print the contagious excitement of discovery.

At this point in our story, however, he was only at the beginning of his career. What part of the NT he should specialize in was clear from the outset. Any overlap with the interests of his senior colleague was excluded. Benoit, however, had never shown the slightest interest in the Fourth Gospel, and this was Boismard's personal preference. He decided to prepare himself thoroughly by devoting two years to textual criticism (in which Benoit wanted him to specialize), two years to literary criticism, and two years

---

4   "Saint Luc et la rédaction du quatrième évangile (Jn, iv, 46-54)," RB 69 (1962) 210.

5   P. Benoit & M.-E. Boismard, Synopse des quatre évangiles en français, Paris: Cerf, 1972, 16, 46-47. This work will be cited as Synopse II.

6   M.-E. Boismard & A. Lamouille, L'Évangile de Jean (Synopse des quatre évangiles en français, III), Paris: Cerf, 1977, 426. The terminology used in this citation is explained below in the section devoted to the Fourth Gospel.

to the theology of the gospel. Only the first part of this comprehensive program worked out as planned.

In January 1948 when Boismard return to the École to teach after his LSS exam in Rome, the academic year had already begun, and the Director, Father de Vaux, dispensed him from classes. In any case the exodus of students began not long afterwards, once it became clear that war was going to break out when the British left in May. Classes resumed only in 1950. Thus Boismard was able to give himself wholeheartedly to textual criticism for the planned two years. He trained himself to work on Greek manuscripts by a making a new collation of all the texts of the Gospel of John. Then there were the versions, which meant that he had to learn Syriac, Coptic, Ethiopian, Armenian, and Persian. As if this were not enough, he prepared himself to reopen the issue of the relevance of patristic quotations to textual criticism by compiling a systematic file of quotations from the Fourth Gospel in the Greek and Latin Fathers of the Church. This provided the material for his next article, "A propos de Jean v, 39. Essai de critique textuelle" (1948). This proved to be the beginning of a saga which is best treated elsewhere (see. p. 89 below).

The years 1948-50 were also the gestation period of the <u>Bible de Jérusalem</u>. Boismard might reasonably have expected to be invited to contribute something in the Johannine corpus, but more senior scholars at least had to be given first refusal. In the end the gospel was assigned to D. Mollat, SJ, and F.-M. Braun agreed to do the epistles. No one wanted the responsibility of presenting the Apocalypse. As often happens in both religious orders and university faculties risky tasks are allotted to the youngest. Not only is it difficult for them to refuse what is presented as an honor, but they have less to loose if things go wrong. And so Boismard was saddled with the most enigmatic of the Johannine writings.

The basic problem with the Apocalypse is the incoherence of its organization. Visions and prophecies are not arranged in any perceptible order, and one often has the impression of returning to a topic which had already been dealt with. German commentators dealt with these difficulties by distinguishing different sources (anything from two to six Jewish texts strung together by a Christian editor, who also made extensive personal contributions). British and French scholars, on the contrary, insisted on the unity of language and style.

Boismard reconciled these two approaches. The extraordinary number of doublets unambiguously indicated two originally independent texts. The style showed them to have been composed by the same author, but at different times if one was to judge by the content. Thus he dated the older text to the end of the reign of Nero (A.D. 54-68) or shortly after, and the second to about A.D. 95 in the reign of Domitian. The two documents were amalga-

Marie-Emile Boismard, O.P.

mated by a Christian editor who added the letters to the churches of Asia about A.D. 100.[7]

With one minor change his list of the component elements of the two texts was printed in the 1949 fascicle edition of the Apocalypse in the Bible de Jerusalem, and was reproduced in all the one-volume editions with the exception of the 1985 Jerusalem Bible. This departure from the conservative norm of a popular Bible accorded de facto legitimacy to source criticism among Catholics, and instructed a wide audience as to its meaning and utility. The pedagogic skill displayed in this presentation inevitably led to invitations to write on the Apocalypse for influential introductions to the Bible.[8]

Despite such literary productivity Boismard was not allowed to forget that he was a member of "The Practical School of Biblical Studies," to give the École its original title. As a student he participated in Roland de Vaux's first season at Tell el-Farah near Nablus in 1946. Thereafter we see him graduate from pottery repairer (1947) to de Vaux's assistant and area supervisor of the necropolis (1950). In 1959 he conducted a brief exploration of western Transjordan with Pierre Benoit.[9] Because of its remoteness and greater variety this region subsequently attracted him much more than Palestine, and he acquired an exceptionally detailed knowledge of its topography. What little knowledge of Greek epigraphy he accumulated on such expeditions was greatly augmented in the spring of 1950 when he and Benoit were commissioned to decipher and record the numerous inscriptions left by pilgrims of the 4th to the 7th centuries A.D. on the walls of a cave near Bethany.[10]

On a completely different level the Dominican community decided that it would be a good idea to keep in touch with ex-students and to inform them of the activities of the École. Such duties inevitably land on the shoulders of the newest staff member, and so in 1949 Boismard became the founder and editor of the Lettre de Jérusalem. Benoit assumed the responsibility in 1950, and remained the editor until his death in 1987. The abrupt change was due to factors outside Boismard's control. In late 1950 his fruitful and varied life in Jerusalem came to an end.

---

[7]   "'L'Apocalypse' ou 'Les Apocalypses' de S. Jean," RB 56 (1949) 507-541.

[8]   "L'Apocalypse," in Introduction à la Bible. II. Nouveau Testament, ed. A. Robert et A. Feuillet, Tournai-Paris: Desclée, 1959, 710-742. "L'Apocalypse de Jean," in Introduction à la Bible. III. Introduction critique au Nouveau Testament, 4, ed. A. George et P. Grelot, Paris: Letouzey, 1977, 13-55.

[9]   "Notes d'archéologie transjordanienne," RB 56 (1949) 295-299.

[10]   "Un ancien sanctuaire chrétien a Béthanie," RB 58 (1951) 200-251. The cave has since been identified as the "guestroom of Martha and Mary" which is mentioned by Saint Jerome; see J. Taylor, "The Cave at Bethany," RB 94 (1987) 120-123.

The University of Fribourg

The spiritual retreat in October was a time of peace and quiet, when the members of the community recuperated from the rigors of the excavation camp at Tell el-Farah and girded their loins for the opening of the academic year in November. That tranquility was shattered by a telegram from the Master General of the Dominican Order. It informed the Director, Roland de Vaux, that Boismard had been named professor of New Testament at the University of Fribourg, Switzerland.

When this institution was founded in 1889 as the de facto Catholic University of Switzerland, the faculty of theology was entrusted to the Dominicans. This honor carried the responsibility of furnishing suitable faculty members, and in 1950 the Master General needed an urgent replacement. The tactic of robbing Peter to pay Paul did not go down at all well at the École Biblique, and de Vaux immediately telegrammed, "Boismard departure impossible. Letter follows." The reply from Rome arrived the next day. Addressed to Boismard personally this time, it read, "Leave immediately for Fribourg." Within the framework of religious obedience this left no alternative, and so on 19 October 1950 he took a flight out of Damascus for Europe.

It was only when he got to Fribourg that Boismard discovered what had happened. He was the victim of a drama centering on the Court of Belgium. When the Second World War began King Leopold III sent his wife and family to Switzerland for safety. A Belgian Dominican, Francois-Marie Braun, who was professor of NT at Fribourg, became their chaplain and eventually a close friend. After the king was liberated from Germany in May 1945, the government did not permit him to return to Belgium; he was thought by some to have been a German sympathizer. Thus he joined his family in Lausanne, where of course he met Braun.

In the plebiscite of 12 March 1950 a slight majority of Belgians (57%) voted for the return of the king, but once the royal family had settled in Brussels (July 1950) there were prolonged violent demonstrations. In this turmoil the royal family felt the need of their old friend and counsellor, and Father Braun was suddenly summoned to Belgium to be the court chaplain. It was a duty that he could not refuse, even though it meant that Fribourg found itself without a professor of NT just at the beginning of the academic year.

To an active and decisive Master General like Manuel Suarez the problem was not a complicated one. He had a contractual obligation to the Ministry of Public Instruction of the Canton of Fribourg. Moreover, students in the theological faculty had to have NT classes in order to meet degree and ordination requirements. At the École Biblique, however, there was no class obligation. Being essentially a research institution it offered no degrees. To Father Suarez, therefore, it appeared the obvious place from which to 'borrow' a replacement for Braun.

That this was his intention is clear from a letter he wrote to Boismard shortly after his arrival in Fribourg, assuring him that his assignation there was only temporary. Good intentions, however, frequently give way to other imperatives. Father Suarez found himself too busy to worry about a permanent successor to Braun. If the École Biblique really wanted Boismard back, his attitude indicated, it could arrange something with Fribourg.

At the university Boismard had the usual heavy class load, and he had to teach the whole NT spectrum in addition to biblical Greek. Since he had taught but very little, everything meant a new preparation and the courses had to be given in Latin. This was justified by the international character of the faculty and students, but the concision and strangness of this artificial form of communication inhibited the flow of verbiage with which a young professor might be expected to pad out his meagre knowledge. Despite this added pressure, Boismard not only survived but flourished.

It was during his Fribourg years that Boismard began his collaboration with the newly founded Lumière et Vie, the theological review of the Lyon province. It was directed to a general audience, and in order to facilitate understanding each issue was devoted to a single theme, and contributors were invited to write on specific aspects of the subject. Thus seventeen times in the next thirty years Boismard momentarily set aside his own research to contribute articles as diverse as "I rencounce Satan and all his works and pomps" (1956) and "Two Examples of Regressive Evolution (Jn 17,3; 1 Jn 5,19)" (1980).

The majority of the topics dealt with fundamental issues -- the divinity of Christ, the return of Christ, faith, baptism, new life, eucharist, etc. -- and the pastoral concern which motivated his acceptance of the invitations animated his writing, thereby creating models of authentic popularisation. These let to other invitations, and in the 1960s he contributed a number of studies to Assemblées du Seigneur, a Belgian liturgical periodical designed to furnish ministers with biblical homiletic material.

From the wide variety of courses he had to teach at Fribourg came articles on Mt 22:14 (1952) and on Rom 1:4 (1953), but the Johannine literature remained Boismard's primary interest. An article on Jn 1:18 (1952) prepared the way for his first book, Le Prologue de saint Jean (1953). It was addressed to "all those, priests or laity, who have the will (and the time) to work at *their* Bible in order to know it better."[11]

I have emphasized the possessive pronoun because it highlights one of Boismard's fundamental convictions, namely, that the role of the expert is not to feed ideas to non-specialists, but to make the latter independent by giving them the freedom of a Book which is above all a source of life. Thus he spared his readers none of the difficulties of the Prologue. Even though

---

[11] Le Prologue, 7.

he proposed solutions, some very original, it is clear that his great pedagogic skills were employed to enable his readers to perceive the problems. It is this gift which has made him such an exciting teacher at all levels. Many professors can make an answer scintillate, but in addition Boismard could make a problem come alive in such a way that the most laborious research became a pleasure. His whole attitude conveyed what Lagrange said regularly to students, "Now you see it! You need not go home and say, 'P. Lagrange said.' You can say: 'I saw it.'"[12]

When nothing had happened about a replacement for Boismard at the end of his first year at Fribourg, the École Biblique became active. It was clear that unless something was done quickly he would become a permanent fixture at the university, where he was very popular both among faculty and students. Benoit in particular realized that Fribourg had no incentive to replace Boismard. He saw that the only solution was for him to find a scholar who would be welcomed in Fribourg and who would be willing to go there.

His choice fell on Ceslas Spicq, O.P., professor of NT at the Saulchoir. In addition to numerous articles, Spicq had published massive commentaries on the Pastoral Epistles (1947) and on the Epistle to the Hebrews (1952). His academic standing surpassed Fribourg's requirements. His willingness to leave France was another question, but his sense of obligation to the École Biblique which had trained him, combined with great generosity of spirit, made him receptive to Benoit's appeal that the École needed young blood and that Boismard would prefer to be in Jerusalem. In the autumn of 1953, therefore, Spicq began a distinguished career at Fribourg, and Boismard returned to the École Biblique

The First Epistle of Peter

After teaching textual criticism and the Fourth Gospel for a couple of years, Boismard felt the need to broaden his horizons, and in 1955-56 he taught an introduction course on the Catholic Epistles. Inevitably he had to deal with the much debated issue of the relation of baptismal materials (homily? liturgy?) to 1 Peter. Given his extraordinary ability to perceive relationships and patterns, Boismard was greatly impressed by E. G. Selwyn's display of the literary contacts between 1 Peter and a range of other NT letters, from which the latter had concluded that all were dependent on a common baptismal catechesis.[13]

Boismard took this argument a step further. Not only were there verbal contacts between 1 Peter, Colossians, Titus, James, and 1 John, but the same structural patterns could be detected, i.e. the repetition of the same

---

12 J. F. McDonnell, O.P., "After Twenty-Five Years ...," Lagrange Lectures 1963, Dubuque: Aquinas Institute, 1963, 20.

13 The First Epistle of St. Peter, London: Macmillan, 1946.

themes in the same order.[14] At the conclusion of this study he suggested that it might be profitable to test Romans for evidence of the same pattern. He took up his own challenge two years later, but in an unexpected way.

From an exegesis course on 1 Peter in 1957-58 Boismard developed a book entitled <u>Quatre hymnes baptismales dans la première épitre de Pierre</u> (1961). The patterns which he had established in his previous article became the key which opened up the letter. Not only did they indicate where hymnic material might be found, but comparison of the different forms enabled him to separate the four original hymns from their editorial additions and/or reformulations. The hymns which he extracted were: I - 1:3-5; II - 3:18-22; III - 2:22-25; and IV - 5:5-9.

The judgment of expert reviewers was divided. Some found only a subtlety so refined as to be self-defeating, whereas others recognized a master literary critic, whose rare capacity for detailed observation was complemented by exegetical insight and creative flair.

In the course of his explanation of these hymns, which for F. W. Beare was "marked by philological exactness, theological weight, and devotional warmth,"[15] Boismard noted contacts between Hymn I and Rom 8:14-25, and between Hymn III and Rom 6:3-12 plus 8:3. In reality these contacts were not very impressive, because the links were too generic. They served their purpose, however, by inspiring him to look for contacts between 1 Peter and Romans outside the hymns. In the conclusion he lists 1 Pt 2:5 = Rom 12:1-2; 1 Pt 3:8-9 = Rom 12:14-17; and 1 Pt 4:7-11 = Rom 12:3-13. In these the contacts are extremely specific. The same terms occur in the same order, and suggest direct dependence.

All this material was reworked and taken up into Boismard's article "Pierre (Première épitre de),"[16] which remains an excellent introduction to this difficult letter, combining as it does a critical assessment of the state of research to 1966 and an original solution. He refused the dominant opinion according to which 1 Pt is made up of a baptismal homily (1:3-4:11) and a letter (4:12-5:14) both composed by the same person. In his view the arguments were not well-founded, and the simplicity of the hypothesis failed to do justice to the complexity of the data. Instead he ranged himself with Selwyn and E. Lohse.[17]

Boismard, however, insisted that it was possible to be more complete then Selwyn and more precise than Lohse. In addition to the four hymns mentioned above, the author of 1 Pt used an outline of a baptismal homily recalling the essential elements of Christian life, and parts of a baptismal

---

14 "Une liturgie baptismale dans la Prima Petri," RB 63 (1956) 182-208; 64 (1967) 161-183.

15 BL 81 (1962) 323.

16 DBS 7 (1966) 1415-1455.

17 "Paränese und Kerygma im 1 Petrusbrief," ZNW 45 (1954) 68-90

creed, which appear in 3:18,21c,22 and 4:6. Boismard accepted Lohse's recognition of the Palestinian coloring of these materials, and then suggested
that, although they may have been given their final form in the church of
Antioch, their roots went back to Jerusalem. This would explain why the
letter was attributed to Peter who had headed that church in its formative
years. In dating the final redaction of 1 Pt, Boismard gave more weight to
the non-liturgical contacts with the authentic Pauline letters than to the type
of persecution suggested by the letter or the late date of the earliest attestation of 1 Pt. Thus, he attributed it to Silvanus, who had been Paul's companion, sometime in the period A.D. 80-95.

The Gospel Synopsis

Significant as was his work on 1 Peter, it represented but a minor dimension of Boismard's literary productivity in the ten years which followed
his return to Jerusalem from Fribourg. The greater part of his energy was
concentrated on the Fourth Gospel, and eight highly original articles consolidated his position as a leading Johannine specialist. Everyone expected
him to produce a major commentary on John which would rival that of
Bultmann. It came as no surprise, therefore, that his next book should have
been a sequel to the one on the Prologue, Du Baptême à Cana (Jn 1,19-
2,11), which appeared in 1956. The book which next appeared, however,
had nothing to do with John. It was an epoch-making literary analysis of the
three synoptic gospels, which appeared in 1972, after a long silence of six
years during which he had not published a single article. What brought
about this abrupt change of direction?

In the late 1950s the École Biblique was invited by Father Chifflot of
Editions du Cerf in Paris to consider the possibility of producing a synopsis
based on the gospel translations in the Bible de Jérusalem, which would
also contain brief notes on the literary relationship of Matthew, Mark, and
Luke. Benoit accepted the offer as a personal project. If Lagrange had
produced a synopsis,[18] it was appropriate that he should also do so. The
École at that stage had an extremely capable secretary, Fawzi Zayadine,
who later became a distinguished archaeologist with a high position in the
Jordanian Department of Antiquities. With solid justification Benoit
deemed him capable of setting out the printed text in parallel columns,
which he would then correct. Finally, the notes would give him the
opportunity to demolish systematically the Two Source Theory.

Once he started work, however, Benoit quickly realized that the project
was neither as simple nor as easy as he had anticipated. The freedom enjoyed by the translators of the Bible de Jérusalem meant that there was no
uniformity in the way a particular word was translated. This slowed the

---

[18] Synopsis evangelica graece, with the collaboration of C. Lavergne, Barcelona:
Éditions 'Alpha', 1926.

work of preparing the synopsis considerably. In order to speed thing up Benoit called on the services of Francois Langlamet, O.P., and L.-M. Dewailly, O.P. But the former, then a student, was destined for OT, and the latter had soon to return to an absorbing ministry in Sweden. Their contribution was of necessity limited. A committment, however, had been made, and Cerf had publically announced the publication of the synopsis. There was no alternative to an appeal to Boismard, whom Benoit had wished to leave free to concentrate on John and textual criticism. With his customary generosity Boismard responded by laying out over 70% of the pericopes in the synopsis.

His adoption of Benoit's principle of giving a complete line to identical material however small greatly facilitated comparison of the different gospels, as did the use of a sign to indicate when the same French word had to serve for more than one Greek word or expression. Another novelty, again with the utility of the student in mind, was the placing of doublets and comparable material within the same gospel in parallel columns, instead of relegating them to footnotes as other synopses did. This frequently meant six columns, and on one occasion seven (section 295). But the ingenuity of the presentation, which owed much to Jourdain-M. Rousee, OP, resulted in pages that were clear, uncluttered, and beautiful, even when they also had to accomodate the more important fruits of Boismard's work in textual criticism.

As the parallel columns multiplied so did the number of pages. By then, however, it had become clear that the synopsis in itself was going to be a major contribution in terms of both design and substance. Thus it was published alone in 1965 as <u>Synopse des quatre Évangiles en français avec paralleles des apocryphes et des Pères: Textes</u>. Immediately it set the standard by which synopses were judged, because clarity of visual display is the only justification for the publication of a synopsis.[19]

At that stage the only up-to-date Greek synopsis was that published by K. Aland in 1963,[20] When judged by this criterion its faults were manifest, notably the placing of the textual apparatus at the end of each pericope, which broke up the page and destroyed any sense of the continuity of the gospels. It was known, however, that H. Greeven had been preparing a new edition of the Huck-Lietzmann synopsis since 1952, and there was some

---

[19] The second edition (1972) was revised by Pierre Sandevoir in the interests of greater literalness. It underwent further revision for the third edition (1981) by Boismard and A. Lamouille who endeavoured always to translate the same Greek term by the same French word. They also added a concordance showing (a) the preferred words of the gospels of Mt, Mk, and Lk; (b) words shared by two gospels but not used in the third; and (c) cases where literalism was not possible.

[20] <u>Synopsis Quattuor Evangeliorum. Locis parallelis evangeliorum apocryphorum et patrum adhibitis</u>, Stuttgart: Würtembergische Bibelanstalt.

hope that it would take advantage of the progress that had been made in synopsis design. It finally appeared in 1981.[21]

Its reception was mixed. It did not contain all of John, whereas that of Benoit-Boismard did, but the parallels given were more detailed than in the latter synopsis. Moreover, the presentation of doublets could run to ten columns (the first prediction of the Passion, pp. 132-133). Such gains, however, were totally compromised by the lay-out, as Boismard wrote, "On opening the Huck-Greeven synopsis for the first time one is immediately and disagreeably struck by the following fact: on many pages the columns reserved to each gospel expand, contract, and intermingle in a most disconcerting fashion."[22] To give but one example, the text of Lk 9:31-32 meanders right across the page with four lines in the Mark column and two lines in the Matthew column (p. 135). In addition the textual apparatus, necessitated by Greeven's reedition, occupies on average half of each page.

At this point Boismard decided to surrender to the numerous and repeated requests that he produce a Greek synopsis which would incorporate all the advantages of the French version. Thus the Boismard-Lamouille synopsis was born.[23] Far from being a simple presentation of the Greek text underlying the French translation, it reflected the experience and insights of twenty years further work on the gospels. It also showed that they could learn from their competitors. Boismard praised the Orchard synopsis for its extraordinary clarity, "Absolute priority is given to the Greek text which occupies the whole page, the only interruption being the very discrete numbers and titles of the pericopes.... The very selective text-critical notes are relegated to the end of the volume in order to give the whole of every page to the Greek text."[24]

Boismard and Lamouille could not follow Orchard on this latter point, because their agenda was more complex. They had points to make in textual criticism, whereas he was concerned exclusively with a particular solution to the synoptic problem. They did, however, reduce known data to the minimum by refusing to duplicate the 26th edition of Nestle-Aland, and used a beautiful small Greek font to minimize the space at the bottom of the page given to the important non-canonical texts. They went a step further than Orchard by eliminating the titles of pericopes, so that no foreign element interrupts the reader's vision of the texts, and remained superior to Orchard by retaining extra columns for doublets within a gospel. In terms of what a synopsis is supposed to do, the Boismard-Lamouille does it best.

---

[21] Synopsis of the First Three Gospels with the Addition of the Johannine Parallels. 13th edition, fundamentally revised by Heinrich Greeven, Tübingen: Mohr (Siebeck).

[22] RB 90 (1983) 443.

[23] Synopsis Graeca Quattuor Evangeliorum, Leuven-Paris: Peeters, 1986.

[24] John Bernard Orchard, A Synopsis of the Four Gospels in Greek arranged according to the Two-Gospel Hypothesis, Edinburgh: Clark, 1983. Reviewed by Boismard, RB 93 (1986) 470-471.

The Synoptic Problem

Reviewing the original French synopsis J. A. Fitzmyer, SJ, commented, "When it is complete, this work will undoubtedly be just another reason why the world of NT scholarship will continue to look with gratitude and indebtedness to the Dominican Fathers of the École Biblique of Jerusalem."[25] The mention of incompleteness was, of course, an allusion to the literary commentary, which by then had been relegated to a second volume. Benoit's conception of these notes as a sustained critique of the Two Source Theory had had to be abandonned very early, not because he had changed his mind on the synoptic problem, but because Boismard had convinced him that they could not be content with a purely negative conclusion. Unless it were supplanted by a more adequate hypothesis, the Two Source Theory, whatever its faults, would continue to hold the field. To be effective, therefore, they would have to elaborate a new synoptic theory.

Benoit declined the challenge on the grounds that he was already committed to a large-scale project, the commentary on the Captivity Epistles, which must have priority. Boismard was left to shoulder the entire responsibility alone. Despite the daunting prospect, his creative spirit exulted at the thought of developing an hypothesis based on a detailed study of all the synoptic material. It had never been attempted before. Like Columbus he did not know what lay over the horizon. As Columbus ignored the warnings that the earth was flat, Boismard took little stock of those who insisted on the NT equivalent; the Two Source Theory no more corresponded to the facts than the Flat Earth Theory. Columbus, however, reached his desired goal a lot more quickly than Boismard. It took him only 71 days to find land in the west, and the dangers he faced were only physical. Boismard's quest lasted six years and brought him to the verge of a nervous breakdown.

It is difficult even for specialists to realise the magnitude of the task he had set himself. He did not start from any preconceived idea. There was no thesis that he wanted to prove. His only assumption was that each gospel was many layered, and his method was to delve as deeply into each text as the matter would allow. As he worked, partial hypotheses were formulated, refined, discarded, or combined. His notes had to be rewritten, again, and again, and again -- and he had no secretarial help.

The strain of trying to discern a pattern in an almost infinite number of variables was compounded by the Six Day War of June 1967. With the other professors and employees he was held for twenty-four hours in the garden, while the École was occupied and looted by the Israeli army. Arab friends of his were killed or ill-treated. The systematic humiliation of the

---

[25]   TS 27 (1966) 153.

conquered proved more than he could handle. His work slowed to a complete stop, and he was ordered to take a complete rest in November 1967.

He returned rejuvenated from Paris on 29 February 1968. He had learnt
that he could not push himself too hard. He helped build the École's tennis
court and began to play regularly. When symptoms of strain manifested
themselves he took a break. This slowed his rhythm and it began to look as
if the project would never be finished. The following academic year the
École released him from the burden of book reviews and classes, and he
worked solidly throughout the winter of 1968-69 in Paris. At that point he
knew were he was going, but he began to fear the danger of subjectivism.
He needed the control and stimulus of a creative challenge to his developing
theory.

He prevailed on Pierre Sandevoir to come to Jerusalem for the academic
year 1969-70. A former student of the École Biblique and a priest of the
archdiocese of Paris, he had been working at Editions du Cerf on the Concordance to the New Testament, which was just about to be published.[26]
This had alerted him to the need for a revision of the French synopsis, and
he made himself responsible for the second edition. Given this framework it
was easy to stimulate his interest in the synoptic problem.

Shortly after Boismard had returned to Jerusalem in early 1969, he was
approached by a Dominican student of the Toulouse Province, who asked
him to direct his Mémoire. This was Arnaud Lamouille who was to become
his principal collaborator. Born in Toulouse on 5 September 1938, he entered the Order in October 1958 immediately after his Baccalaureat. After his
ordination on 4 July 1965, he completed the usual theology cycle, and spent
eight months in Germany to learn the language before coming to Jerusalem
in the autumn of 1968. His mémoire on the complex pericope of the Ga-
darene Swine (Mk 5:1-20 and parallels) revealed him to be a gifted literary
critic, whose subtle approach to the text was very close to that of Boismard.

After the memoire had been approved at Easter 1970, he was invited by
Boismard to stay on for a further year to help him complete the commentary. He did so, and it was he who made it possible for Boismard, not only
to complete his project, but to envisage others. Lamouille, however, had no
desire to become a professor at the École Biblique. So when the last proofs
were completed in July 1971 he returned to France to begin a fruitful biblical apostolate. He thought that he had finished with the École Biblique, but
Providence decreed otherwise.

Those who approach a gospel passage wearing the blinkers of the Two
Source Theory invariably begin by comparing the two, three or four ver-

---

[26] Concordance de la Bible. Nouveau Testament, par Soeur Jeanne d'Arc, M. Bardy, O.
Odelain, P. Sandevoir, R. Seguineau, Paris: Cerf/Desclee, 1970. See RB 78 (1971)
438-442.

sions of the pericope. In fact it is even taught as a principle of method.[27] The most obvious flaw in such a methodology is that it is inapplicable to texts which have no parallels. Boismard, on the contrary, believed that each version should be analysed in and for itself before any notice is taken of the parallels. In many sections of Synopse II it is possible to follow the process wereby he reached his conclusions, whereas in others clarity demanded that he present his conclusion first and then the supporting arguments.

To work through a selection of passages was an instructive experience for students, but at a later stage Boismard and Lamouille simplified the process by publishing a short do-it-yourself manual of literary criticism.[28] They begin by explaining a number of the clues which indicate that a gospel passage is not a literary unity, namely, internal tension or contradiction, a commentary-like note, a reprise,[29] a break in the thought, a verbal or structural doublet, a change in vocabulary and/or style, different theological perspectives, textual variants (showing that scribes saw a problem). They then show, by working through a series of passages from Mark, Luke, John, and Acts, how these keys are used to open up the literary history of a text.

It was by systematically exploiting such clues in every synoptic pericope that Boismard finally worked out an hypothesis which did full justice to all the data. Not surprisingly it is much more complex than the simplistic Two Source Theory. In Synopse II he distinguishes three stages in the written gospel traditon, of which the third and last is represented by the four gospels in their present form. On the first and most primitive level he discernes four documents, which he terms A, B, C, and Q. The last mentioned is one of the key elements of the Two Source Theory, in which it explains most of the double tradition. Boismard, however, diverges from the consensus by attributing to Q certain passages found only in Lk or Mt, and by refusing to Q some parts of the double traditon. He further confesses himself unable to decide whether Q formed a well-defined unity.

Documents A, B, and C, on the other hand are homogeneous units, which he does not hesitate to call gospels.

Document A was composed in Palestine in a Judaeo-Christian community. In general its narratives are simple and concrete, and are often composed on the basis of the framework of an OT story. There are few explicit OT quotations, but allusions to the Hebrew text of the OT are frequent.

---

[27] See, for example, H. Zimmermann, Neutestamentliche Methodenlehre: Darstellung der historisch-kritischen Methode, Stuttgart: Katholisches Bibelwerk, 1967.

[28] La vie des évangiles. Initiation à la critique des textes. Paris: Cerf, 1980. Translated into German and Spanish but unfortunately not into English.

[29] Boismard has written an important article on this redactional technique, "Un procédé rédactionnel dans le quatrième évangile: la Wiederaufnahme," in L'évangile de Jean. Sources, rédaction, théologie (BETL 44), ed. M. de Jonge, Gembloux-Leuven, 1977, 235-241.

This document was then reinterpreted in a Gentile Christian milieu, thus giving rise to Document B, which among other features cites the OT according to the Septuagint version. Boismard claims that Paul knew Document B when he wrote Romans. This permits him to date it prior to A.D. 57. Since Document A must be earlier, he dates it about A.D. 50.

Document C was entirely independent of the other two, and reflects different and older traditions. Because it gives prominence to Peter, Boismard suggests that this document might be the "Teaching of Peter" known to Ignatius, or the "Recollections of Peter" of which Origen spoke.

For Boismard, the second or intermediate stage in the written gospel tradition is also constituted by four documents.

Intermediate-Mark had as its principal source Document B, but also used Document A, and to a lesser degree Document C. The editor did not simply combine these documents. He carefully organized them in order to highlight certain theological themes. He had a marked interest in exorcisms, and most of Jesus' orders to keep silent about his ministry were introduced by him. He gave special prominence to faith, and to the related themes of the rejection of the Jews as the chosen people and the call of pagans to salvation. The prominence given this latter theme, when coupled with the way the editor modified and explained his sources in order to make them more intelligible to non-Jewish readers, indicated that Intermediate-Mark was written for converted pagans.

Intermediate-Matthew drew on only two sources, Q and Document A, the latter being the more important. The chief concern of this editor was to set in relief the teaching of Jesus by showing that it preserved what was essential in the Mosaic Law, while opposing the narrow interpretation of the Scribes and Pharisees. Such interest in the Law revealed that Intermediate-Matthew was composed in Judaeo-Christian circles, but outside Palestine, because the OT is cited according to the Greek versions attributed to the Septuagint and Theodotion. Since this editor was strongly influenced by the Treatise on the Two Ways, which was widely known in Egypt and in particular at Alexandria, Boismard suggested this city as the place of composition, and would date the document before the fall of Jerusalem in A.D. 70.

Intermediate-Matthew was the principal source of Proto-Luke, which also depended on Q, Document B, and Document C. Like many others Boismard was led to postulate a Proto-Luke in order to explain the agreements of Luke and John, and the agreements of Matthew and Luke against Mark. Despite the differences in theological perspective between Proto-Luke and Luke, Boismard attributes both to the same author, because they exhibit identical style and vocabulary.

Boismard further insists that some sections belonging to Proto-Luke were abandonned at the time of its last redaction. They were preserved in John, of which Proto-Luke was one of the principal sources, the others being Documents B and C. Boismard was careful to point out, however, that these conclusions regarding the Fourth Gospel depended only on those sections which John had in common with the Synoptics. The hint that they might need modification was in fact verified when he completed his study of the whole of John.

The final stage of the written tradition is represented by the final redactions of the four gospels, whose structure (John excepted) was determined by that of Intermediate-Mark.

The final edition of Mark was influenced, not only by this key document, but also by Intermediate-Matthew and Proto-Luke. In the style of the final editor Boismard detected what he called 'Paulinisms' and 'Lukanisms' and in consequence attributed the final form of Mark to a disciple of Luke.

The last editor of Matthew knew only Intermediate-Matthew and Intermediate-Mark, and he systematically brought the former into line with the latter. In addition he grouped the stories and sayings of his sources, and so increased to five the number of discourses he found in Intermediate-Matthew. The style and vocabulary of the final Matthean redactor, according to Boismard, exhibited the same type of 'Lukanisms' which he had found to be characteristic of the final editor of Mark. Hence, he claimed that they were one and the same person or, at the very least, members of the same Lukan school.

The work of the final redactor of Luke consisted in completing Proto-Luke in function of Intermediate-Mark. Boismard suggested that originally Proto-Luke and the Acts of the Apostles formed a single document. When Luke got to know the contents of Intermediate-Mark, he decided to expand the portion of his work concerned with the ministry of Jesus. The bulk of the expanded document made it too unwieldy, and Luke split it into two books. This necessitated both a conclusion to the gospel and an introduction to Acts; these are in effect a doublet.

The final redaction of John was not very extensive. The redactor contented himself with the introduction of elements drawn from the final version of Matthew.

How did the scholarly world react? There were those who found it possible to ignore such a massive achievement, thereby implicitly acknowledging the force of its arguments.[30] There were also those who considered the theory and flatly denied it, e.g. Bruno de Solages, who insisted that more weight should be given to the order of pericopes than to their detail.[31]

There were those who found such attention to detail productive only of an unacceptable complexity. H. F. D. Sparks, himself the editor of a synopsis, surely spoke for many in writing, "The greatest stumbling block in the

---

[30] E.g. J. A. Fitzmyer, SJ, The Gospel according to Luke (I-IX) (AB), Garden City: Doubleday, 1981, 63-106.

[31] "Une question de méthode: A propos de la théorie synoptique du P. M.-E. Boismard," BLE 74 (1973) 139-141.

path of the theory, however, is its complexity. If the prehistory of the gospels was indeed as complicated as Père Boismard supposes (and there is no valid a priori reason why it should not have been), the question inevitably arises whether it is possible for any twentieth-century scholar, whoever he may be, to unravel its intricacies as precisely and as successfully as Père Boismard claims to have done. And, if it is not possible, the moral would appear to be that the more complicated the theories to explain the interrelationship between the gospels become, the more questionable and less obviously compelling they necessarily are; though to say this is not to say that they are therefore further from the truth than the much simpler theories to which we have all been accustomed for so long. In other words, it is likely that in the future we shall either have to be content with one of simpler solutions or admit frankly that on the basis of the existing evidence alone the problem is insoluble."[32] In brief, a bad hypothesis as long as it is simple is preferable to any complicated hypothesis! The position of partisans of the Two Source Theory could hardly have been put more delicately.

Theories, however, must be judged, not in terms of the energy and comfort of the interpreter, but in terms of their adequacy to the data. The positive side of Sparks' reaction was articulated by W. Wink, "We always knew the issue might be more complex than we had conceived; we were right to try to reduce the complexity to a minimal pattern. If that attempt has failed, then we must be willing to face that complexity head-on until it submits to some intelligible and generally commendable pattern."[33]

Wink was but one reviewer to recognize that, whatever one thought of Boismard's own theory, he had convincingly demonstrated the need for a more sophisticated vision of gospel prehistory.[34] Wink proved this to himself by doing what less critical reviewers failed to do. "In the compass of a brief review, I cannot possibly reproduce the trial tests I have run on B's thesis. I can only indicate the procedure and results. First, I selected 30 pericopes and tested B's explanation of their development against the phenomena as I saw them in Aland's Synopsis. Then I asked if the two-document hypothesis could explain the same phenomena as well or better. Then I tried the Griesbach hypothesis on the same material. In about two-thirds of these passages, I found B's explanations convincing or at least completely conceivable, and superior to either alternative."[35]

---

[32] JTS 25 (1974) 486.

[33] CBQ 34 (1973) 225.

[34] E. P. Sanders wrote that he shared "Boismard's view that we have reached the stage at which complex solutions to the synoptic problem should be considered. It is useful to have before us a view which permits the student to think that, in any given passage, influences among the gospels could have run in any one of several directions, or even in more than one direction." (JBL 94 [1975] 130). Similarly S. Legasse, BLE 74 (1973) 152.

[35] CBQ 34 (1973) 224.

He thus confirmed the judgment of X. Jacques, SJ, that Boismard had produced "a magisterial work, a new and important landmark in the study of a difficult question,"[36] and vindicated those who had compared his book to Bultmann's History of the Synoptic Tradition.[37] It did not open a new field of investigation as this classic work did, but it offered the same comprehensive coverage of the gospel tradition, the same quality of original insight, the same courage in daring hypotheses, and the same challenging lack of ambiguity in presentation.

At this level of research being right is of less importance than being a stimulating part of an ongoing quest. What Boismard's provocative, but in no way arbitrary, hypothesis called for was "a spate of dissertations and a decade of debate."[38] Only after such prolonged and intense interaction between text and thesis could an adequate judgment emerge on a work of such wide-ranging vision and minute detail. Why it should not have taken place is difficult to explain, but it is not unrelated to the failure of French scholarship in general to command a hearing. The only detailed discussion of Boismard's hypothesis has focused on particular aspects.[39]

The Fourth Gospel

After the publication of his synoptic theory in 1972 Boismard's attention returned to the Gospel of John. Not only was it his first love, but he had worked on the pericopes which had synoptic parallels, and he was keen to extend the same type of literary analysis to the whole of the gospel. In the course of the synoptic project, however, he had learnt two things, the limits of his own strength and the advantages of working with a partner. Thus he invited Arnaud Lamouille to return to the École from France in order to coauthor a book on John.

While awaiting the response of the Toulouse province, Boismard's reflections on the problems of the gospel produced two articles, a study of Jn 10:24-39 for the Schnackenburg Festschrift,[40] and an unusual combination of topography and theology designed to reinforce the identification of

---

[36] NRT 94 (1972) 807.

[37] E. P. Sanders, JBL 94 (1975) 128; see also RB 79 (1972) 435.

[38] W. Wink, CBQ 34 (1973) 225.

[39] F. Neirynck, "La matière marcienne dans l'évangile de Luc," in L'évangile de Luc. Problemes littéraires et théologiques. Mémorial L. Cerfaux (BETL 32), ed. F. Neirynck, Gembloux: Duculot, 1973, 158-201, esp. 162-166; id. "Urmarkus Redivivus? Examen critique de l'hypothèse des insertions matthéennes dans Marc," in L'évangile selon Marc. Tradition et rédaction (BETL 34), ed. M. Sabbe, Leuven: University/Gembloux: Duculot, 1974, 103-145.

[40] "Jésus, le Prophète par excellence, d'après Jean 10, 24-39," in Neues Testament und Kirche, ed. J. Gnilka, Freiburg: Herder, 1974, 160-171.

"Aenon", at which John the Baptist ministered, with Ain Farah in the middle of Samaria.[41]

Eventually Lamouille's agreement and the authorisation of his province came through, and in the late summer of 1973 they began their study of John. This time, however, they worked in very close collaboration, so close that in the preface to the magnificent volume <u>L'Evangile de Jean</u> (1977) Boismard wrote, "It is impossible to specify what each of us contributed to the final product. Each note was rewritten four or five times as our general theory became more precise, and reflects the contribution of both of us in varing degrees."[42] Nonetheless, as far as Boismard was concerned, this book was the culmination of thirty years work on the Fourth Gospel. It reflected approaches and options made long before.

(a) Textual Criticism

In the preface just referred to Boismard pointed out that he bore the full responsibility for the notes on textual criticism. A little later he explained his method, "As a general rule one should select the more difficult reading, the one which contradicts the smoothing tendency of copyists, the one which can account for the origin of the other readings, even if it is attested by only a small number of manuscripts, or even by the ancient versions or patristic citations alone."[43] By this assertion that he preferred to weigh each variant rather than merely count manuscripts, Boismard identified himself as an eclectic, and thus ranged himself with a minority of specialists working in this field.[44] His final words, however, excluded him from even that tiny group, although they would have assured him a warm welcome by a number of celebrated scholars of the past.

At the beginning of the twentieth century F. C. Conybeare in England and F. Blass in Germany had insisted on the importance of patristic citations for the recovery of authentic readings which had been lost in the manuscript tradition. Their efforts won them little more than an amused smile. At best, the authorities pontificated, patristic evidence could be used to strengthen a manuscript reading.[45] At the very outset of his career Boismard threw down the gauntlet to the text-critical establishment. In 1948 when studying Jn 5:39 he discovered that the best reading in terms of intrinsic probability

41 "Aenon, près de Salem (Jean, iii, 23)," RB 80 (1973) 218-229.

42 L'Évangile de Jean (Synopse des quatres évangiles en français, III), avec la collaboration de G. Rochais, Paris: Cerf, 1977, 7.

43 Évangile de Jean, 11.

44 See for example, J. K. Elliott, "Plaidoyer pour un éclectisme intégral appliqué a la critique textuelle du Nouveau Testament," RB 84 (1977) 5-25.

45 For a brief history, see J. Duplacy, "Les citations grecques et la critique du texte du Nouveau Testament: Le passé, le présent, et l'avenir," in La Bible et les Pères, ed. A. Benoit, Paris: Presses Universitaires de France, 1971, 187-197.

appeared in no gospel manuscript but was amply attested by the versions and the Fathers.[46]

The significance of the Fathers received much greater emphasis in his next, programmatic, article in which he laid down the radical thesis that reopened an important debate, "Anyone who takes the trouble to collect systematically the biblical quotations of the Fathers observes that there is a double textual tradition, that of the Fathers and that of the manuscripts, and that the latter is not always the best."[47]   In order to prove his point he discussed a series of examples (Jn 1:12-13; 12:32; 14:2,23; 17:5,21) in which he observed that what he considered the preferable reading was shorter than the received text. Not surprisingly, this article was followed by one entitled "Lectio brevior, potior" ('The shorter the reading the better'; 1951) in which he showed that certain versions and Fathers attested a shorter text of John 7. The same phenomenon appeared in a further article analysing Jn 6:23-24; 11:48-50; 13:10,24; 19:34, [48]

One would have expected such a systematic proposal concerning the text of a gospel to create a certain stir in the world of NT scholarship. In fact it barely created a ripple. M. J. Suggs noted, "his astonishing acquaintance with the Fathers," and commented, "If Boismard is correct in his estimate of the significance of this testimony, then it is a mistake to try to understand at least some patristic evidence in terms of the fourth-century recensions."[49]   J. Duplacy claimed that Boismard's articles "probably constitute the most original contribution of these last years to the history of the gospel text [of John].To an usual degree the author combines a mighty quest for data with methological reflection."[50] But apart from some general remarks about how judicious should be one's judgment in a matter so delicate he let the matter drop.[51]

It is not too difficult to detect a note of thinly veiled scepticism. Obviously the text-critical establishment thought that by ignoring Boismard's troublesome theories they could relegate him to obscurity, as they had done to Blass and Conybeare. It must have come as a chilling surprise when finally -- almost two decades after the event -- they became aware of the fact that Boismard's hypothesis of a short text as the original text of John had strongly influenced a highly popular modern translation of the Bible.

---

[46]   "A propos de Jean v, 39. Essai de critique textuelle," RB 55 (1948) 5-34.

[47]   "Critique textuelle et citations patristiques," RB 57 (1950) 388.

[48]   "Problemes de critique textuelle concernant le quatrième évangile," RB 60 (1953) 347-371.

[49]   "The Use of Patristic Evidence in the Search for a Primitive New Testament Text," NTS 4 (1957-58) 144-145.

[50]   Où en est la critique textuelle du Nouveau Testament?, Paris: Gabalda, 1959, 49.

[51]   Op. cit., 36-37.

In his introduction to the first fascicle edition of John in the Bible de Jérusalem, D. Mollat wrote, "In the course of its transmission a dense and
concise text appears to have been overloaded and weakened by a parasitic
vegetation of 'auxilary words' -- pronouns, adverbs, adjectives, subjects,
verbs -- designed to make it more intelligible. Sometimes a forceful word
was watered down by a fearful copyist. Without claiming to have revised
the text of the Fourth Gospel extinsively, we have reexamined a certain
number of variants, and have come to the conclusion that in more than one
case it is possible to recover well-attested short readings which restore to
the style of St. John its orignal concision and vigor."[52] Boismard could
hardly have put it better himself!

This of course put the cat among the pigeons, or to use the words of G.
D. Fee, it took "Boismard's theories out of the laboratory and into the market place in a permanent form."[53] Serious criticism was now imperative,
even though it came eighteen years after the event. Fee's critique of Boismard, however, is not very serious. He attacks a few texts where Boismard's
arguments are weak, deplores his heavy reliance on Chrysostom and Nonnus, and provides some sententious advice on methodology which repeats
that of Suggs and Duplacy.

Fee's suggestion that Boismard's case in great part rests on the witness of
only two Fathers is inexcusable unless he actually read only the article
"Lectio brevior, potius," where in fact Chrysostom and Nonnus play a major
role. Boismard had always been concerned to provide multiple attestation in
order to avoid the obvious danger that a patristic variant might be due to a
slightly inaccurate memory or to a conscious effort to adapt a saying of Jesus to a new situation. It was precisely his quest for such evidence that
brought him face to face with the problem. "When we speak of the patristic
tradition, it is not a question of a few isolated variants attested by two or
three Fathers based in this or that region of the Christian world, but of almost entire verses attested by 25 to 35 Fathers ranging in date from the 2nd
to the 8th century and scattered throughout the whole Christian world of
that time, Europe, Africa, Alexandria, Palestine, Syria, Cappadocia,
Constantinople, Armenia, Ethiopia. This is a most remarkable fact which
we must try to explain."[54]

This is the challenge that none of Boismard's critics have ever accepted.
The Neirynck team of the University of Leuven, for example, merely compounded Fee's error by transferring the criticism to Boismard's programma-

---

52 La Sainte Bible, traduite en français sous la direction de l'École Biblique de Jérusalem:
    L'évangile et les épîtres de saint Jean, Paris: Cerf, 1953, 65.

53 "The Text of John in the Jerusalem Bible. A Critique of the Use of Patristic Citations
    in New Testament Textual Criticism," JBL 90 (1971) 165.

54 "Critique textuelle et citations patristiques," RB 57 (1950) 397.

tic article, "Critique textuelle et citations patristiques."[55] The facts, however, for the texts treated in this article are: Chrysostom is cited for four out
of the five texts considered, and Nonnus for only one, but the average number of Fathers cited for each text by Boismard is *nineteen*!

Having read Boismard much more carefully, B. Metzger was conscious
of the weight of the number of Fathers that Boismard was able to draw together. Apropos of Jn 14:2 he noted that Boismard's position was supported by
thirty-four Fathers, but could only reply, "When one examines each of
Boismard's references in its context, one is struck by the paucity of evidence
that the Father, in any single case, intended to quote the full text of the
verse.... In these cases one can discern no reason why a given Father should
have been obliged to refer to more than the gist of the text."[56] Apart from
the *petitio principii* that the manuscript tradition represents the authentic
text, which is precisely what Boismard does not accept, it is clear that Metzger has missed the significance of the numbers. Is it conceivable that so
many Fathers of different centuries would *all* quote the gist of a text in *precisely* the same way?

Since the methodological criticisms of his position seemed to be no
more more than an excuse to remain with familiar illusions, it is understandable that Boismard was not at all deterred. In fact quite the opposite.
He extended his research to include the Synoptics! It had long been recognized that when a Father consistently cites a gospel saying with the same
variations from the accepted text, or when a number of Fathers who were
not dependent on one another all cite the same variant from the received
text, one must postulate that he and they are dependent on a document.
What sort of a document was this, and how was it related to the canonical
gospels? In an article which gives a very useful history of the wide variety
of answers given to these questions, Boismard analysed Mt 5:16,17 and 37,
and concluded that the document was independent of canonical Matthew,
because it contained a more archaic form of the logia, and that it was probably a catechism for the instruction of candidates for baptism.[57]

If the ill-founded criticism of his work was rightly ignored by Boismard,
there were others less competent who took it more seriously, and pressure
was brought to bear on Father Mollat to move to a more centrist position.
Thus in the third edition of John in the Bible de Jérusalem (1973) we find
the sad little note, "It will be remarked that, in terms of text-critical options,

---

[55] F. Neirynck, J. Delobel, T. Snoy, G. Van Belle, F. Van Segbroeck, Jean et les Synopti-
      ques. Examen critique de l'exégèse de M.-E. Boismard (BETL 49), Leuven: University
      Press, 1979, 29.

[56] "Patristic Evidence and the Textual Criticism of the New Testament," NTS 18 (1971-
      72) 390.

[57] "Une tradition para-synoptique attestée par les Pères anciens," in The New Testament
      in Early Christianity (BETL 86), ed. J.-M. Sevrin, Leuven (in press).

in more than one case this edition represents a step backwards by comparison with the preceding one."[58]

In his commentary on John Boismard moved in the same direction, but in this case the reason is clearly given. "By and large our textual criticism has remained very moderate, and we have not made use of a number of habitually neglected variants. We did not wish to develop our literary hypothesis on the basis of a text that many would not have hesitated to criticize."[59]

Just in case it might prove an easy way to demolish the Boismard-Lamouille explanation of the genesis of the Fourth Gospel, the Neirynck team at the University of Leuven took a very close look at their textual options.[60] If one sifts through the mass of niggling and often irrelevant criticism of detail, it becomes clear that no fundamental or serious objections have been raised.

On the contrary, it is recognized that Boismard had fulfilled his promise of moderation by not drawing on seventeen variants in whose favor he had argued in previous publications. Moreover, he had not abused the patristic tradition. Out of the 107 cases in which he diverged from the 26th edition of Nestle-Aland, there were only three instances in which he based himself exclusively on citations from the Fathers. In addition, he had not neglected external criteria, but even granted them a decisive role in certain circumstances. Finally, he had followed the rule of all the manuals from Hort to Metzger by actually doing what others only talked about; he used the style of the NT author as a criterion in the appreciation of variants.[61] More than that, A. Lamouille had actually drawn up the first complete and scientifically based list of Johannine stylistic characteristics, thereby furnishing scholars with a unique tool.

(b) Literary Criticism

Despite Boismard's willingness to abandon or modify his position in the light of new evidence, there was always a fundamental consistency in his approach which would have enabled those familiar with his publications to predict certain aspects of his literary history of the Fourth Gospel.

---

58 La Sainte Bible, traduite en français sous la direction de l'École Biblique de Jérusalem: L'évangile et les épîtres de Jean, Paris: Cerf, 1973, 71.

59 Évangile de Jean, 12.

60 Examen critique de l'exégèse de M.-E. Boismard, 23-40 and 205-226.

61 Since it is difficult to dig out the key conclusions from the mass of verbiage, the page references in Examen critique de l'exégèse de M.-E. Boismard, are 27, 28-29, 32, 39, 220, 225.

On a number of occasions he had postulated an Aramaic substratum as the most probable explanation of the origin of textual variants.[62] The recognition that a single author might have translated different Aramaic sources was an important factor in Boismard's refusal to be overwhelmed by E. Ruckstuhl's demonstration of the ubiquity of a unique style throughout the Fourth Gospel; a book which inhibited most Catholic scholars from taking up the challenge of Bultmann's great commentary.[63]

In his very first article Boismard had accepted the existence of different literary levels in John, and this aspect appeared in his every publication on the subject. Of particular importance, however, were a series of studies which demonstrated various forms of evolution within the Fourth Gospel. The thought of the gospel exhibited development in the treatment of eschatological themes, in the traditions concerning John the Baptist and Jesus, and in the understanding of Jesus' washing of the feet of his disciples.[64]

His recognition of Baptist and Christian missions in Samaria laid the groundword for the admission of Samaritan influence,[65] particularly as regards the vision of Jesus as the Prophet-like-Moses.[66] But he also detected the influence of the Targums in the translation of certain OT texts used in John.[67]

Such details, however, acquired their proper shape only within the framework of the whole. In his first book Boismard divided the gospel into seven weeks,[68] which he was to follow up by a detailed analysis of the first week.[69] Finally, he had also had occasion to speak of John in Synopse II. On the basis of those passages which John has in common with the Synoptics he had concluded that there were three literary levels in the Fourth Gospel.[70]

---

[62] "A propos de Jean v, 39: Essai de critique textuelle," RB 55 (1948) 5-34; "Importance de la critique textuelle pour établir l'origine araméenne du quatrième évangile," in L'Évangile de Jean. Études et problèmes (RechBib 3), ed. F.-M. Braun, Brugge, 1958, 41-57.

[63] Die literarische Einheit des Johannesevangeliums (SF 3), Freiburg in der Schweiz: Paulusverlag, 1952. Reviewed by Boismard in RB 59 (1952) 425-427.

[64] "L'évolution du thème eschatologique dans les traditions johanniques," RB 68 (1961) 507-524; "Les traditions johanniques concernant le Baptiste," RB 70 (1963) 5-42; "Le lavement des pieds (Jn, xiii, 1-17)," RB 71 (1964) 5-24.

[65] "Aenon, près de Salem (Jean, iii, 23)," RB 80 (1973) 218-229.

[66] "Jèsus, le Prophète par excellence, d'après Jean 10, 24-39," in Neues Testament und Kirche. FS R. Schnackenburg, ed. J. Gnilka, Freiburg: Herder, 1974, 160-171.

[67] "'De son ventre couleront des fleuves d'eau' (Jo., vii, 38)," RB 65 (1958) 523-546; "Les citations targumiques dans le quatrième évangile," RB 66 (1959) 374-378.

[68] Le Prologue de saint Jean (LD 11), Paris: Cerf, 1953, 136-138.

[69] Du Baptême à Cana (Jean, 1,29-2,11) (LD 18), Paris: Cerf, 1956.

[70] Synopse II, 16.

While all these partial studies have left their mark on L'Évangile de Jean, they were inevitably nuanced and sometimes transformed in being absorbed into a complete hypothesis according to which the Fourth Gospel in its present form is the term of a four-stage evolution.

Stage 1. About A.D. 50 a complete gospel written in Aramaic appeared in Palestine. It may have been written by the Beloved Disciple, who was either John son of Zebedee or Lazarus. It should be called John I because neither style nor vocabulary distinguish it from subsequent stages, but it is identical with what Boismard called Document C in his study of the Synoptics, and he preferred to retain this name in order to highlight the links between all four gospels. In this primitive gospel pride of place was given to five miracles, 'signs' performed by Jesus, which served as the basis of faith. The influence of Samaritan theology was underlined by the presentation of Jesus as the Prophet-like-Moses.

Stage 2. Some ten to fifteen years later, still in Palestine, this material was reworked in Greek by the main Johannine author, whom Boismard called John II. Identified as 'John the Presbyter', of whom Papias spoke, he produced two editions of his gospel (John II-A and John II-B) as well as the three Johannine letters. In his first edition (John II-A) he kept the order of Document C, while adding two miracles (from Document A) to bring the number up to seven, the call of Andrew and Peter, and a few dominical discourses. He toned down some of the Samaritan traits of Document C, but identified the opponents of Jesus as 'Jews'. He developed further the apologetic use of miracles to promote faith in Jesus as the Prophet par excellence, but at the same time introduced Wisdom christology. His use of chaism and misunderstanding revealed a creative literary spirit.

Stage 3. John II eventually emigrated from Palestine and settled in Ephesus, capital of the province of Asia. There he came into contact with Essene groups and with the Pauline church. It was there that he discovered the works of Matthew, Mark, and Luke. He also encountered new problems, notably, the opposition of Judaeo-Christians which heightened tensions within the community, and the problem of faith among second-generation Christians.

Thus in the last decade of the first century he decided to update his gospel and produced John II-B, which incorporated the new theological ideas to which he had been exposed, and strove to respond more adequately to the needs of a church very different to that for which John II-A had been written. He replaced the geographical framework of Document C by a schema of eight weeks in which Jewish feasts played a key role. Since there were no longer miracles to generate faith, he changed the relationship; a miracle was asked for out of faith based on the word of Jesus. Moreover, miracles were but fragments among long discourses of Jesus. The christology reflected the developing insights of the church and portrayed Jesus as a pre-existent figure. Its pastoral needs were catered for by an explicit sacramental theology. The polemic against the 'Jews' became much sharper.

Stage 4. The editor who gave the gospel the shape in which we have it today, John III, was a fussy old antiquarian of the Johannine school in Ephesus at the beginning of the second century. Even though John II had set aside (as no longer relevant) portions of Document C and of John II-A, John III was determined to preserve them for posterity. He did so by inserting them into John II-B, thereby creating archaizing doublets. Even less intelligently, he changed the original order of what are now chs. 5 and 6. He also added explanatory glosses which on more than one occasion obscure rather than clarify.

As with all great pioneering works, L'Évangile de Jean was not received with universal applause. It did, however, receive the accolade of the longest and fastest review ever written. The imprimatur was granted on 16 June 1977 and in December of that same year the Neirynck team at the University of Leuven published a 115 page assessment.[71] Such speed was possible only because Neirynck had requested and received the proofs of the book and so did not have to wait for its appearance on the market.[72] Such generosity must not go unremarked, because Neirynck had been severely critical of the first two volumes of the Synopse,[73] and Boismard had no reason to expect better treatment, knowing Neirynck's refusal to abandon positions he has once adopted.

Yet, as he and Lamouille stressed in their preface, no one was more conscious than they of the hypothetical character of their conclusions. They freely admitted that even they were unhappy with some of the notes, notably those concerning the final discourse of Jesus. They made no claim to have produced the definitive answer to the Johannine problem. In their view they were simply making an innovative contribution to the on-going debate. Their courageous tentativeness, however, was met by a defensive certitude.

Instead of a serious attempt to look at the gospel in a new way, which is the essence of genuine dialogue, the Neirynck team retreated behind a bar-

---

[71] "L'Évangile de Jean. Examen critique du commentaire de M.-E. Boismard et A. Lamouille," ETL 53 (1977) 363-478. Thus it beat by two pages and a couple of years J. Strugnell's review (RevQ 7 [1970] 163-276) of J. Allegro, Qumran Cave 4, I (4Q158-4Q186) (DJD 5), Oxford: Clarendon, 1968. In contrast to what we are at present considering, Strugnell's review was much more intelligent and creative than Allegro's book.

[72] In the first note of the article referred to in the previous footnote we read, "We thank the author and Father F.-R. Refoulé of Éditions du Cerf for their generosity in making this book available to use as soon as it was ready (dès son achèvement)." The deliberate ambiguity of the final phrase is to be noted, as is the disappearance of even this grudging expression of gratitude in the expanded version of this review which was published as a book, F. Neirynck, J. Delobel, T. Snoy, G. Van Belle, F. Van Segbroeck, Jean et les Synoptiques. Examen critique de l'exégèse de M.-E. Boismard (BETL 49), Leuven: University Press, 1979.

[73] See the reprints in Examen critique de l'exégèse de M.-E. Boismard, 289-387.

rier of minutiae. The atmosphere of their critique is perfectly conveyed by the patronising shallowness of their conclusion, "We have learned much in reading this book [Évangile de Jean], but we have also judged it useful to relate it to earlier works of Boismard and to show how the positions of the latter have evolved. The Commentary itself does not adequately inform its readers of such matters, nor indeed of the opinions of his predecessors; when these are cited it is in too general a manner, and what he owes to each one is not specified.... As regards the arguments of internal criticism and the use of stylistic characteristics, we have verified that their application demands more nuances than Boismard accords them, and that in John one needs to take into account a good number of variations and synonyms.... The principal contribution of the Commentary is the very detailed inventory of the characteristics of the vocabulary and style of John,.... We have completed these observations by adding those of other authors whom he has neglected.... We have not hidden our misgivings with regard to the literary theory, and for many passages we have proposed a different exegesis.... The examination of this book has permitted us to improve and explain our personal approach to the Fourth Gospel."[74]

It is not really surprising that those so committed to exactitude in detail should have omitted the name of Lamouille, who had particular responsibility for the preparation of the list of Johannine stylistic traits. In 286 pages -- the book expanded the original ETL article -- there is not a single generous, warm, human gesture of gratitude or encouragement. The tone of magisterial sententiousness evokes, not a partner in dialogue, but a don putting out a contract!

Understandably, therefore, X. Léon-Dufour, SJ, thought it necessary to highlight a presupposition (hinted at in the last sentence of the above citation) and to articulate a warning. "Neirynck refuses to distinguish different levels in the redaction of John, estimating that it is much too complicated to do so; he prides himself on explaining everything by the direct literary dependence of John on the Synoptics. From this point of view, which I believe to be wrong, it would be abusive to judge the monumental work of Boismard exclusively on the basis of the detailed studies of Neirynck."[75]

This is not to imply, however, that Léon-Dufour agreed with Boismard-Lamouille. On the contrary, he questioned the very legitimacy of source criticism, "Can one claim guaranteed objectivity in the detail of sources and text?"[76] Were 'guaranteed objectivity' a criterion for the publication of exegetical theories, there would be no books, and certainly no book reviews! Léon-Dufour nonetheless ended on a positive note, "The major contribution

---

[74] Examen critique de l'exégèse de M.-E. Boismard, 285-286.

[75] RSR 68 (1980) 284.

[76] RSR 68 (1980) 282.

of Boismard will be to nuance the description of the Johannine community proposed by J. L. Martyn and R. E. Brown."[77]

The allusion is to the latter's The Community of the Beloved Disciple (1979), which Léon-Dufour reviewed in the same bulletin. This book develops a broad four-phase hypothesis to explain the evolution of the Johannine church. Léon-Dufour called it seductive, but he asked, "Is it conformed to the reality? Many, probably, will consider the historical underpinning too fragile. In the last analysis, the panaroma is reconstructed on the basis of a few rare texts, such as 5:18 or 9:22; 12:42; 16:2."[78]

It is precisely here that we begin to perceive the real difference between Boismard-Lamouille and their contemporaries. The ostensible difference is the complexity of their theory. According to R. Kysar, "The proposal is unnecessarily complex."[79] R. E. Brown was rather more brutal, "The theory of Johannine composition, like the earlier theory of synoptic interrelationships, is so detailed, so complicated, and so idiosyncratic that I suspect that it will have little influence."[80] Why Brown should consider such a remark as valid objection is difficult to fathom because his own theory involves at least five stages, one more than Boismard-Lamouille![81] In response to criticism, after pointing out that little in NT studies is provable, Brown said, "I would argue that the really convincing theory in relation to the Fourth Gospel is the one that most plausibly accounts for the present gospel and has at least some antecedent in biblical composition as we know it from OT or NT (I have been amused by critics who dismissed my own theory of five steps of composition when similar five steps are widely accepted by OT scholars in discussing the composition of Jeremiah!)."[82]

The real test of an hypothesis, as Brown recognizes when it is question of his own work, is not simplicity but adequacy. Complexity alone does not put Boismard-Lamouille outside the mainstream of Johannine studies, as some reviewers have tried to suggest. What really sets them apart from their contemporaries (with the exception of R. T. Fortna) is their willingness to be highly specific.

While fully aware of the artificiality of the enterprise, they offer detailed reconstructions of sources and editorial additions in order that their readers may be in no doubt as to exactly what they mean. Thereby of course they

---

[77] RSR 68 (1980) 283.

[78] RSR 68 (1980) 287. Boismard came to exactly the same conclusion in his review. "Brown has accustomed us to more rigor in his demonstrations. I doubt that his book will convince those who seek the proofs which support the statements of its author." (RB 88 [1981] 471).

[79] JBL 98 (1979) 607.

[80] CBQ 40 (1978) 627.

[81] The Gospel according to John (I-XII) (AB 29), Garden City: Doubleday, 1966, xxxiv-xxxix.

[82] JBL 96 (1977) 146.

give hostages to fortune. They can be proved wrong in details or in the general picture. Such gallantry unfortunately is an affront to those who rely on their position or reputation to sustain vague generalisations, which would be dismissed as fantasies if proposed by lesser scholars. So they bridle defensively and bleat that all the complications of various editions of the gospel of John would be avoided if a greater role were given to oral tradition.[83]

To try to pindown such theories is like trying to capture smoke, which regretfully is the whole point. The hypotheses are so fluid that they cannot be disproved, and thus become exempt from serious discussion. Even if the proposal of Boismard-Lamouille is not accepted, its mere existence serves as a prick to the professional conscience by its thoroughness and completeness. It sets a new standard for the rigorous clarity with which an hypothesis should be presented, in addition to being a distinguished theological commentary.[84]

A Leuven Doctorate

The intellectual attitude of the Neirynck team to the ideas of Boismard-Lamouille did not extend to their persons. On the personal level friendship dominated and bore extraordinary fruit. In order to honor Boismard for his great contribution to NT scholarship they proposed him for an honorary doctorate, which was conferred at Leuven on 25 October 1988. On that occasion the *Laudatio* was pronounced by F. Neirynck, whose generosity was equal to the demands of the literary form. With grace and wit he explained why Leuven was so quick to criticize. After mentioning the number of times that Boismard had lectured at Leuven, he continued, "One almost has the impression that before each of his major publications Professor Boismard intended to come to Louvain to give us a foretaste.... In response to these premiers accorded to Louvain we have attempted each time to offer him the antidote of a first critical examination of his hypotheses." The doctorate ceremony also doubled as a party to launch Boismard's latest book, Moïse ou Jésus. Essai de christologie johannique, which had just been published in the most prestigious series of the Theological Faculty. Therein he explained the major themes of Johannine christology, Jesus as Prophet, Wisdom, Word, and Only-Begotten, and brought them into a new synthesis.

The Acts of the Apostles

After the Synoptics and John only one other literary mountain remained to be climbed. Its attractiveness was all the greater in that Boismard had not

---

[83] See in particular E. Cothenet, "L'Évangile de Jean," RThom 78 (1978) 629, but also A. Jaubert, RHR 196 (1979) 98; R. Kysar, JBL 98 (1979) 607.

[84] It took a German reviewer to point out the L'Évangile de Jean is the first major commentary on John to appear in French since that of Lagrange in 1925 (J. Hainz, MTZ 31 [1980] 92).

yet even approached its foothills. The Acts of the Apostles was the one topic on which he had never written an article! Moreover, the Acts of the Apostles was one of the major sources for the history of the early church. There were points, however, on which it did not agree with the data of the Pauline letters. This made it imperative to determine the sources on which Luke had drawn, and how he had treated them. But which text should be analysed, the long Western Text or the shorter Alexandrian Text?

(a) Textual Criticism

At the beginning of critical study it was felt that no choice between the Western and Alexandrian Texts was necessary. Eminent names were convinced that both texts came from the pen of Luke, who had revised his own work. If there was any dispute it concerned which text was the older. In the 20th century the hypothesis of two Lukan editions was abandoned. For a short period the Western Text enjoyed popularity as the authentic text, but it was quickly supplanted by the Alexandrian Text, which today serves as the basis of the 26th edition of Nestle-Aland, the reigning critical edition of the NT.

Naturally, such a simplistic choice attracted opposition, and a considerable number of scholars refused to give automatic preference to either text. While in theory they insisted on a consistent eclecticism, it was clear that in practice their choices were dictated by an undeclared preference for the Alexandrian Text. Others reacted against this bias by showing that the vocabulary and style of the Western Text were authentically Lukan. To this the partisans of the Alexandrian Text retorted that the second century A.D. editor of the Western Text had imitated the style of the original document best represented by the Alexandrian Text.

Boismard and Lamouille immediately saw the fallacy of this reponse. It is easy to talk about a distinction between an author's style and its imitation by someone else, but that is all. To develop criteria which would demonstrate the distinction would be so difficult as to be impossible. The imitation hypothesis, therefore, should be ignored because it is incapable of verification. The question of the Lukan style of the Western Text then became a matter of paramount importance, and Boismard and Lamouille saw that they would have to solve this fundamental problem before undertaking any literary analysis of Acts. To this they devoted the next five years (1978-83), and the fruits of their labors appeared in 1984 under the title <u>Le texte occidental des Actes des Apôtres. Reconstitution et réhabilitation.</u>

Their first problem was to find the Western Text. The principal witness is the Codex Bezae (D), but they were easily able to confirm its inadequacy. All their extraordinary erudition was brought into play in a comprehensive interrogation of other witnesses in Greek, Latin, Coptic, Ethiopian, Syrian, Armenian, and Arabic, not to mention such esoterica as medieval translations in Provençal, Dutch, German and Bohemian. This quest yielded a vast jungle of possible readings. How were they to discriminate between them?

On the basis of a purified Alexandrian Text and the Third Gospel Lamouille in particular developed a list of almost a thousand characteristics of Lukan style ranging from single words to complex expressions. This is an extraordinary exegetical took which in both scope and detail far surpasses all previous efforts to tabulate the style of Luke. It is indispensable for future critical study of both Luke and Acts. Given the extent and complexity of the task, it would be surprising if these listings were immune to error. Certain corrections and refinements have in fact been suggested,[85] but these are so minor as to be a most convincing tribute to the care and thoroughness of Boismard and Lamouille. Their work will stand as a benchmark in Lukan studies and as a model for the stylistic analysis of other sacred authors.

These stylistic trail-markers enabled them to find their way through the jungle of variant readings to the El Dorado of the original Western Text. The Western Text which they have reconstructed is undoubtedly authentically Lukan. This is clear in the long readings, where the consistency of style renders the hypothesis of an imitator implausible. Even more noteworthy is the fact that when the Western Texts parallels the Alexandrian Text the former is almost always shorter then the latter.

This is likely to prove the most debatable feature of their work, because in certain instances the readings adopted are attested by only a very limited number of witnesses. A case in point is their choice of an ultra-short text of Acts 27-28 on the basis of two Ethiopian MSS of the 14-15th centuries and the Latin palimpsest of Fleury. Generally these witnesses have been ignored, because it was assumed that the translators could not understand the highly technical nautical terms employed in the account of Paul's sea journey to Rome, and so simply omitted whole sections. As reconstructed by Boismard-Lamouille, however, the text has a consistency which is incompatible with a mutilated document; on occasion the style is manifestly Lukan.

Once again Boismard and Lamouille are likely to annoy their colleagues by the clarity and firmness of their reconstruction of the Western Text, but they make no claim to have established the definitive Western Text. "Let us say rather that we wanted to present to specialists an 'experimental' text, whose traits we have accentuated to the maximum, and which should be submitted to a close analysis."[86]

---

[85] F. Neirynck with F. Van Segbroeck, "Le texte des Actes des Apôtres et les caractéristiques stylistiques lucaniennes," ETL 61 (1985) 304-339.

[86] Le Texte Occidental des Actes des Apôtres (Synthèse 17), Paris: Éditions Recherche sur les Civilisations, 1984 (= 1985), I, x.

From the reviews it is clear that specialists are not clear how to accept this challenge. J.-C. Haelewyck put his finger on the difficulty, "It would be impossible to verify everything. Yet merely to take soundings would be unworthy of the magnitude of the work accomplished." and so he confined his remarks to some important comments on the use of the Latin versions.[87] "Such a thesaurus of Western readings has not been available hitherto and is a monument of abiding significance, regardless of one's judgement on B + L's text." is the assessment of J. K. Eliott, but he does not commit himself to a judgment on their text.[88] In fact it would be very difficult to do so, because it is rare for their conclusions to rest solely on the number and date of witnesses. In a significant number of cases they are able to show that their preferred short readings provide the most probable explanation of the inversions which appear in one or the other grouping of better known and more widely accepted witnesses.

The only adequate critique, therefore, will be to produce better explanations of highly complex bodies of data. The challenge is a stimulus to the science of textual criticism, but if specialists accept it and indeed do better, it will certainly be due in great part to the vast body of evidence so conveniently assembled by Boismard-Lamouille and to the critical tools which they have developed for its dissection.

(b) Literary Criticism

As might have been expected from their work on the Synoptics and John, the Boismard-Lamouille analysis of the Acts of the Apostles is complex; more so, however, in the interplay of relationships than in the number of documents they discern.

At the most primitive level they postulate three documents. Document P (the Petrine document) was the continuation of a gospel which served as a source of Luke and John, namely, Document C in Boismard-Lamouille's synoptic theory. The prominence given to Peter might suggest that this document could be the "Recollections of Peter" mentioned by Origen. It was written about A.D. 50 in a community of converted Hellenized Jews. Document J (the Johannite document), on the other hand, was an elaboration of themes which appear in the "Benedictus" (Lk 1:68-79). Written in a group dependent on John the Baptist, it depicted the latter as the one who would restore the kingdom of Israel. Finally, there was a Travel Diary which was written by a companion of Paul, probably Silas. It covered a journey mainly by sea from the port of Antioch via Troas and back to Caesarea Maritima, which was followed by a second voyage from Caesarea via Malta to Rome.

---

[87] "Le texte occidental des Acts des Apôtres. A propos de la reconstitution de M.-E. Boismard et A. Lamouille," RTL 19 (1988) 342-353, here 343.

[88] NT 29 (1987) 285-288, here 287.

This corresponds to the collection journey mentioned by Paul in Rom 15:22-29.[89]

The first editor of such diverse material, <u>Acts I</u>, was not interested in writing history. He divided Document J into three parts, which he incorporated into the key speeches of Peter (Acts 3), Stephen (Acts 7), and Paul (Acts 13), but he reacted against its basic thesis. He used Document P, which stressed the importance of the resurrection to show that Jesus, not John the Baptist, was the new Elijah who would return to restore the kingdom of Israel. This document furnished him with all the material for the Petrine section (Acts 1-12 minus 9:1-35). In the Pauline section (Acts 13-28) he used the Travel Diary to create a framework for Paul's ministry, and to provide him with ideas for his own sea stories. Acts I was not interested in Paul as an apostle to the gentiles; he is presented exclusively as a missionary to Jews, who refused his preaching again and again. In consequence, Acts I believed, God would retaliate by destroying Jerusalem.

The second editor, <u>Acts II</u>, knew not only the work of Acts I, but also two of its sources, Document P and the Travel Diary. These he often cites where Acts I merely alluded to them. The inevitable result was a certain number of doublets (e.g. the double presentations of the Ascension and the gift of the Spirit). He was also ideologically opposed to Acts I. In his view the idea that the kingdom of Israel would be restored had been superseded. The kingdom was already present in the gift of the Holy Spirit, which is given to all humanity. The horizon of Acts II is much wider than the Jewish people. Thus he also corrected the portrait of Paul. If he preached to Jews, his ministry was above all to gentiles. Moreover, Acts II was interested in Paul as a person. He drew on the Pauline letters, notably Galatians but also the Corinthian correspondence, to provide biographical details about the Apostle. Finally, Acts II insisted on the importance of the organisation of the church and its sacramental life. This edition was contemporary with the redaction of the Pastoral Letters, and was the work of Luke, probably about A.D. 80.

The final editor, <u>Acts III</u>, to whom we owe Acts in its present form, drew sometimes on Acts I, and sometimes on Acts II, whose style he improved.

Since Boismard and Lamouille's book will appear roughly at the same time as this survey of their accomplishments, it is too early to speak of its impact. One thing is sure, it breaks new ground in the study of the Acts of the Apostles, because it is the first systematic source analysis to be based on a detailed analysis of the entire work.

Many as his laurels are Boismard does not intend to rest on them. Once the proofs are read and the volume published, he plans to begin a comprehensive text-critical study of the Gospel of John.

---

[89] Justin Taylor made a significant contribution to the detection and reconstruction of the Travel Diary source.

Chapter 5

JEROME MURPHY-O'CONNOR, O.P.

by Justin Taylor, SM

The first non-Frenchspeaker to be appointed to the faculty of the École Biblique was Jerome Murphy-O'Connor. He was born in Cork, in what is now the Republic of Ireland, on 10 April 1935, the first of four children of Kerry Murphy-O'Connor, a wholesale wine and spirit merchant, and his wife Mary McCrohan. He was educated by the Irish Christian Brothers in Cork, and by the Vincentians at Castleknock College in Dublin as a boarder. Before he finished his schooling he had already made up his mind to enter the Dominican Order, and his parents gave him the freedom of living at home and attending a day school in his last year. He left school in 1953 with an Honours Leaving Certificate.

In appreciating Jerome Murphy-O'Connor the scholar and writer, it is important to know something of the man. He is a big man in physique and in temperament, in his youth an ardent rugby player who had a reputation for being able to take and give hard knocks, and throughout his life a keen hiker. He has applied his energy and determination to intellectual effort, but he has never tired of walking around the Holy Land with a curiosity that is always able to discover something new. He enjoys "laughter and the love of friends," and has found in their company and conversation the challenge of fresh points of view and many of the questions which he has tried to answer in his articles and books. It is important also to reckon with the Irishness of Murphy-O'Connor. He has the characteristically Irish delight in the play of wit and language, in story-telling, and in vigorous argument. He has also shared the destiny of so many of his compatriots to live outside their native land.

Formation

In the Ireland of the 1950s no one would have been surprised by the young Murphy-O'Connor's decision to become a priest. Many of his uncles and cousins were secular priests, but it was not to the diocesan priesthood that he was drawn. He would say he had a fear of living alone, and so instinctively found the idea of life in community more congenial. Later on, he was to find in "community" the key to understanding not only religious life but also the theology of St Paul. As for the Dominicans, they were a religious Order which he knew from attending their church, St Mary's, in Cork. He did not realise they had an intellectual tradition, and even had he known, that would not have interested him greatly at the time.

Murphy-O'Connor entered the Novitiate in Cork in September, 1953, when his baptismal name of James was changed to Jerome. The choice of the patron saint of Biblical studies in the Western Church was purely fortuitous and indicated no intention, either on his part or on that of his superiors, that he should make such studies his life's work. But in this case, nomen est omen. He remained in Cork for his first year of philosophy, then went to the Dominican House of Studies at Tallaght near Dublin for his second and third years of philosophy and his first two years of theology.

By then he realised that there were too many priests in Ireland, and consequently there was too little work for religious priests in parishes. He thought he would like to become a professor and teach in the House of Studies. He opted for Scripture, because that was the field in which creative work was being done at the time. In particular, his imagination was caught by the work produced at the École Biblique.

In the summer of 1959 Murphy-O'Connor had a stroke of luck. It became clear that when the philosophy students came up from Cork, there would not be enough room for all at Tallaght, so ten of the seniors were scattered throughout Europe. Murphy-O'Connor was sent to the University of Fribourg in Switzerland, where he spent three years from 1959 to 1962. He was ordained priest on 10 July 1960 and received the Licentiate and Lectorate in Theology in 1961.

At that stage the Provincial of Ireland asked him to stay an extra year in Fribourg to get a doctorate, if possible. In those days one would not think of questioning the wisdom of such a decision, and in any case Murphy-O'Connor felt he was well on the way to the goal. He had already produced a thesis of 100 pages for the Lectorate, which was received by the Faculty "Summa cum Laude." The subject, "St Paul's Conception of Preaching," indicated what was to prove to be a lifelong interest in St Paul; it indicated also that this interest would not be only academic but would be in close touch with the needs and concerns of the pastoral ministry.

From his work on this first dissertation, Murphy-O'Connor knew what further questions needed to be answered and saw how it could be expanded into a doctoral thesis. Moreover, he intended to continue working with the great Pauline specialist Ceslas Spicq, O.P., who had directed his earlier research, and knew that Spicq read quickly and corrected thoroughly. The thesis was accepted "Summa cum Laude" on 9 July 1962 with the title, "The Activity of an Apostle. A Study of Saint Paul's Conception of Missionary Preaching."

During his year in Fribourg, Murphy-O'Connor got to know a number of Dominican Sisters who were fellow graduate students. One of these was Sr Kaye Ashe, O.P., of the Sinsinawa Congregation, who became a lifelong

Jerome Murphy-O'Connor, O.P.

friend. Murphy-O'Connor has expressed his gratitude for her help and encouragement by dedicating several of his books to her.

The year 1962-1963 was spent in Rome preparing for the Baccalaureate in Sacred Scripture from the Pontifical Biblical Commission. Then to Jerusalem, as St Paul's contemporaries might have done, by boat from Naples via Alexandria to Beirut; but whereas earlier travellers would have walked from Beirut or ridden a camel or a donkey, in 1963 one took a service taxi ($3.) So Jerome Murphy-O'Connor arrived at the École Biblique which had fired his enthusiasm as a student in Ireland. He did not realise it yet, but he had found his vocation.

During his first year as a student at the École, Murphy-O'Connor's Fribourg Th.D. thesis was published under the title Paul on Preaching.[1] The author declared his aim to address a contemporary pastoral problem in the Church, namely the revitalisation of preaching, which was by common consent regarded as generally poor. Reading the Introduction one breathes again the heady atmosphere of the years just before and during the Second Vatican Council: "That action (of the Spirit,) as manifested by the movements stirring within the Church today, indicates that all renewal must be a rediscovery and a recapturing of the pattern, structure and ideals that existed at the beginning. In other words, it must be effected by a return to the sources. And when it is a question of a renewal of preaching, no further apology need be made for an effort to share the insights of the preacher par excellence, St Paul" (p.xv.).

Paul, of course, nowhere gives us a developed view of preaching or of the preacher; it was necessary to infer what he thought from remarks scattered throughout his letters and from the general lines of his theology. Murphy-O'Connor's procedure reminded more than one reviewer of a detective at work. The resulting synthesis of Paul's insights was, as one Protestant reviewer put it, a "high view" of preaching, which is thus summarily stated on p.25: "Hence, not preaching as such, but preaching as the intimation of a choice made from all eternity in Christ Jesus (Eph. 1.4), is the point of contact between the objective and subjective orders of redemption. It puts individuals into contact with the merits of Christ's passion only in so far as it embodies an eternal call addressed to them." The book first examines the place of preaching in the plan of salvation, then the prophetic ministry, with a study of the various titles which Paul applies to the preacher. Preaching, it emerges, is for St Paul nothing more nor less than a prolongation of the ministry of Christ. There follows a study of the power of the word, an idea which would have been relatively unfamiliar to Catholics at the time, but was soon to be enshrined in the documents of Vatican II. Murphy-O'Connor deals also with the proposal of the word by the preacher and its acceptance or refusal by the hearer, and finally discusses preaching as a "liturgical act."

---

1   Paul on Preaching, London and New York: Sheed and Ward, 1964.

To reread Paul on Preaching after getting to know the later writings of
Murphy-O'Connor is to recognise much that is familiar. It is a work of biblical theology, rich and inspiring, yet based on careful exegesis. It is not
written primarily for other exegetes, but for non-specialists, in this case
preachers, in the hope that it may be useful to them in their ministry. It is
about St Paul, and many Pauline themes are introduced which will be developed in the future. On the other hand, it belongs in many ways to another
world. The theological categories in which the thought is expressed are
scholastic. The author had not yet acquired a perfect ease of style nor the art
of writing what the reader needs to know, which is not everything the writer
knows. One looks in vain in the index for the word "community" which had
not yet found its place in Murphy-O'Connor's thinking.

The book was widely reviewed in English language periodicals and ma-
gazines on both sides of the Atlantic. Protestant reviewers gave it a genuine,
if at times patronising, welcome; Catholics were generally more deferential.
Most paid tribute to the author's learning, though some felt that at times it
got in the way of his message. The most important review was that of P.
Benoit,[2] who congratulated the author "on having been able to draw from
an academic exercise a work which is highly theological, spiritual and apostolic." He too noted that the book had rather too much of the doctoral dissertation about its presentation, but was sure that it possessed all that was
needed "for this excellent study to bring light and profit, not only to Biblical
scholars and theologians, but also to the vast audience of all those to whom
God continues to address his word."

Benoit saw to it that the book was translated into French and published
in 1966 in the Cahiers de la Revue Biblique.[3] On the whole the book was
taken more seriously in French than in English and was reviewed in major
French, German and Swiss periodicals, as well as in the Catholic Biblical
Quarterly, whose reviewer thought it "deserves rapid publication in English" (the same periodical had already reviewed the original.) Reviewers
were generally favourable: Ch. Matagne, S.J., in Nouvelle Revue Théologique described the book as "a fine study, enriching and timely." For Joachim
Gnilka in Theologische Revue "This work is doubly stimulating: it concerns
a central problem in Pauline theology, and it has much to offer every pastoral theologian and preacher." In the view of Francois Bovon in Theologische Zeitschrift, the book presents "a respectable exegesis of various Pauline texts on preaching and good syntheses of Biblical theology on the subject"; but it was regrettable that "the author ignores a great part of what has
been produced in Germany and does not enter into dialogue with contem-

---

[2]   RB 71 (1964) 465-466.
[3]   La Prédication selon saint Paul, Paris: Gabalda, 1966.

porary theologians of the Word of God (Barth, Bultmann, Ebeling, to name only those)." A German version of Paul on Preaching appeared in 1968. [4]

It was a good beginning. During his first year at the École Murphy-O'Connor wrote a mémoire on "La vérité chez saint Paul et à Qumran" which was received with a "mention très honorable" and published in the Revue Biblique for 1965. The choice of subject indicated that he was continuing the line of Pauline studies and at the same time announced a new interest, Qumran. The article takes for granted that there are traces of Essenian influence in the Pauline corpus which cannot be explained simply in terms of shared Old Testament background, and tries to determine in one area the precise extent and form of this influence. The concept of "truth" was chosen for comparison because it is important both in the Pauline corpus, where the noun *aletheia* occurs 44 times, and in the Qumran literature, with at least 120 occurrences of the theme. Murphy-O'Connor concludes that affinities between Paul and Qumran with respect to various aspects of the concept of "truth" are to be found, not scattered throughout the Pauline corpus, but grouped according to the great divisions of the Pauline writings. This suggested either that Paul was at different moments emphasising one or other facet of the idea in reaction to Qumran, or that those who wrote the epistles under his aegis were influenced in different ways by the Essenian concept. The latter hypothesis was to be preferred in the case of Ephesians. This last point provided material for a popular article in which he argued that the writer of Ephesians was a disciple of Paul who had himself been an Essene.[5]

Benoit clearly had his eye on this promising young Dominican who had already produced writings of high quality. The future of the École depended on regular recruitment of new Faculty members. Although the École Biblique possessed a definite French identity and had up till then drawn on the French provinces of the Dominican Order for its professors, there was no legal obligation imposed either by the Order or by the French Republic which restricted recruitment to them. Benoit could certainly not be suspected of denying or trying to weaken the French tradition of the École. Even so, it seemed to him, the time had come to look more widely for new professors, and Murphy-O'Connor seemed the right candidate. Benoit had already been discreetly guiding his career in the direction he thought it should go.

In the summer of 1964 Benoit asked Murphy-O'Connor if he would like to stay on as a professor. Murphy-O'Connor replied in the negative. He did not think that he was qualified to teach on that level or that he had the creativity necessary for genuine research. Nor did he think he wanted to spend the rest of his life at St. Etienne. Benoit overrode his refusal and went

---

4 Neubelebung der Predigt. Die Predigt bei Paulus, dem Verkünder, Luzern and München: Rex-Verlag, 1968.

5 "Who Wrote Ephesians?" Bible Today, April 1965, 1201-1209.

straight to the Master General of the Order, Father Michael Browne. The latter was an Irishman who knew that the Irish province was well equipped with exegetes and so he was forearmed against any objection which the Irish Provincial might be expected to make. Browne immediately acceded to Benoit's request, and Murphy-O'Connor found himself a professor-designate of the École Biblique.

Murphy-O'Connor's second student year at the École (1964-65) was chiefly devoted to preparing for the Licence examination before the Pontifical Biblical Commission. During the course of it, however, Benoit asked him to write the article on Philippians for the Dictionnaire de la Bible Supplément, as he was running out of time and wanted to concentrate on Colossians and Ephesians. It was an unusual request to make to a student preparing important professional examinations, but one which Murphy-O'Connor could hardly refuse; besides, it implied recognition of him by Benoit, and eventually by others, as a fellow exegete of established status. In the article,[6] Murphy-O'Connor argued that Philippians is a compilation of three letters, which he dated - against Benoit's own views - to the period of the great Epistles. He also passed his Licence examinations.

Benoit wanted Murphy-O'Connor to take on the teaching of Intertestamental Literature, which was not then covered by the courses offered at the École. Since this branch of study had not yet formed any serious part of his training, Murphy-O'Connor asked for study leave to prepare himself. There followed a two year period of post-doctoral research in Germany (1965-67.)

The Dead Sea Scrolls were the intertestamental documents most discussed at that period, and the best work was being done under Karl Georg Kuhn at the University of Heidelberg. So it was to Heidelberg that Murphy-O'Connor went in 1965. There, in addition to working with Kuhn's team in the Qumranforschungsstelle, he sat in on the lectures of Dieter Georgi, Hans von Campenhausen, and Gerhard von Rad.

During the year at Heidelberg (1965-66) Murphy-O'Connor also got together the material of what became Paul and Qumran. Studies in New Testament Exegesis (Chapman, 1968). The object of this collection of translated papers, all of which had appeared separately in French or German, was to help bridge the gap between specialists who had been working on the Scrolls for 20 years and an interested public who had no direct access to the results of their research. Everyone knew that the Qumran writings had some bearing on the study of the New Testament and of Christian origins, and in the absence of readily available documentation, rumours and speculation abounded. "Pan-Qumranism" flourished, and certain writers would have had their readers believe that everything in primitive Christianity, including Jesus, really came out of the Essene movement; many affected to believe that delays in the publication of the Scrolls meant that there was something to hide. It was to restore balance and perspective that Benoit had delivered

---

6　　"Paul: Philippiens (Épître aux)," DBS 7 (Paris 1966) cols. 1211-1233.

his reflection on "Qumran and the New Testament" at the closing session of the Meeting of the SNTS at Aarhus in 1960, and it was fitting that this should form the first chapter. There follow eight studies of various points of comparison between Paul and Qumran, concluding with Murphy-O'Connor's own "Truth: Paul and Qumran"; the other contributors are Joseph A. Fitzmyer, Joachim Gnilka, Mathias Delcor, Walter Grundmann, Karl Georg Kuhn, Joseph Coppens, and Franz Mussner. Paul and Qumran made an excellent companion to The Scrolls and the New Testament edited by Krister Stendahl in 1957.

During the summer semester Kuhn suffered a heart attack, and it seemed unlikely that he would be teaching at Heidelberg in the following year. Murphy-O'Connor was in no hurry to return to Jerusalem, so he decided to transfer to Tübingen. There in 1966-67 he made up the deficiencies noted by Bovon in his knowledge of German and specifically German Protestant exegesis and theology. The master whom he found at Tübingen was Ernst Käsemann. Murphy-O'Connor attended all Käsemann's classes and seminars and learned from him a "genuinely critical approach to the New Testament," which, he now believed, was indispensable to the Church.

In the summer of 1966 Murphy-O'Connor gave a paper on "Sin and Community in the New Testament" at the Maynooth Summer School, Ireland, which was centred on the theme "Sin and Repentance".[7] In the following year he gave it as a paper in Käsemann's Ausländerkolloquium at Tübingen and then published it in French.[8] It is interesting to see for the first time in a title the word "community" which became a key-word for Murphy-O'Connor; interesting, too, that in this article he relates sin and community, as he was to do so frequently in later writings. Certain other themes which will become familiar make their first appearance. On the other hand, the reader is aware that the view of both sin and of community in the article is not yet that which Murphy-O'Connor holds and develops in his later works. A number of characteristic elements of his thought are still missing.

One of these elements was discovered while at Heidelberg. It was impossible to study theology in the Germany of the 1960s without coming to terms with Rudolf Bultmann, and to understand Bultmann one had to know what existentialism was about. To enlighten himself, Murphy-O'Connor went out and bought John Macquarrie's An Existentialist Theology, which was first published in 1955. There he found the best account that had yet appeared in English of the theology of Rudolph Bultmann and of the philosophy of Martin Heidegger which provided Bultmann with the hermeneutic principle underlying his interpretation of the New Testament. From Bultmann - mediated and criticised by Macquarrie - he learned a new way of

---

[7]   "Sin and Community in the New Testament," in Sin and Repentance, ed. Denis O'Callaghan, Dublin: Gill, 1967, pp. 18-50.

[8]   "Péché et communauté dans le Nouveau Testament," RB 74 (1967) 161-193.

understanding the New Testamant writings, and in particular St Paul. When Paul speaks of "life" and "death" he seems frequently to mean something very like what existentialist thinkers call "authentic" and "inauthentic" existence; Sin is alienation from God and from the authentic self; Christ is the fully authentic human being; the salvation brought by Christ is the possibility, not merely theoretical or "ontological" but real or "ontic", of living an authentically human existence; this authentic human existence can only be lived in a community, in which human beings realise that "being-with-others" which Heidegger thought impossible of achievement.

These ideas came to Murphy-O'Connor as a revelation. They shed a new light on the elements of Paul's thought which he had hitherto studied and enabled him to assemble and present them in a new synthesis. Murphy-O'Connor's theology at last had its characteristic vocabulary and master ideas. Not only did he now have a theological vision; he also had the urge to communicate it. Paul, he was convinced, had a message for the people of today: he addressed their situation and spoke a language which they could understand. The sharpening and deepening of this theological vision and the effort to communicate it to those who needed it were to become his principal endeavour.

Not all the influences upon Murphy-O'Connor have come from books and fellow academics. Some of the most important have come from contacts with a wide range of people in many different countries, and especially in America. In the summer of 1966 he was invited to lecture in the United States, through the Dominican Sisters who had been with him at Fribourg. He taught St Matthew's Gospel at Rosary College in Chicago, and that began a tradition which he has maintained every summer. Other invitations to teach in American institutions followed. Most of these have been summer schools, but from January to June 1984 he was the John A. O'Brien Professor of New Testament at the University of Notre Dame, Indiana. He has also lectured in Australia and New Zealand, the Philippines, Japan, Taiwan, South Korea, Canada and South America. Prophets often tend to get more recognition the further they are from their own land: Murphy-O'Connor has taught only twice in Great Britain, and twice in Ireland.

Colleagues have sometimes found it difficult to understand all this travelling, which to them appears to be a distraction from the main business of academic life. For Murphy-O'Connor, however, it provides a much needed outlet for pastoral activity which is restricted in Jerusalem, and it gets him away from the tensions there. It can also be seen as exercising a profoundly formative influence on him as a man and as a scholar. In the United States and elsewhere he is continually faced with the challenge of fresh experiences and other points of view. He is also in regular touch with the American Church as it works out its own way of being Catholic. Above all, on his travels he is talking mostly with non-specialists, religious, laity, priests in pastoral ministry, missionaries. It is they, he believes, who have the questions which the academics have the time to try to answer. In other words, the agenda of academic research should not be set by the academics themselves; the priorities of the University are not necessarily the priorities of the Church.

The Dead Sea Scrolls

In October 1967 Jerome Murphy-O'Connor returned to the École Biblique to take up his post as a professor. The Jerusalem he had left in 1965 was now much altered. After the Six Days War it was no longer possible to arrive in the Holy City by taxi from Beirut and Amman. East Jerusalem found itself under Israeli control. Members of the École could now move freely in Israel as well as the West Bank (and, for a time, in the Sinai), as well as on both sides of what had been the "No Man's Land" dividing the city. On the other hand, travel to Arab countries was much more difficult; the days when the École "caravan" could make its way throughout the Near East were over.

Murphy-O'Connor's first course was on "The Testaments of the Twelve Patriarchs," and he published an article on this document in the following year in the Haag Bibel-Lexicon. In the following year he switched to the Dead Sea Scrolls, and from 1968-1972 taught a course entitled "Qumran and the New Testament," in which he analysed the Manual of Discipline (1QS) and the Damascus Document (CD). He was the first to apply source criticism systematically to these documents. In a series of articles mainly in the Revue Biblique he presented his findings to the scholarly world.[9] They established him as a leading Qumran specialist.

In 1972-73 Murphy-O'Connor taught a course on "Biblical Commentaries from Qumran," in which he paid special attention to the historical allusions contained in the Scrolls.[10] For a time he interested himself in the history of the Essenes and in the problems of relating the evidence of the Scrolls and of the excavations at Qumran with the testimonies of ancient authors, principally Philo, Josephus, and Pliny the Elder, who mention the sect. In 1973 "The Essenes and their History" was delivered in Dublin as the prestigious Boylan Lecture.[11] This study dissented in several important

---

[9] "La génèse littéraire de la Règle de la Communauté," RB 76 (1969) 528-549; "An Essene Missionary Document? CD 2:14-6:1," RB 77 (1970) 210-229; "A Literary Analysis of Damascus Document 6:2-8:3," RB 78 (1971) 210-232; "The Original Text of CD 7:9-8:2," HTR 64 (1971) 379-386; "The Translation of Damascus Document 6:11-14," RevQ 7 (1971) 553-556; "The Critique of the Princes of Judah (CD 8:3-19)," RB 79 (1972) 200-216; "A Literary Analysis of Damascus Document 19:33-20:34," RB 79 (1972) 544-546.

[10] See his "Demetrius I and the Teacher of Righteousness (1 Macc 10:25-45)," RB 83 (1976) 400-420.

[11] "The Essenes and their History," RB 81 (1974) 215-244.

respects from the consensus view on the history of the Essenes, in particular by assigning their origins to Babylon rather than Palestine.

After 1975 Murphy-O'Connor stopped teaching Qumran. He had by then exhausted the sectarian materials which alone interested him. Further source critical work on other intertestamental writings was hampered by lack of critical editions of most of the texts, and he himself did not have the knowledge of the wide range of languages which would be required in order to undertake the needed textual criticism. He still continued to publish on Qumran, both for fellow scholars and for a wider public.[12]

In "Qumran and the New Testament"[13] Murphy-O'Connor surveys the scholarly productions of the past thirty years concentrating on the most important areas of the New Testament which are thought to have been illuminated by the Scrolls. Within Palestine, these areas are Palestinian Aramaic, John the Baptist, Jesus, and the Early Church. On these last three topics, Murphy-O'Connor finds evidence of relatively few contacts between Essenism and early Christianity. Typical is his judgment regarding the Early Church: "Many analogies have been seen between the vocabulary, practices, and organisation of the church in Palestine and those of the Essenes .... Few, if any, stand up to close examination,and scholars have become progressively more prudent regarding the affirmation of any direct Essene influence on the early church." On the other hand, the closest analogies to Essene doctrines are to be found in Christian documents composed outside Palestine, and Murphy-O'Connor surveys the results of comparisons made with the Pauline and Johannine literature, and with the Epistle to the Hebrews.

By way of conclusion Murphy-O'Connor offers a number of methodological observations which reflect his general assessment of this area of research. With Benoit, he insists that the influence of Qumran on the New Testament becomes possible only when the proposed parallel cannot be accounted for in terms of their common background in the Old Testament and in Second Temple Judaism. On the other hand, plausibility should not be confused with probability, and the dependence of one document on another has to be shown to be the most likely explanation of the parallel. Here much work has been vitiated because of an uncritical approach to the Qumran documents, which have been treated as a homogeneous body of literature, by ignoring internal tensions and traces of development, in a manner which

---

12 "Judah the Essene and the Teacher of Righteousness," RevQ 10 (1981) 579-585; "The Damascus Document Revisited," RB 82 (1985) 223-246; "The Manuscripts of the Judaean Desert," in Early Judaism and Its Modern Interpreters, ed. G. Nickelsburg and R. Kraft, Chico and Philadelphia: Scholars Press and Fortress Press, 1986, 125-165; "The Essenes in Palestine," BA 40 (1977) 100-124.

13 The New Testament and Its Modern Interrpreters, ed. G. MacRae and E.J. Epp, Chico and Philadelphia: Scholars Press and Fortress Press, 1989, 55-71.

would be judged naive and precritical, if not fundamentalist, were it to be applied to the New Testament documents.

The Synoptic Gospels

Murphy-O'Connor wanted to move into mainstream New Testament studies, where he would find a much greater opportunity for pastoral application of his exegetical work than he had with the Scrolls. There was too the question of a successor for Benoit, who was nearing the age of retirement. In fact Murphy-O'Connor had all along kept in touch with the New Testament. On one level, there was his teaching in the United States every summer. This was paralleled by classes held every Wednesday evening in Jerusalem which were attended by many religious and laity. (They ceased in 1981 when it was evident that the need for such teaching was being met elsewhere.)

In 1969 seminars were introduced at the École Biblique to supplement the "cours magistral," and since then Murphy-O'Connor has conducted a seminar on the literary criticism of the Synoptic Gospels. In it he has imparted the classical method of source criticism as applied to the Synoptics. He has also instilled into many generations of students his own rigorous standards of argumentation. He insists that mere possibilities are not enough; one must have probability. An hypothesis is never anything more than a possible explanation; real probability demands the demonstration that one hypothesis is more likely than all the alternative explanations of the same phenomenon. The other thing he insists on is that one must come down clearly in favour of a position. He has no patience with academic timidity which wants at all costs to cover itself against the risk of being found wrong. It is the contrary quality - the willingness to assert an opinion and open oneself to enemy fire - that he particularly admires in Boismard and Käsemann. This does not, of course, mean that one should be dogmatic or overstate one's case. All necessary qualifications are to be made, but still one must be decisive; otherwise, one is wasting the reader's time. In his seminars, Murphy-O'Connor makes no concessions to his students but pays them the compliment of treating them as equals - an experience which not all find very comfortable.

It is surprising that, despite many years of involvement with the Synoptic Gospels, Murphy-O'Connor has produced only three articles in this field. In one[14] he examined the structure of the narrative material in St Matthew's Gospel separating the Parable Discourse (ch. 13) and the Community Discourse (ch. 18.) He was especially interested in the methodological problems involved, namely the relation of redaction criticism to source criticism, and the importance to be attached to details. These problems present

---

14   "The Structure of Matthew XIV-XVII," RB 82 (1975) 360-384.

themselves all the more acutely in this section of Matthew in which the order of episodes is the same as that in Mark 8-9.

M.-E. Boismard had already suggested in Synopse II that Luke's account of the Transfiguration contains the earliest Gospel material on this episode. Murphy-O'Connor took this up and sought to determine the historical event which gave rise to the Transfiguration narratives.[15]	He also published a popular article explaining redaction criticism to the general reader.[16]

The Corinthian Correspondence

Murphy-O'Connor has identified himself especially with Pauline studies. In the academic year 1975-76 he began to teach the "Corinthian Correspondence," a course which he has continued to give regularly since then. This has meant working his way through the two Epistles to the Corinthians and tackling each exegetical problem as it occurs. As he has studied the Corinthian correspondence, he has gradually formulated his own ideas on the historical situations in which the letters of St Paul to the Christians of Corinth were written, and on the issues involved. This basic exegetical work on Paul's texts has underpinned his discussion of larger questions.

From his work on 1 and 2 Corinthians has come a long series of articles, in each of which he has given a new answer to an old problem.[17] Most of these deal with precise points of interpretation of texts. In the articles on 2 Corinthians, Murphy-O'Connor has developed his view of the *pneumatikoi*

---

[15]	"What Really Happened at the Transfiguration?" Biblical Review 3/3 (1987) 8-21.

[16]	"What is Redaction-Criticism?" Scripture in Church 5 (1974-75) 78-92.

[17]	"The Non-Pauline Character of 1 Corinthians 11:2-16?" JBL 95 (1976) 615-621; "1 Corinthians 5:3-5," RB 84 (1977) 239-245; "Works Without Faith in 1 Corinthians 7:14," RB 84 349-361; "Corinthian Slogans in 1 Corinthians 6:12-20," CBQ 40 (1978) 391-396; "1 Corinthians 8:6 - Cosmology or Soteriology?" RB 85 (1978) 253-267; "Freedom or the Ghetto (1 Cor 8:1-13; 10:23-11:1)," RB 85 (1978) 543-574; "Food and Spiritual Gifts in 1 Corinthians 8:8," CBQ 41 (1979) 292-298; "Sex and Logic in 1 Corinthians 11:2-16," CBQ 42 (1980) 482-500; "Tradition and Redaction in 1 Cor 15:3-7," CBQ 43 (1981) 582-589; "The Divorced Woman in 1 Corinthians 7:10-11," JBL 100 (1981) 601-606; "'Baptized for the Dead' (1 Cor 15:29) - A Corinthian Slogan?" RB 88 (1981) 532-543; "Paul and Macedonia: The Connection between 2 Cor 2:13 and 2:14," JSNT 25 (1985) 99-103; "Interpolations in 1 Corinthians," CBQ 48 (1986) 81-94; "Being at home in the body we are in exile from the Lord' (2 Cor 5:6b)," RB 93 (1986) 214-221; "Relating 2 Cor 6:14-7:1 to its Context," NTS 33 (1987) 272-275; "Pneumatikoi and Judaizers in 2 Cor 2:14-4-6," AusBR 34 (1986) 42-58; "A Ministry beyond the Letter (2 Cor 3:1-6)," Paolo Ministro del Nuovo Testamento (2 Co 2,14-4,6), ed. L. De Lorenzi, Roma: Benedictina Editrice, 1987, 104-157; "Pneumatikoi in 2 Corinthians," PIBA 11 (1988) 59-68; "Philo and 2 Cor 6:14-7:1," RB 95 (1988) 55-69; "1 Corinthians 11:2-16 Once Again," CBQ 50 (1988) 265-274; "Faith and Resurrection in 2 Cor 4:13-14," RB 95 (1988) 543-550.

at Corinth. These were, he argues, a group who had been influenced by the thought of Philo, no doubt understanding him no more accurately than they understood Paul. They had formed a certain opposition to Paul at Corinth, and in 1 Corinthians 2 he had sought to dismiss them as purveyors of a "wisdom" which had nothing to do with the folly of the Cross. Subsequently he changed his tactics. In part this was in recognition of the mischief the *pneumatikoi* were doing by offering an opening at Corinth to the Judaizers. Besides, contact with Apollos at Ephesus had acquainted Paul with Philonian terms and concepts. So in 2 Corinthians 3:6-17, Paul argues with the *pneumatikoi* on their own ground in defence of his Gospel and against the Judaizers' attempt to present the Law as the supreme Wisdom.

Three articles discuss 1 Corinthians 11:2-16, a text which has often been used to argue that Paul regarded women as subordinate to men and wished this subordination to be reflected in Christian worship. Murphy-O'Connor was well aware of the difficulty of this passage, which many Christians find embarrassing in this age of the movement for the recognition of women's equality with men. Even so, in "The Non-Pauline Character of 1 Corinthians 11:2-16?", he was unable to accept the "radical surgery" proposed by Wm.O. Walker, Jr., who had argued that (a) the whole section is an interpolation, (b) that it is composed of three originally separate texts, and (c) that none of these texts is from the pen of Paul. In "Sex and Logic in 1 Corinthians 11:2-16," he showed the internal coherence of the passage. To perceive Paul's logic, one must understand the problem he was facing. By comparing Paul's language with that of a number of ancient writers, Murphy-O'Connor was able to demonstrate that the problem was that of men wearing long hair, which gave them an effeminate appearance, and of women not wearing their long hair wrapped around their head in plaits, in the accepted feminine way. The Christians at Corinth were thus blurring the distinction between the sexes in an effort to prove their liberation from mere conventions. Paul was no doubt worried that this behaviour would shock outsiders and give the community a bad name, and may also have been concerned lest male homosexuality become a problem among his converts.

Paul responded to this situation by arguing that men should look like men and women should look like women. He sought to prove this from the order of creation (vv. 3,7-12,) from the teaching of nature (vv. 13-15,) and from the custom of the churches (v. 16.) It is the first argument which gives the most difficulty, and especially v. 3 with its statement that "man is the head of woman." Murphy-O'Connor showed that "head" here does not mean authority, but source. The rest of Paul's elaborate argument presupposes the equality and complementarity of the sexes in the order of nature and "in the Lord." Paul also takes it for granted that women have the same role as men in Christian worship: both equally pray and prophesy. In "1 Corinthians 11:2-16 Once Again," Murphy-O'Connor replied to the criticisms of Joël Delobel and clarified his earlier arguments, especially those regarding vv. 7-12.

Michael Glazier's invitation to write the commentary on 1 Corinthians in the popular New Testament Message series gave Murphy-O'Connor the opportunity to present his interpretation of the epistle to a wider circle of readers. It also enabled him to formulate a general view of this letter with whose details he had been occupied for so long. No words are wasted in this book of 162 pages (one reviewer described it as "lean and muscular")[18] in which Paul is shown striving with realism, a sense of humour, and great powers of persuasion to keep the disparate elements at Corinth in one Christian community. Murphy-O'Connor himself describes 1 Corinthians as "perhaps the greatest example of the pedagogy of love."

Close application over a number of years to the Corinthian correspondence awoke Murphy-O'Connor's interest in the city which was home to Paul's converts and made him realise that reading the letters against the background of ancient Corinth not only brought them to life but also pointed the way to solving more than one exegetical problem. He began to collect material on Corinth from ancient writers and archaeological reports and present it in class where it would throw light on the Pauline text under discussion. It was, of course, in the best tradition of the École Pratique des Études Bibliques to bring together in this way text and monument and to do exegesis in close contact with archaeology, history and topography. Then he realised that readers would appreciate having this material made available to them. The result was St. Paul's Corinth. Texts and Archaeology (Glazier, 1983).

In Part One, The Ancient Texts, Murphy-O'Connor brings together twenty one Greek and Roman writers from the 1st century BC to the 2nd century AD who describe or mention the Corinth which St Paul knew. The passages from their works are given in English translation and accompanied by commentaries which are designed to clarify the meaning or to highlight the importance or implication of what is being said. The literary evidence is also confronted with the results of the excavations of Corinth, Isthmia, and Cenchreae. Part Two, When Was Paul in Corinth?, discusses two problems of Pauline chronology which concern Paul's ministry in Corinth, namely the expulsion of the Jews from Rome by Claudius and the Proconsulate of Gallio. He has no new hypothesis to offer in either case, but presents and discusses the relevant texts, notably the Gallio inscription from Delphi. Part Three, Archaeology, deals not with the general archaeology of Corinth but with the light which excavations have thrown on particular passages in the Corinthian letters: dining rooms in private houses; public dining rooms attached to temples; workshops near the agora; honorific inscriptions. The book has been widely appreciated as a valuable companion to the letters to the Corinthians (though not all have been convinced by the suggestion that Paul was inspired to make his famous comparison of the Church to a human

---

[18] The First Epistle to the Corinthians (New Testament Message 10), Wilmington: Glazier, 1977, revised and expanded 1982.

body by seeing anatomical ex-voto offerings displayed in the temple of Asklepios.) It was soon translated into French.[19] Murphy-O'Connor also published an article bringing together all the evidence relating to the manufacture of the famous "Corinthian bronze" - the only work of "pure erudition" he would say he has ever produced.[20]

Pauline Studies

St Paul is the other field, besides Qumran, in which Murphy-O'Connor has become known internationally. As well as his work on the Corinthian correspondence he has also published on Philippians, Colossians and Philemon, and on 1 Timothy.[21] His interest in historical and chronological problems involved in reconstructing a biography of St Paul led him to write on the subject of Pauline missions before the Jerusalem Conference[22] and on travel and transport on and around the Mediterranean in the 1st century AD.[23]

As early as 1969 Murphy-O'Connor wrote several articles on particular points of St Paul's theology.[24] He was not yet ready, however, to write a developed study of Pauline theology. He had come back from Germany with an existentialist hermeneutic to interpret Paul, and his detailed work on the Corinthian correspondence was giving him an intimate acquaintance with Paul's thought. He still needed a central idea around which to construct an original synthesis. Eventually he found it in the notion of "community".

To understand the genesis of this insight we need to follow Murphy-O'Connor's intervention in the post-Vatican II debate on religious life. In the late 1960s and early 1970s religious were faced with a twofold crisis of confidence. One aspect of this was theological: in the light of the Council's insistence on the universal call to holiness, what was the justification of religious life? On the other hand Orders and Congregations were frequently

---

[19] Corinthe au Temps de saint Paul, d'après les textes et l'archéologie, Paris: Cerf, 1986.

[20] "Corinthian Bronze," RB 90 (1983) 80-93.

[21] "Christological Anthropology in Philippians 2:6-11," RB 83 (1976) 25-50; the article on Philippians in DBS has already been noted; contributions on "Colossians" and "Philemon" to A New Catholic Commentary on Holy Scripture, 2nd ed., London: Nelson, 1969; "Colossians" and "Philippians" in Scripture Discussion Commentary, XI; London: Sheed and Ward, 1971; "Community and Apostolate: Reflections on 1 Tim 2:1-7," Bible Today, October 1973, 1260-1266; "Redactional Angels in 1 Tim 3:16," RB 91 (1984) 178-187.

[22] "Pauline Missions before the Jerusalem Conference," RB 89 (1982) 71-91.

[23] "On the Road and on the Sea with St Paul," Bible Review 1 (Summer 1985) 38-47.

[24] "The Presence of God through Christ and in the World," Concilium 10 (1969) 54-59; "The Christian and Society in St Paul," New Blackfriars 50 (1969) 174-182; "Letter and Spirit: St Paul," New Blackfriars 50 (1969) 453-460.

finding that their traditional works of teaching or nursing were being taken over by others: what was their raison d'être? Murphy-O'Connor believed he had something to say and in 1967 published an article in the Irish Dominican publication Doctrine and Life on "Religious Life as Witness."

An eventual fruit of this article was an invitation to preach a retreat for the Dominican Sisters of Sinsinawa, Wisconsin. In this retreat, which he gave in August 1972, Murphy-O'Connor sought to rethink the structures of religious life in terms of the New Testament concept of community. In the following year, the text of the retreat was published as a whole issue of Supplement to Doctrine and Life (1973) under the title "What Is Religious Life? - Ask the Scriptures" and was promptly translated into Portuguese in Brazil.[25] Murphy-O'Connor saw the point of religious life to be its witness to the possibility of a living Christian community. "What is important is that religious recognise that the primary service they render to the Church and to the world is the witness of their life together as a community" (p. 14.)

This view of religious life was based upon a theology of salvation, sin and grace which Murphy-O'Connor found in the New Testament, and in particular in St Paul. The salvation brought by Christ consists in rescuing human beings from the prevailing environment of destructive selfishness and greed (Sin) and establishing them in a community where they can grow in love and freedom. Such a community is portrayed in the early chapters of the Acts of the Apostles. Where is it to be found today? Theoretically, in the local church. But the diocese, or even the parish, is too large to be a real community in the New Testament sense. In reality, only the family and the religious community can be living witnesses to the values of the Christian community. Of these the religious community is the more striking because less ambiguous: there unity and unselfish love cannot be explained away as manifestations of sexual attraction or natural affection. "In terms of altruistic love, of mutual sharing of goods, and of submission to the call of God in Christ the religious community is what the diocese and the parish are called to be" (p. 12.)

Various consequences follow logically from this position. Service in the form of particular works, such as teaching or nursing, is not the real raison d'être of religious life. The crisis facing so many active Congregations who saw their traditional works disappearing was in fact an "undisguised blessing" since it forced them to look deeper into the nature and purpose of religious life. It followed too that the community is for the individual, rather than the other way round.

In later chapters Murphy-O'Connor reassessed some of the most important institutions of religious life in the light of his vision of religious life as witness to the possibility of community. Authority should be that of example rather than of command. Prayer of petition is normally to be answered

---

25 Os Religiosos na Igreja Particular, Sao Paolo: Edicoes Paulinas, 1974.

by members of the community for one another. Poverty is the sharing of resources, psychological and spiritual as well as material, among members of the community and with the needy. Celibacy is to be lived by mutual love within the community. A final discussion on "tension and community" affirms the value of a certain healthy tension between the ideal and the real, the individual and the community, and among individuals within the community.

Such a radical rethinking of religious life could not go unchallenged. A series of articles in Supplement to Doctrine and Life gave some of Murphy-O'Connor's critics the chance to state their objections, to which he was given the right of reply. In general the tone of the debate was courteous and positive on all sides. Murphy-O'Connor commended E.J. Fox for his "effort at sympathetic understanding, the care to give credit where it is due, and the closely-reasoned clarity with which an opposing view is expressed," and on several occasions thanked his critics for obliging him to restate his views more adequately or to correct any lack of balance in their presentation. Once or twice he betrayed his constitutional inability to suffer fools gladly. It is interesting that no women took part in the debate. A few years later, the original articles together with those on both sides of the debate were republished together in Ireland and in the United States as What Is Religious Life? A Critical Reappraisal.[26]

Thinking his way through the theology of religious life reinforced Murphy-O'Connor's belief that "community" was the key to a correct understanding of Paul's theology. He became totally convinced after working with Irish missionaries in Sao Paolo, Brazil, in the summer of 1974. They had seen the relevance of his idea of the religious community to the work they were doing in animating basic Christian communities. Now through their eyes Murphy-O'Connor was able to see a Pauline church at work, and community was the fundamental element.

In the meantime Murphy-O'Connor was writing a book which he called "Moral Imperatives in St Paul" and which was eventually published in French under the title L'Existence Chrétienne selon saint Paul (Cerf, 1974). He described it as "an attempt to give an answer to the question: - exactly what value does Paul give to the moral imperatives of which his epistles are full?" (Avant-Propos.) The question and his answer had their origins in a session on moral theology in 1970 at Stonehill College, North Easton, Mass., in which he had taken part along with R.E. Brown, Charles Curran, and Richard A. McCormick. His views were further developed in a series of articles in Doctrine and Life in 1971, and in lectures which he had given at Milltown Park, a consortium of religious orders in Dublin, in 1973.

In the first part of the book Murphy-O'Connor works out in greater detail the theology of St Paul which he had already stated more briefly in

---

26 What Is Religious Life? A Critical Reappraisal, Dublin: Dominican Publications, 1976
    and Wilmington: Glazier, 1977, with an Introduction by Sr. Kathleen Ashe, O.P.

What Is Religious Life? He asserts strongly the centrality of the Christian community: "... Paul believes that the community constitutes the person in his or her authenticity" (p. 83.) That is the single most important statement in the book, and everything else is a consequence of it. The community is, or should be, an environment in which no one sins, in which all are authentic. Sin, by contrast, is a social force engendered by the inauthenticity of individuals in the course of history. It is in and by the community that the individual is saved, and one of its fundamental functions is to protect the individual from the hostile forces of the environment. On the other hand, the freedom of individuals to realise their human potential is conditioned by the authenticity of the other members of the community.

If human beings are liberated from Sin, they are, according to St Paul, emancipated also from the law. This does not mean, Murphy-O'Connor explains, that concrete moral directives no longer have any interest for the authentic human being. The law from which human beings are emancipated is a structure of inauthentic existence, not by reason of its content, but by reason of the fact that it is imposed by an inauthentic environment. Murphy-O'Connor could say: "... Paul's teaching does not simply contain the seed of antinomianism, as some have suggested, it is fundamentally antinomian" (p. 127.)

Where then is there a place in Paul's teaching for the moral imperatives in his letters, and what is their force? Murphy-O'Connor refers back to the real situation of the Christian who is always in a state of development and always threatened by the hostile environment of the world. In certain cases Paul put forward specific directives as remedies for moral sickness which had broken out in a particular community. In other cases his moral precepts are designed to help form the ethical judgment of recent converts and so have an essentially pedagogical function. In no case were they imposed as absolutely binding. If Paul regarded the Christian as emancipated from the Law of Moses, it cannot be thought that he regarded his own precepts as having absolute force. He appealed to his own authority only in order to give a solution to pressing practical problems.

On examination, Paul's moral directives turn out to be drawn indifferently from the sacred writings of his own people, from the ethical maxims of the Greek world, and from the tradition of the teaching of Jesus. He does not appear to have attached greater weight to one source rather than to another. The inference is that he regarded them all as indications of how the authentic human being will behave. They do not constitute a body of binding law or of absolute ethical precepts. At the centre of Paul's vision stands the person of Christ who alone manifests fully the humanity willed by God for the human being. Christ gives to human beings the possibility, now restored, of a truly human life, whose demands he himself embodies.

Was Paul then a "situationist"? Murphy-O'Connor's reply is carefully nuanced. In so far as Paul considered the demand of God to be manifested in the concrete situation, he was a situationist. On the other hand, Paul's concept of the moral subject differed widely from that held by the modern proponents of "situation ethics." For them, the moral subject is the individual in isolation; for Paul it is the individual-in-society. His moral subject is constituted by a relationship to community. So the freedom of the individual is not absolute, but is conditioned by the requirements of authentic existence in community. The spiritual knowledge which discerns the will of God is mediated by the community, not under the form of inspired directives, but in sharing an existence filled by the Spirit. The individual's quest for an adequate response in each situation must be undertaken in freedom, but his or her reflexion on the elements of the problem is sharpened and encouraged by the moral consciousness of the community.

This was a book which Murphy-O'Connor had wanted to write, and it was a disappointment to him that repeated attempts to find an English language publisher failed. It was, however, published not only in France but also, once again, in Brazil.[27] Subsequent discussions with audiences in Ireland and the United States, in Peru and Brazil, in Australia and in New Zealand revealed that the first part of the book, which dealt with what it means to be human and with the structures of authentic and inauthentic existence, was much more relevant to the contemporary situation of the Church than the discussion of Paul's moral imperatives. Murphy-O'Connor decided to develop this part further and to publish it separately "in the hope that it will be of some service to those who are trying to build the church in the modern world." The result was Becoming Human Together which was published in the United States and in Ireland in 1977 and reappeared in a second revised edition in 1982.[28] This was a book which others wanted him to write, and perhaps for that reason it is better than its predecessor. Murphy-O'Connor himself regards it as his most important contribution.

Becoming Human Together

The title, Becoming Human Together, does not immediately indicate the subject of the book. In the 1970s it could well have been the title of a book on group dynamics, and in an Irish newspaper it was reviewed with great bewilderment as a book on marriage. Once one has read the book, however, the title appears to describe its contents admirably.

The first part of the book, entitled "Human Being" explores what it means to be fully human, according to the intention of God. This intention is to be seen in Christ, who is, according to ch. 2, the Criterion. Murphy-O'Connor disagrees with those who seek to discover the meaning of Christ's

---

27 A Vida de Homem Novo, Sao Paolo: Edicoes Paulinas, 1975.

28 Becoming Human Together. The Pastoral Anthropology of St.Paul (Good News Studies 2,) Wilmington: Glazier and Dublin: Veritas, 1977, 2nd rev. ed. 1982.

humanity by surveying the qualities of humanity in general. Rather, the humanity of Jesus is to be found in his fulfilment of the original vocation of the human being to be the "image of God." To be the image of God is to participate in God's creativity, and for the human being this means to offer "a new possibility of existence to others" (p. 36.) Murphy-O'Connor frames his study of Christ the fully human being with a chapter (1) discussing what Paul knew of Jesus and another (3) on how Paul viewed the relationship between Christ and God; both these chapters were considerably developed in the second edition. A fourth chapter outlines the interpretation of the basic Pauline concepts of "Life" and "Death" in terms of Heidegger's "authentic" and "inauthentic" existence. Murphy-O'Connor's starting point is still Macquarrie's An Existentialist Theology, which he had discovered in Heidelberg in 1965, but the ideas now sit more comfortably and the language is less obviously borrowed. Long acquaintance with the existentialist categories and repeated efforts, in speech and in print, to relate them to Paul's thought and to the contemporary situation have made them his own.

The second part of the book, "Society", describes the effects of failed human beings to exploit the opportunity to participate in God's creative activity. Sin - spelt with a capital letter and personified - frustrates the human potential by choosing to protect and promote the self rather than the other. This leads to a reliance on law (human, divine, or ecclesiastical) for security and results in a world full of division, distrust and destructive competition. Paul's description of the society he had to deal with could be applied to our own. A little later in the book Murphy-O'Connor makes it clear that in many respects it could also be applied to the church of today: "The value-system by which Christians really live is that of the 'world.' Within the church and outside we find the same lack of concern for the poor and underprivileged, the same desire for material possessions, the same hostilities and bitterness" (pp. 171-172.)

In contrast to this picture of freedom abused Murphy-O'Connor sets out Paul's ideas about "Community" (Part Three.) To be a Christian means to embrace, by personal witness and preaching, the selfless and loving attitudes of Jesus. But the individual cannot do this without the witness and support of a community. To be "in Christ" or "in the Spirit" (the terms are mostly used synonymously by Paul) means to be in the community. In contrast to a dramatic society which is brought into existence by its members, the Christian community brings its members into existence as authentic human beings, creative and free. The contemporary Christian is not to assume that he or she is in such a community just by the fact of belonging to the church. "Christians cannot take it for granted that they are free. The magnificent assertions of Paul have been reduced to the status of promises because his vision of the true nature of Christian community has been lost sight of" (p. 172.) With this statement we come around again to the point where Murphy-O'Connor began his reflexions on the point of religious life ten years previously.

Much of the material on Paul's ethical teaching which appeared in L'Existence Chrétienne selon saint Paul finds its place in Becoming Human Together, but now put much more succinctly. The Christian is free from law, though moral directives have their place as guide-lines. On the other hand, the Christian is not an isolated and autonomous individual but is with and for others. The moral choice of the Christian is so orientated towards the other that it can only be understood in terms of creating or destroying community. The book ends with a finely drawn portrait of "the model of an authentic decision," namely that of Paul himself in Phil 1:20-25 where he debates whether he should wish to die and be with Christ or to live and stay with his converts: "Paul decides for the complexity of the real, and so participates fully in the 'mind of Christ' whose standard is provided by the sacrifice of the Cross, whose depth is derived from the accumulation of lived community experience, and whose clarity is refined by continued sharing in love" (p. 217.)

Becoming Human Together was widely acknowledged to be a profound and stimulating synthesis of Pauline theology. It brought to completion a long process of maturing thought in which existentialist theology, detailed exegesis, and contact and discussion with Christians trying to spread the Gospel and build up the church in many parts of the world, had all interacted. It represents a high point in Murphy-O'Connor's career as an exegete and theologian, for which, it can be seen, many aspects of his life and work until then had prepared him.

Frequent visits to the United States and the influence of K. Ashe had made Murphy-O'Connor aware of women's issues in the church. One effect was to sharpen his sensitivity to the use of exclusive or inclusive language, a development which one can trace in reading the books he wrote in the course of twenty years. It is significant that among the changes he made to Becoming Human Together between the first and second editions was to add a section on "Women in Christ" (pp. 193-197) to the chapter called "The Living Christ." These pages follow a section on "This Is My Body" in which he had argued that in the view of St Paul the "selfishness of the Corinthians is the antithesis of what should be and so makes the celebration of the Eucharist impossible" (p. 190; cf. 1 Cor 11:17-34.) He remarks: "In today's church it would be highly unusual for any community to tolerate the blatant discrimination in terms of food and drink that negated the Eucharist at Corinth. There are, however, other forms of discrimination which manifest the same lack of love, and it is only love that transforms the assembly into the community that is Christ." He goes on to claim that "The most widespread discrimination in the contemporary church is evident in the official attitude towards the active participation of women in the liturgy," and wonders if this "may be the explanation why the Eucharist produces so few fruits!" It is important to determine what was the attitude of Paul towards women, and in particular towards their participation in the liturgy. Here he repeats the substance of his argument in "Sex and Logic in 1

Corinthians 11:2-16. Murphy-O'Connor was not endorsing the ordination of women - in fact he does not expressly mention the issue - but no doubt those who were campaigning for women's ordination would have drawn aid and comfort from his remarks. About the same time he also wrote an article-length favourable, though not uncritical, review of Elizabeth Schussler Fiorenza's In Memory of Her. A Feminist Theological Reconstruction of Christian Origins.[29]

In 1970 Murphy-O'Connor started doing archaeological visits and lectures for the United Nations Truce Supervision Organisation, and in 1971 became the leader of the Sunday Group, friends of different nationalities and professional positions, who liked to hike and explore. He was thus prepared to take over the École field trips when François Lemoine, O.P., died in May 1975, and he remained responsible for them until Marcel Beaudry took over at the beginning of the academic year 1982-83.

It was on the basis of this practical knowledge of the terrain that Canon John Wilkinson, then director of St George's College in Jerusalem, suggested Murphy-O'Connor's name when in 1977 Oxford University Press were looking for someone to write an archaeological guide book to the Holy Land. Negotiations dragged on until the summer of 1978. Then with a firm commitment from OUP and with Alice Sancey, the wife of a "cooperant" seconded to the École by the French Government, to do the drawings, he went to work and finished it by Easter 1979. It was published in 1980 and translated into German (1981) and French (1982). A second edition, revised and expanded with the help of Marcel Beaudry and with new drawings by Caroline Florimont, appeared in 1986.[30] This was not the first guide book produced by a professor of the École. It has a precedent in the third edition of the Guide Bleu on Palestine which was the work of P. Abel. The Holy Land was received with enthusiasm, and many tourists have obeyed the injunction of one reviewer that it "should be in the luggage of every visitor to the Holy Land."

In his middle 50s, Murphy-O'Connor has arrived at the age when exegetes commonly reach their maturity. Given good health, he has many years of productive life ahead of him. What can we look for from him? He has exhausted the vein he exploited in the trilogy What Is Religious Life?, L'Existence Chrétienne selon saint Paul, and Becoming Human Together. He has not written a major commentary on the Corinthian correspondence and has not shown any inclination to write one. It is possible to think that he needs to find another big subject. Going on his past record, it will be a subject suggested not by purely academic interest but by pastoral need and will

---

29 RB 91 (1984) 287-294 = "A Feminist Re-reads the New Testament," Doctrine and Life 34 (1984) 398-404, 495-499.

30 The Holy Land. An Archaeological Guide from Earliest Times to 1700, London: Oxford University Press, 1980; 2nd edition revised and expanded 1986.

be developed in dialogue not only with texts and other specialists but also with actively engaged Christians in many parts of the world.

Chapter 6

FRANÇOIS-PAUL DREYFUS, O.P.

All of François-Paul Dreyfus' predecessors on the faculty began their careers at the École Biblique. He was already 50 when he became a member of the staff, and he already had a full life behind him.

He was born on 9 August 1918 into a Jewish family of Mulhouse, Alsace. His parents, Jules, an industrialist, and Emma did not practice their religion apart from the observance of certain fundamental traditions. In consequence, he was 14 or 15 when he discovered the Bible. The indifference of his family provoked a reaction which had serious consequences. He took the Scriptures seriously and, simply because the Bible was a Christian one, he worked his way through the New Testament when he had finished the Old. He was deeply impressed by the moral teaching of the gospels which he saw as the splendid fulfilment of what was only sketched in the Jewish Scriptures. The seed thus sown remained dormant for a number of years.

After his Baccalaureat (Latin, Greek, Mathematics, Philosophy), he spent two years preparing the highly compeditive exam for entry into the celebrated École Polytechnique (1935-37). He was successful, and graduated with distinction in 1939, just in time to be swept into the French army at the beginning of the Second World War as an engineer officer. Captured by the advancing Germans in 1940 he ended up in a prisoner of war camp. In July of that year the Jewish officers in the camp were invited to declare themselves. He raised his hand, a note was taken, and he went back to his barracks expecting the worst. To while away the time he borrowed a Bible from his company commander, who happened to be a Dominican, and read his favourite passages, Leviticus 19 and the Sermon on the Mount. When the Germans did not follow up the information that he was Jewish, he took instructions and was baptized in prison in 1941.

He remained a prisoner until the end of the war in 1945, but he and his companions were treated as officers, and were free to develop an intense intellectual life. Discussions were stimulated by presentations by scholars of the caliber of M.-H. Vicaire, O.P., professor of Church History at the University of Fribourg, and the world-renowned theologian Yves Congar, O.P. Dreyfus helped the latter perfect his Hebrew, and the web of relations thus built up in captivity is nowhere better illustrated by the words used by Congar to inscribe his translation of A.-M. Hunter's The Unity of the New Testament for Dreyfus, "To Father Paul Dreyfus, my comrade, my brother, my disciple, my master!"

From his baptism Dreyfus had been drawn to the religious life and, given such influence, it is not surprising that he should have entered the Dominican Order in 1947, after working for two years as an engineer in the Department of Bridges and Highways. On receiving the habit in the noviciate at St. Jacques in Paris Paul was added to his secular name. His philosophical and theological studies at the Saulchoir (1948-54) were guided by some of the most brilliant minds in France. The Dominican professors there were preeminent among the progressive theologians who prepared the way for the Second Vatican Council.

Despite the capacity for biblical studies manifested in his Lectorate thesis, "The Remnant of Israel in the Old Testament,"[1] the Provincial of the Paris province, Father Avril, destined him to the cofounder of Isaiah House in West Jerusalem with Bruno Hussar, O.P. He did in fact go to Jerusalem in 1954, but not in that capacity.

When Ceslas Spicq, O.P., moved to the University of Fribourg in 1953 to replace Boismard (see above p. 77), his place at the Saulchoir was taken by Andre Viard, O.P. Despite his competence as a scholar, it quickly became clear that Viard was not going to be a success as a teacher. The new Provincial, Father Ducatillon, designated Dreyfus as his successor. Thus he spent two years (1954-56) as a student at the École Biblique. At that stage the École was in the Arab sector of Jerusalem, and memories of the debacle of 1948 were still vivid. The name Dreyfus was a guarantee of difficulties, and so for the duration he became Father Trévoux.[2]

The year after his return to the Saulchoir he completed his doctorate, which was a greatly expanded version of his Lectorate thesis. The published portion revealed an unusual talent.[3] This served him well in the following ten years which he spent as professor of New Testament at the Saulchoir, during which he published two important articles.[4]

In the mid-1960s both Benoit and Boismard were exceptionally busy. The former was preoccupied by the affairs of Vatican II, and the latter was deeply involved in the preparation of the French Synopsis and the writing of the literary commentary. The result was a tremendous backlog of book reviews. These could not be neglected, because the École needed to retain the good will of publishers. Books that arrived free for review meant a

---

1   This provided material for his first article "La doctrine du Reste d'Israel chez le prophète Isaïe," RSPT 39 (1955) 361-386.

2   Dreyfus is considered to be the medieval Jewish form of the name of towns now known as Trier, Troyes, and Trévoux.

3   "Le thème de l'héritage dans l'Ancien Testament," RSPT 42 (1958) 3-49. Only much later did he publish a more comprehensive study, "Reste d'Israel," DBS 7 (1966) 414-437.

4   "L'argument scripturaire de Jésus en faveur de la résurrection des morts (Marc, iii, 26-27)," RB 66 (1959) 213-224; 'Maintenant la foi, l'espérance et la charité demeurent toutes les trois' (1 Cor 13, 13)," SPC, I, 403-412.

significant saving in the acquisitions budget of the library. Thus in 1967 Benoit invited Dreyfus to come to Jerusalem to write book reviews. This time he did not have to change his name, since Israel had taken East Jerusalem in the Six Day War. For the next two years he spent alternate semesters at the École Biblique and at the Saulchoir, and reviewed 150 books!

This led to an invitation to remain at the École Biblique as professor of Biblical Theology (1969) in place of Jean-Paul Audet, O.P., who had been coming from Canada for one semester a year since 1959, and who found this system seriously disruptive of his teaching at Ottawa and Montreal.[5]

Academic versus Pastoral Exegesis

Dreyfus' appointment gave him a mandate to delve into both OT and NT. His specific object, however, made him particularly sensitive to a problem of communication. Books such as Walter Wink's The Bible in Human Transformation. Toward a New Paradigm for Biblical Study (Philadelphia: Fortress, 1973), and articles like F. Refoulé's "L'exégèse en question" (VSpirSup n. 111 [1974] 391-423) argued that the historical-critical method was bankrupt. It had a value; there were still areas that it could explore. But it was not doing what readers of the publications of experts expected of it. It was not making the Bible come alive in a way that fed the life of faith and illuminated the present and the future.

One might reply that the producers knew best what they were about. They, after all, were the qualified specialists! As an exegete whose role was theological, Dreyfus was not prepared to take this line, pointing out very reasonably that unless the consumers agree to buy, the producers will go out of business. If the consumers feel that exegetes do not write for them but for a small circle of their colleagues, there is something wrong. If the consumers perceive exegetes as concerned exclusively with the past, which they articulate in unintelligible jargon, this is unhealthy. If the consumers see themselves as excluded from the privileged group of interpreters of the Bible, a dangerous situation develops. In order to clarify this problem and to suggest how it might be remedied Dreyfus wrote an important series of five articles between 1975 and 1979.

He began by distinguishing between academic and pastoral exegesis.[6] The former is a recognized professional discipline concerned with the Bible

---

5   Audet was known particularly for his La Didachè. Instructions des apôtres (EB), Paris: Gabalda, 1959, and while at the École published a number of articles relevant to the NT, "'De son ventre couleront des fleuves d'eau'. Le soif, l'eau et la parole," RB 66 (1959) 379-386; "Qumran et la notice de Pline sur les Esséniens, " RB 68 (1961) 346-387; "L'hypothèse des Testamonia. Remarques autour d'un livre récent [P. Prigent, Les Testimonia dans le christianisme primitif], RB 70 (1963) 381-405.

6   "Exégèse en Sorbonne, Exégèse en Église," RB 82 (1975) 321-359.

François-Paul Dreyfus, O.P.

and on a par with the critical study of any other body of literature. It abstracts from any personal religious committment on the part of professor or student. It treats the biblical text as an historical document no different from any other of its type or period, and studies it under all possible aspects with all possible scientific resources. Only methods yielding verifiable knowledge are considered legitimate, and the resulting knowledge is valued as an end in itself. Whether it is useful to anyone outside academe is irrelevant.

Pastoral exegesis, on the other hand, treats the biblical text as a unique sacred document whose meaning is vital to a religious community. It is therefore an ecclesial ministry dedicated to the service of the people of God in its pilgrimage to the Kingdom. Its practitioners must be committed to the finality of the text. A coldly objective attitude is excluded. The same interpretative techniques as in academic exegesis are used. But they are means, not ends, and nonrational knowledge is not excluded. It appeals to faith at certain stages

While academic exegesis can treat the biblical text as polyvalent, i.e. open to many possible meanings, none of which is privileged with respect to the others, pastoral exegesis recognizes that the biblical text is designed to communicate certain convictions and to promote a specific type of behaviour. What the author intended to say, therefore, is of crucial importance, and must be the prime concern of pastoral exegesis. It cannot, however, be content with merely reaching this meaning, it must present it to a very different world in such a way as to release its life-giving power.

But how can the word of God addressed to a different people in another age and culture be made a vital force today? To answer this question Dreyfus turned first to the Bible.[7] It reflects a history of over 2000 years, and the ways in which the word of God was kept alive through succeeding generations should furnish the basis of a methodology which can control, stimulate, and guide the pastoral exegete.

Within the Bible the continuing vitality of the word of God is rooted in the organic unity of the People of God of both Old and New Testaments. Those of one generation see themselves as vitally involved in what happened to their predecessors; that past is a constitutive element of their present. It is in virtue of this unity that the word of God addressed to one generation is valid also for all succeeding ages.

What has to be made alive is not primarily a written text, but a tradition recounting an event which is related (as preparation, consequence, etc.) to God's saving action on behalf of his people. The privileged place of this vitalisation is the cultic celebration of the events of salvation. It is possible elsewhere, but in the cultic act time, as it were, stands still.

There are two important modes of vitalisation. The most fundamental takes place in and through an event. Within the OT new situations challen-

---

7   "L'actualisation à l'intérieur de la Bible," RB 83 (1976) 161-202.

ged received interpretations and revealed unrecognized virtualities. For Christians the resurrection of Jesus both interpreted Scripture and was interpreted by it. It was the prism which refracted and the lens which refocused the millenial word of God and brought it to bear on a new world. Such vitalisation does not falsify the original message. It may develop a secondary aspect or enhance a hidden dimension or rearrange the elements in the pattern, but contradiction is excluded by the fact that author and interpreter are both interconnected cells within the same organic unity, the collective personality of the people of God.

The final stage of Dreyfus' demonstration was to apply this methodology to the pastoral exegesis of the Bible in the current situation.[8] The collective personality, which made vitalisation possible within the Bible, has now been transformed into the Body of Christ in which believers are members of him and of one another. What is vitalized, however, is no longer an event but a person, the crucified and risen Christ living in the church. As the incarnation of the Eternal Word he is the unique and perfect word of God to whom all other imperfect expressions (events and texts) are referred for their true meaning.

In the eucharist Jesus becomes really present in the community, thus confirming the liturical assembly as the privileged location in which vitalisation takes place. The homily on the scriptural readings, in consequence, is the principal goal of pastoral exegesis. If it is to prepare the community for full participation in the eucharist, its fundamental task is to relate the readings to the paschal mystery. This it does typologically by underlining the resemblances between then and now. Such similarities are validated by the consistence of God in the working out of his plan of salvation, and by the basic consistency of human nature in its individual and social manifestations. They are legitimized by precedents in the vitalising tradition of the Bible and the Church.

The Bible itself and the patristic tradition insist on the essential role played by the Holy Spirit in the true understanding of the Scriptures. The Spirit who gave birth of the Scriptures must be at work in those who desire to grasp their profound meaning. This involves a prayerful listening to the voice of the Spirit in the past and present of the church, which makes itself heard in the tradition of its practice and the pronouncements of the Magisterium.

The number of texts whose meaning has been defined by the Magisterium is very small, but this is not to say that the church has neglected its duty to propound the authentic meaning of Scripture. It does so indirectly, and much more frequently, by specifying a reality with which one or more texts are concerned. Thus, for example, when the Council of Trent defined

---

[8]   "L'actualisation de l'Écriture. I: Du texte à la vie," RB 86 (1979) 5-58; "II: L'action de l'Esprit," RB 86 (1979) 161-193; "III: La place de la Tradition," RB 86 (1979) 321-384.

the relation of celibacy to marriage it at the same time indicated the church's understanding of 1Cor 7:25-40.

This summary does scant justice to the complexity of Dreyfus' thought. Nor does it evoke the intense pastoral fervor with which the whole series of articles was permeated. As was pointed out at the beginning, it was an effort to enable academic exegesis to escape from the impass in which it found itself. But as the series progressed it became clear that Dreyfus was also concerned to bridge what many people saw as a growing gap between the results of critical exegesis and the traditional teaching of the church.

On the one hand, Dreyfus insists on the hypothetical character of all literary conclusions, no matter how rigorous the methodology or complete the data, and on the other hand, he highlights the certitude of the church's understanding of the realities underlying the Scriptures, which is manifested by the sensus fidelium and eventually articulated by the Magisterium. In pastoral exegesis the faith dimension must supply what is lacking in the historical-critical method, because only a clear and unambiguous interpretation can release the life-giving power of a biblical text.

Did Jesus know that he was God?

These reflections on a vitally important contemporary problem never received the attention they deserved. Since the articles were never collected into a book, no reviewers were constrained to confront the challenge they posed. This certainly was not true of Dreyfus' next publication. Not only was it translated into the major languages, but one reviewer (J. Galot, SJ) dealt with it on at least three different occasions!

The topic was Jesus' knowledge of his divinity, which Dreyfus posed in the following terms. "Let us suppose that Jesus of Nazareth in the course of his earthly life got his hands on a copy of John's gospel. How would he have reacted on reading certain statements attributed to him by the evangelist, such as, 'Not that anyone has seen the Father except him who is from God; he has seen the Father.' (6:46); 'Before Abraham was, I am.' (8:58); 'I and the Father are one.' (10:30); 'Father glorify me with the glory which I had with you before the world was made.' (17:5)? Would Jesus have recognized in such affirmations words that he said, or at least could have said, because they corresponded to what he thought of himself, of his person, and of his mystery? Or would he have proclaimed them to be blasphemy, and agreed with those who, according to the evangelist, wanted to stone him after one of these declarations? Their reproach was unambiguous, 'being only a man, you make yourself God' (10:33)."[9]

Dreyfus then went on to say that up to the middle of the last century Christians of all denominations would have answered the first question in

---

[9]   Jésus savait-il qu'il était Dieu? Paris: Cerf, 1984, 7.

the affirmative and the second question in the negative, whereas in recent times the responses would be reversed. This assessment is certainly correct, and the shift could be explained in a number of ways. Dreyfus, however, saw it as an architypical example of the tension between the minimalizing conclusions of academic exegesis and the traditional faith of the church.

His experience as a popular lecturer had shown him that this tension created a serious pastoral problem, and so he wrote the book to show nonspecialists that no reinterpretation of traditional teaching was necessary, because the arguments which could be brought forward to justify the position of the church were stronger than those employed by academic exegesis.

His first concern was to establish the position of the church, and his conclusion is without ambiguity. "The affirmation that Jesus knew he was God is part of the deposit of faith of the church."[10] He admits that it has not been formally defined. But he insists that it has been taught consistently by the ordinary magisterium since the first century, and that such teaching was not unreflective repetition, but a deliberate choice in response to formal negations. The most important link in this dogmatic chain is the first. "In opposition to those who denied the mystery of the incarnation, John wrote his gospel to prove that Jesus is the Son of God, God himself, and that this conviction is rooted in the teaching of Jesus himself, whose truth is attested by the miracles, the 'signs', the 'works' which Jesus did."[11]

To support this position Dreyfus argues that John wanted to give a substantially historical portrait of Jesus, and that he would not have dared to put words claiming divinity into Jesus' mouth unless he were utterly convinced that Jesus had in fact said those or similar words. And Jesus cannot have been a liar, because God granted the miracles which confirmed his teaching.

Thus, according to Dreyfus, the believing exegete must begin from the conviction that the church demands, not only that he believe that Jesus was God, but that he believe that Jesus knew he was God. In the second part of his book Dreyfus transforms this belief into the sort of working hypothesis that any historian could accept, and then examines the NT for any data which would indicate the inadequacy of the hypothesis. This is precisely the way in which any serious scholar would deal with the claim to divinity made by a number of Roman emperors.

If Jesus was convinced that he was divine, Dreyfus asks, how could he have communicated this self-understanding? Obviously if he had said straight out "I am God", he would immediately have been written off as a lunatic. All those who are seriously concerned to communicate adapt their statements to the capacity of their audiences, and this is what Jesus did. Dreyfus distinguishes three categories among those who heard Jesus speak.

---

10   Jésus savait-il qu'il était Dieu?, 38.

11   Jésus savait-il qu'il était Dieu?, 37.

When Jesus preached to the first category, the crowds, he did not say all that could be said. He limited himself to what could be accepted and assimilated without error given the current mentality. He did try to move them beyond their expectations, which gave rise to charges of blasphemy.

Some emerged from the crowds into the second category. They became followers of Jesus. To those who accepted him as their leader Jesus was able to reveal more of the intimacy of his relationship with God, e.g. he called God 'Abba', which claimed an intimacy to which no other human being had aspired. These disciples may not have fully grasped what Jesus was trying to convey, but they retained the formulae, whose meaning they gradually came to appreciate.

Among the disciples there was a privileged inner circle made up of Peter, James and John. To these Jesus spoke much more plainly. There is no explicit evidence that Jesus told them of his divinity. Dreyfus, however, deduces that he must have done so. At a very early stage, represented by the Pauline epistles (Phil 2:6-11; 1 Cor 8:6; 2 Cor 8:9), Christians believed in the divinity and preexistence of Christ. They did not receive such ideas from paganism, and they could not have received them from Judaism. Hence, says Dreyfus, they must have received them from Jesus himself.

Jesus, in other words, did what divine condescension had done in the progressive revelation of the OT. He adapted his message to the varying capacities of those to whom he ministered. What he communicated even to those best equipped to understand was limited by the inability of the human mind to articulate clearly the intuitive knowledge by which Jesus grasped the beatific vision. The knowledge which the mystic has of God is but a pale analogy of Jesus' awareness of his own person.

Having thus established his working hypothesis as the best possible explanation of the NT evidence, Dreyfus turns to objections to his position based on texts which betray ignorance on the part of Jesus. Jesus attributed to David a psalm which he did not write (Mk 12:36). He took Jonah's sojourn in the whale's belly as an historical fact (Mt 12:39-41). He said that he did not know the date of the last judgment (Mk 13:32). He feared death (Mk 14:32-42), and on the cross experienced the ultimate desolation (Mk 15:34).

In each case Dreyfus gives the same basic response. When understood within the framework of Jesus' knowledge of his divinity, these texts "permit us to understand much more profoundly the psychology of Jesus who, in order to save us, took upon himself not sin but its most painful consequences."[12] Hence, Dreyfus concludes, "If during his earthly life Jesus had read the Fourth Gospel, he would have said, 'This is really me.'"[13]

---

[12] Jésus savait-il qu'il était Dieu?, 128.

[13] Jésus savait-il qu'il était Dieu?, 129.

Brickbats and Bouquets

Within days of publication this book was a success. In the space of nine months it was reprinted twice, which is most unusual for a religious book in France, and was awarded a prize by the most prestigious institution in the country, the French Academy. It both touched a nerve and answered a deep need.

There were negative assessments which expressed nothing but the extreme irritation of the reviewer,[14] while others saluted the book as "reassuring and illuminating for the faith."[15]

This latter reaction was explained by Jean Galot, SJ, "It is a healthy and welcome reaction to the tendency of recent studies to reduce the affirmations of the Christian faith by a reinterpretation of Scripture and the Councils."[16] To which Christoph Schönborn, O.P., added, "The success of this book is to a great extent explained by the surprise of many Christians on hearing this question [concerning the divinity of Jesus] raised by theologians, who moreover give it a negative, or at least a hesitant, answer."[17]

These two citations summarize a broad spectrum of reviews. The book was warmly welcomed by those who perceived the honest hesitations of scholars as a pastoral problem. The faithful were not being given the brief straightforward answers which their piety and lack of theological sophistication demanded. From this perspective Dreyfus' book seemed like manna from heaven. It was a perfect example of the sort of unambiguous response which pastors needed to stem the rising tide of uncertainty among their flocks. "A breath of fresh air dispelling the mists of doubt" was the cliché which appeared regularly in such reviews.

On a more academic level the book was greeted with the sense of relief which characterizes the reception of a defector from the other side at a critical moment in the struggle. Those who were committed to the immutability of church statements had always seen exegetes as destructive subversives.[18] If they could change the meaning of the Bible, what might they not do to conciliar decrees or papal pronouncements? Thus a number of reviewers praised Dreyfus' bravery. "We can only applaude the courage of this ex-

---

[14] E.g. E. Trocmé of the University of Strasbourg in RHPT 66 (1986) 226-227.

[15] L. A. Erchinger, Église en Alsace, n. 84, 50.

[16] Esprit et Vie 94 (1984) 627.

[17] Sources 11 (Sept-Oct 1985) 228.

[18] B. Bro, O.P., was far from being untypical in writing, "On the pretext that if he knew that he was the Son of God, Christ would have been less a man, the response of exegetes has surreptitiously and cleverly brought doubt into contemporary thought." (France Catholique Ecclesia, 27 April 1984, 16.

egete who has not feared to infringe the code of the tribe,"[19] by "throwing this exegetico-theological 'bomb', this book which is so much at odds with the current ethos."[20] In their eyes it exploded the myth of 'scientific' exegesis by revealing the subjectivity of its preconceptions and the precariousness of its logic. Thereby it won for Dreyfus the accolade of Jean Guitton, "I see in him a sort of Amos, namely, a little prophet, who announces to the heavens in Jerusalem the theologian-exegetes of the future."[21]

Not all reviewers were as complimentary. Some were so disconcerted that they contented themselves with a simple summary without a single word of evaluation.[22] The majority were rather generic in their criticism, pointing out the neglect of the Synoptics, and stressing the distance between Dreyfus and the main body of NT scholarship, of which of course he was perfectly well aware.[23]

The most serious exegetical critique came from his colleague at the École Biblique, M.-E. Boismard.[24] He attacked two key points in Dreyfus' demonstration, namely, the assertion that 'Son of God' had a transcendant value in Jn 20:31, and the view that the Pauline letters betrayed a belief in the divinity of Christ.

A survey of 'Son of God' in the Fourth Gospel indicated to Boismard that it means either the King-Messiah or the Just man protected by God, except in 10:36 and 19:7, where it is used by the Jews in a transcendant sense because they accuse Jesus of blasphemy. The point made by Jesus in reply to such accusations is that 'Son of God' does not necessarily have this meaning; a caution which gravely diminishes the probative value of Jn 20:31.

As regards the second point, Boismard argues that in the Pauline epistles pre-existence is related, not to 'Son of God', but to 'Wisdom' as in the sapiential literature. It is, therefore, a Jewish concept, and as such cannot imply that a being other than God is divine. Moreover, in Col 1;15 Christ is explicitly said to be a creature. Thus, Boismard does not accept that the bending of the knee in Phil 2:6-11 is a salute to divinity, or that the name there given to Jesus is Yahweh. The name is 'Lord' which has only a functional value. In consequence, Boismard denies that there is any evidence to

---

[19] D. Ols, O.P., Angelicum 62 (1985) 338.

[20] B. de Margerie, SJ, Science et Esprit 36 (1984) 381.

[21] France Catholique Ecclesia, 11 May 1984, 11. B. de Margerie was equally effusive, "Father Dreyfus has written ... the book that Saint Thomas would have loved to give us, were he still among us." (Science et Esprit 36 [1984] 381).

[22] E.g. S. Legasse, BLE 87 (1986) 144-145.

[23] E.g. N. McEleney, CBQ 48 (1986) 137-138; R. Haubst, TRev 81 (1985) 43-44; W. Tillmanns, Bijdragen 46 (1985) 9.

[24] RB 91 (1984) 591-601.

show a very early belief that Jesus was God. Without this belief there is no reason to think that Jesus ever spoke of his divinity to a group of disciples.

In the average faculty such devastating criticism by one member of a book written by another would not find its way into print in the periodical edited by the faculty. Even though people might feel very strongly about the book, the requirements of long-term coexistence would ensure that it be ignored or assigned to someone outside the faculty for review. The École Biblique, however, is not just any faculty. The bonds which bind its members together are of a completely different order to the contractual arrangements typical of a university. They are members of a religious community whose committment to one another is total and lifelong.

If such a group is to survive healthily, honesty is imperative, but it flows from a Christlike charity which guarantees that intellectual criticism carries no disparagement of the person. Boismard's critique of Dreyfus had a precedent in Benoit's refutation of Vincent's location of the Praetorium (see p. 37f above), and it was taken in precisely the same spirit. Freedom of research and expression at the École Biblique are not insidiously restricted by insecure personal relationships.

A year later Boismard made a request to the community for a subsidy in order to keep the price of his book on the Western Text of the Acts of the Apostles within reasonable limits. During the discussion as to where the money was to come from, Dreyfus suggested that the profits from his book should be used to assist Boismard!

Boismard's criticism had focused on what he saw as the weak points in Dreyfus' argumentation. He concluded that the latter had not proved his case, and left it at that. Other reviewers, however, saw that a negative response to Dreyfus' thesis carried with it the obligation to provide an alternative answer to the question "Who did Jesus think he was?" Thus, G. Rochais offered some brief reflections on Jesus' consciousness of having a filial relationship to God before concluding, "The exegete has no trouble in concluding that the early church in calling Jesus 'Son' adequately translated the particularity of his unity with God. Arrived at that point, he can pass the problem to the speculative theologian ...."[25] It is difficult to imagine a more blatant way of avoiding the issue.

The same accusation cannot be levelled against R. E. Brown who produced the most thoughtful response to Dreyfus' provocation.[26] Noting that Dreyfus did not discuss how first century Jews would have understood divinity,[27] Brown suggests that for them it would have meant 'the Father in

---

25 "Jésus savait-il qu'il était Dieu? Réflexions critiques à propos d'un livre récent," SR 14 (1985) 106.

26 "Did Jesus know he was God?" BTB 15 (1985) 74-79.

27 Dreyfus' ahistorical Trinitarian approach is reproduced in the first proposition of the International Theological Commission, "La conscience que Jésus avait de lui-même et

heaven'. In first century terms, therefore, Dreyfus' question would have meant 'Did Jesus know that he was the Father in heaven?'; it could only have generated obscurity and confusion. It was Christian theology that eventually expanded the meaning of 'God' so that it became possible to include the Son on earth as well as the Father in heaven.

In this the resurrection played a role, whose importance Dreyfus unduly diminished, but Brown agrees with him that the speed and extension of the Christian tendency to accord divine honors to Jesus must have been rooted ultimately in the personality of the latter. While concurring with Dreyfus that Jesus was not only God but knew his identity, Brown refuses to admit that he would have articulated it in the terms of the Fourth Gospel.

Dreyfus appeared to assume that self-identity was a matter of conceptual knowledge, whereas it is in fact a direct intuitive appreciation which is virtually impossible to articulate conceptually. Brown, therefore, answered Dreyfus' question in the following terms. "Jesus' intuitive knowledge of his self-identity would have been a knowledge of what we call in faith being God and being man, and certainly such self-knowledge can have been no less difficult to express than our knowledge of being human. I regard the term 'God' applied to Jesus to be a formulation of Christians in the second half of the first century seeking to express an identity that Jesus knew better than they and which is scarcely exhausted by the term 'God'.... Yet if I judge unsatisfactorily obscure the question 'Did Jesus know he was God?', I am more disconcerted when Christians give the answer 'No.' Some who give that answer think that they are being alert to the historical problem; in my judgment their denial is more false to the historical evidence of Jesus' self-awareness than the response 'Yes.' The affirmative response may be wrong linguistically if it assumes that Jesus must have had the ability to express his self-identity; the negative response may also be wrong in a second way if it assumes that Jesus did not have knowledge of his self-identity or thought he was simply another prophetic emissary."[28]

To judge by the number and variety of the reviews, Dreyfus certainly succeeded in drawing attention to a problem that exegetes would prefer to sweep under the carpet. Even those who disagreed with him recognized the value of being forced to reflect on the conscious or unconscious bias with which such fundamental questions are approached.[29]

Although he reached retirement age in 1988 Dreyfus continues to teach. He is at work on a book on Hell, which is likely to produce as many sparks as the one on Jesus.

---

de sa mission. Quatre propositions avec commentaire," Gregorianum 67 (1986) 417-418.

[28] "Did Jesus know he was God?," 78.

[29] L. Legrand, Indian Theological Studies 22 (1985) 117-118.

Chapter 7

THE NEW GENERATION

The two latest additions to the NT faculty have much in common, even though they come from the opposite ends of the earth. Both speak English as their first language, but are able and willing to teach in French. Both are past students of the École Biblique, and acquired first-class doctorates at prestigious secular universities. Both taught for a number of years at seminary and university levels before returning to take up permanent residence in Jerusalem.

Benedict T. Viviano, O.P.

A chance encounter at a biblical meeting at the University of Louvain in the summer of 1982 brought the first American professor to the École Biblique. Benoit had immensely strengthened the NT department by the addition of Boismard, Murphy-O'Connor, and Dreyfus, but an important gap still remained. No one was specializing in the Synoptic Gospels, which had been taught by Benoit himself until he retired. Thus, when he ran into Benedict Viviano, a Dominican of the Chicago province, who had written a well-received doctorate on Matthew, and had just begun a sabbatical in Germany during which he intended to concentrate on that gospel, Benoit spontaneously asked if he would be interested in teaching at the École Biblique. Viviano's affirmative reply set in motion a series of amicable official moves which resulted in his assignation to the École in time to begin the academic year 1984-85.

Born in St Louis on 22 January 1940, he was the first child (of three) of Frank Gaetano Viviano, a wine and spirit importer, and Carmeline M. Chiappetta. Before his graduation from high school in 1957 he had realized that his vocation to be a Christian teacher and scholar would be best fulfilled within the framework of an intellectual religious order. The Benedictines were excluded because of their lack of mobility, as were the Jesuits because of their strict discipline and non-liturgical spirituality. That left the Dominicans and, after the mandatory two years of further education (at Loras College, Dubuque, Iowa), he entered the midwestern novitiate at Winona, Minnesota, where he received the name Benedict.

From 1960-63 he studied philosophy at the Dominican House of Studies, River Forest, Illinois, graduating with an M.A. and a pontifical Licentiate in Philosophy for a thesis on "John Stuart Mill's Concept of Liberty."

The following three years at the Aquinas Institute of Theology, Dubuque, Iowa, culminating in an M.A. in Theology, revealed his capacity for higher studies. This led to him being assigned to the Pontifical Faculty of the Immaculate Conception in Washington, DC, for the academic year 1966-67, which enabled him to acquire the Licentiate in Sacred Theology for a thesis on "The Righteousness of God in Paul according to Ernst Käsemann." The subject indicated that he was destined to specialize in Sacred Scripture. A year of biblical languages at Harvard University (1967-68) prepared him for the Pontifical Biblical Institute, Rome, which granted him the Baccalaurate in Sacred Scripture in 1969.

That fall he entered the doctorate program in religious studies at Duke University, Durham, North Carolina. During his previous studies he had been strongly influenced by J. Jeremias, B. Gerhardsson, and R. LeDeaut, all of whom had used Jewish literature to illuminate the gospels. The best Christian expert in the English speaking world on the rabbinic background to the NT was W. D. Davies of Duke, and it was with him that Viviano wanted to work. He spent two years at Duke as Davies' research assistant, and on completion of his doctorate examinations was awarded the James A. Montgomery Fellowship of the American Schools of Oriental Research, which enabled him to spend the academic year 1971-72 in Jerusalem. Though he participated in the activities of the American School, he lived and studied at the École Biblique where he began work on his thesis. Reality asserted itself in the fall of 1972 when he was appointed to teach NT at the Aquinas Institute of Theology, Dubuque, Iowa. Nonetheless he completed his dissertation on "Aboth and the New Testament" in three years, and his Ph.D. was conferred in 1976.

As with most dissertations, this one was justified by the fact that no full study had yet been devoted to the topic, but in Viviano's mind it also had a pastoral dimension, which he thought was important for the Catholic church in America. Study as Worship, the title of the published version (1978), highlighted the Pharisaic conviction, articulated in Aboth, that study was the essential precondition for progress in holiness. Such an attitude was diametrically opposed to the anti-intellectualism of American Catholics, who tended to equate untroubled simplicity with authentic piety.[1] Viviano hoped that his academic work might, as a by-product, furnish elements for a biblically based justification for the sanctifying value of study, which was also the Dominican ideal.

Naturally this dimension was not worked out explicitly in the dissertation which remained strictly on the historical level. The Pharisees elevated study to the status of worship, because exact observance of all the prescrip-

---

[1]   This was a matter of intense debate at the time as the result of John Tracy Ellis' devastating critique American Catholics and the Intellectual Life, Chicago: Heritage, 1956. The discussion is documented in American Catholics and the Intellectual Ideal, ed. F. L. Christ and G. E. Sherry, New York:Appleton-Century-Corfts, 1961.

tions of the Law -- the sole way to sanctity -- was possible only when they were understood thoroughly. The Pharisees, however, did not invent this attitude. They merely intensified it. Viviano showed that the virtual identification of the Law as Wisdom, and the ideal of the Jews as a learned people, was of great antiquity, and so widespread that it must have formed part of Jesus' religious presuppositions.

Jesus would have felt closer to the Pharisees than to any other Jewish group, precisely because of his love and respect for the Law, and for the great and sacred realities to which it gave access. But, Viviano was at pains to point out, Jesus opposed the trivializing atomization of the Law through ever more refined jurisprudence. This marginalized all those who were either unable or unwilling to become fulltime lifelong students of the Law.

Jesus' familiarity with the Law betrayed the value he accorded it, but he would not make its study either a measurement of sanctity or a condition of salvation. Instead he took the responsibility of developing a new halacha designed to make it possible for those immersed in the ambiguities of the struggle for existence to live an authentically religious life. His attitude towards Sabbath observance was typical of his stance.

Scholarly reactions to Study as Worship were generally favorable. One reviewer, however, pointed out that the book offered less than the subtitle promised. It did not really deal with "Aboth and the New Testament" but with Aboth and Matthew.[2] This indicated a bias in favor of the First Gospel, which in fact became Viviano's preferred area of specialization.

His first scientific article was entitled "Where was the Gospel According to St. Matthew Written?"[3] The answer of the majority would have been 'Antioch-on-the-Orontes' in western Syria, but a surprising number of scholars remained noncommittal. From a number of recent studies Viviano had picked up hints which pointed to Palestine as the place of origin. In consequence, he suggested that Caesarea Maritima fulfilled all the conditions to explain the complex genesis of the First Gospel. As Alexander Sand recognized, this hypothesis is difficult to demolish.[4] For Viviano, however, it is less an apodictic claim than an expression of his conviction that Matthew's church was in dialogue with the rabbinic academy of Jamnia.

This in itself betrays the fundamental orientation of his commentary on "Matthew" in the New Jerome Biblical Commentary (1989). He distances himself from a recent tendency to divorce Matthew entirely from Judaism, and returns to an enriched form of the older consensus, according to which

---

2   M. J. Cook, JBL 99 (1980) 637. In his preface Viviano had made the obvious point that "To keep the study within reasonable bounds has meant having to renounce full consideration of the contributions of Paul and John. These may be reserved for a later study." (p. x).

3   CBQ 41 (1979) 533-546.

4   Das Evangelium nach Matthäus (RNT), Regensburg: Pustet, 1986, 32-33.

Matthew is a gospel written for a predominantly Judaeo-Christian community, which is both in tension with its Jewish heritage and open to the gentile mission. The format of the NJBC imposed extreme concision, but Viviano managed to be both scientific and pastoral.

While a professor at the Aquinas Institute of Theology (1972-84) Viviano's recognition of the Jewish dimension of Matthew led him regularly to direct a seminar on rabbinic Judaism and to teach a course on Aramaic. During his first sabbatical (1977-78) he got the Licentiate in Sacred Scripture from the Pontifical Biblical Commission, but the bulk of his time was spent at Louvain reading targums. One by-product was a paper on the use of 'rabbi' in the Transfiguration account (Mk 9:5), which he read at the 1978 meeting of the Society of Biblical Literature. It resulted in his becoming editor of the Newsletter for Targumic and Cognate Studies (1978-81), on whose board he still serves.

The pastoral concern manifest in Viviano's choice of a subject for his doctoral thesis continued to assert itself because of, rather than despite, his interest in Aramaic paraphrases of the OT. He needed to relate his studies to contemporary Christian concerns. In the early 1970s in the United States the most urgent of these was seen to be social justice both at home and abroad. Structures had to be changed and new values assimilated. Rightly convinced that charity alone was not enough to make the movement authentically Christian, Viviano determined to make his contribution by underlining the importance of the kingdom of God, which of course is one of the major themes of Matthew's gospel. This he did in conferences and workshops. His interest was not merely in the exposition of the meaning of the concept in the first century, but also in the way in which it was used and misused throughout history. The first fruit was an article "The Kingdom of God in Albert and Thomas" (1980), which subsequently became part of an award-winning book The Kingdom of God in History (Glazier, 1988).[5]

In it Viviano begins with a succinct yet profound effort to determine the meaning of the concept in the NT. "To attempt to define the indefinable, we could say that the kingdom of God is a future apocalyptic divine gift not built by human beings directly but given as a response to hopeful prayer, longing, and hastening struggle. It is the final act of God in visiting and redeeming his people, a comprehensive term for the blessings of salvation, that is, all the blessings secured by that act of God."[6]

From the close of the NT canon to about A.D. 1000 Viviano discerns four currents of interpretation and realization. The first is the eschatological, which carries on the authentic NT doctrine. The second is the mystico-spiritual, according to which the kingdom is identified either with some present spiritual good in the soul of the believer or with a future blessed state of the

---

5   It was chosen by the editors of the New Theology Review (1 [1988] 74) as the best book to appear in its field in 1988.

6   The Kingdom of God in History, 29.

faithful. The third is the political, which saw the kingdom realized in a political entity such as the Holy Roman Empire in the West and the Christian Empire of Constantine in the East. The fourth is the ecclesial, which identified the church with the kingdom of God on earth.

The understanding of the kingdom of God developed by the great theologians of the High Middle Ages was complicated by the need to react to the three-state theology of history of Joachim of Fiore. Bonaventure was disposed to be ambiguous in order to hold the Franciscan Order together. Thomas Aquinas was inhibited in his understanding of the gospel by the anti-mendicant controversy, which threatened the very existence of the Friars, and which in consequence made it unwise to talk about a kingdom of God whose coming would herald radical social changes. Albert the Great was the least touched by Joachism, but his approach was that of Platonizing Christian spirituality which identified the kingdom with God himself.

Viviano's breadth of culture is displayed to best advantage in his treatment of the early modern period. Utopian visionaries like Savonarola rub shoulders with Anabaptists who were interested in a social revolution inspired by the biblical promise of the kingdom of God. He gives pride of place, however, to Immanuel Kant, who in 1793 by a little book entitled Religion Within the Limits of Reason Alone reminded theologians and philosopheres of the central hope of the Synoptic Gospels, the kingdom of God on earth. He saw it as an ethical commonwealth which could be built by human energy without the grace of God. This led to the Social Gospel movement in the 19th century, whose influence on Catholicism is evidenced by labor movements and social encyclicals.

This then set the stage for the rediscovery of the eschatological vision of the eschatological vision of the kingdom of God in the 20th century. With scholars like J. Weiss, A. Schweitzer, and K. Barth, the kingdom again becomes God's to bring and build, but humanity can prepare the way, and perhaps even hasten its advent, by removing obstacles to the reign of love. The hope of humanity is centered in the kingdom of God.

While at the École Biblique Viviano has served as the NT editor of The Illustrated Dictionary and Concordance of the Bible (1986), and from his teaching have come a series of articles in which he explored the Essene use of the kingdom of God concept,[7] the contemporary relevance of the dominical directive "Render unto Caesar the things that are Caesar's",[8] and the implications of the amputation of the ear of the servant of the High Priest for Mark's anti-Temple polemic.[9]

---

[7]   "The Kingdom of God in the Qumran Literature," in The Kingdom of God in 20th Century Interpretation, ed. W. Willis, Peabody: Hendrickson, 1987, 97-107.

[8]   "'Render unto Caesar': Power and Politics in the Light of the Gospel," The Bible Today 26 (1988) 272-276.

[9]   "The High Priest's Servant's Ear: Mark 14:47," RB 96 (1989) 71-80.

Justin Taylor, S.M.

Justin Taylor, a New Zealand Marist, is not the first non-Dominican to join the NT faculty of the École Biblique. That honor belongs to Thomas Calmes, a French Picpus Father, who was invited by Father Lagrange in 1900, and who taught a course in 1901-02. His superiors, however, permitted him to stay only a single year, an attitude that stands in vivid contrast to the generosity of the New Zealand Marist province.

Born on 26 August 1943 in Wellington, New Zealand, to John J. Taylor, a civil servant, and Margaret Lilias Beard, Taylor completed his primary and secondary studies in his native city. He gave up a University National Scholarship to join the Society of Mary in 1960. After his philosophical and theological studies at Mount St. Mary's Seminary outside Napier, New Zealand, he was ordained a priest on 2 July 1966, and was assigned to Cambridge University, England, for graduate work. He took him a year to get there, because he divided his time between France and Germany in order to perfect his knowledge of those languages.

He entered Cambridge in 1967 to read for the Modern History Tripos leading to the B.A. Honours degree. But during the course of his first year Dr. W. H. C. Frend recommended that he be transferred to research for the Ph.D., and the Board of Graduate Studies concurred. Frend's fields were Roman history and archaeology and early church history. Taylor fully expected to be assigned to him as a student, but the History Faculty directed him to the Professor of Ancient History, the celebrated A. H. M. Jones, whose great work The Later Roman Empire had just appeared.

Taylor's new status was recognized by Downing College which first elected him into a Bye-Fellowship (1969-70), and then into a full Research Fellowship (1970-73), which carried with it an M.A. and membership of the Governing Body of the College. In 1972 he was awarded the doctorate for a dissertation on "The Papacy and the Eastern Churches from 366 to 417," parts of which were published in a series of articles.[10] While working on his thesis, he also did a certain amount of tutorial work for Downing and other colleges, and delivered a series of lectures in the History Faculty on "Popes and Emperors in the Early Byzantine Period."

On his return to New Zealand in 1973 he taught at Mount St. Mary's Seminary and at Massey University, and was a visiting lecturer at the Pacific Regional Seminary in Figi. Gradually it was recognized that he was nee-

---

[10] "Eastern Appeals to Rome in the Early Church: A Little-known Witness," DRev 89 (1971) 142-146; "St. Basil the Great and Pope St. Damascus I," DRev 91 (1973) 187-203, 262-274; "The Early Papacy at Work: Gelasius I (492-6)," JRH 8 (1975) 317-332; "The Founding of the New Rome," Prudentia 7 (1975) 111-116; "East and West in the Church: In the Beginning," Prudentia 8 (1976) 91-98; "The First Council of Constantinople (381)," Prudentia 13 (1981) 47-54, 91-97.

ded more as a professor of NT than as a professor of church history. To this period belong two popular books, Introducing the Bible (1981), which was reedited by Paulist Press, New York, in 1987 as As it was Written: An Introduction to the Bible, and Alive in the Spirit (1984) on the working of the Holy Spirit in the Christian life.

Although widely read in the field and well equipped linguistically, Taylor felt the lack of at least some professional formation in biblical studies. So when he got a study leave in 1983-84 he came to the École Biblique. He returned again in 1985-86. His first Mémoire examined Mt 18:3 and Jn 3:3 with other related texts including the Coptic Gospel of Thomas, and concluded that they wer all converging versions of a single saying of Jesus on "becoming a child again." Duting that year he also published an article "The Johannine Discourses and the Speech of Jesus: Five Views."[11] For his second Mémoire he compared several texts of the Sermon on the Mount with corresponding passages in Justin Martyr and other early writers, and postulated that these Fathers had drawn on an extra-canonical tradition of the sayings of Jesus.

The talent for textual criticism exhibited in these papers and his previous formation as an historian drew him into the work that Boismard and Lamouille were doing on the Acts of the Apostles (see pp. 102-103 above). They invited him to return for three months in 1987 in order to research certain historical points which impinged on their literary analysis of the Acts of the Apostles. This brought home to the faculty the value of having an historian of the NT period on the staff. The contributions of Abel and Savignac before the Second World War had somehow been forgotten. An honorable tradition came to life again when Taylor was invited to remain permanently at the École Biblique. The parallel with Abel is made all the stronger by the fact that Taylor wrote "Khirbet es-Samra dans l'histoire," the opening chapter in the École's forthcoming publication on that site in Jordan.

Taylor's first course (1988-89) dealt with the historical background to Paul's missionary journey in Acts 13-14. The material will eventually feed into the historical commentary, which is planned as a companion volume to the literary and theological commentary being written by Boismard and Lamouille. He also contributed to that work, not only by dealing with historical issues, but also in the generation and development of some of the literary hypotheses.

His ability to extract spiritual material from literary criticism is well illustrated by a paper on "The Jerusalem Church in the Acts of the Apostles, 2:42-47 and 4:32-35," which was delivered to the Second International Colloquium on the Study of Marist History and Spirituality held in Rome in March 1989. On a very different level, his exceptional memory enabled him to remark resemblances between Mt 24:9-13 and Tacitus, Annals 15:43-44,

---

11   Scripture Bulletin 14 (1984) 33-41.

Benedict T. Viviano, O.P.

Justin Taylor, S.M.

which caused him to conclude that in this passage Matthew was referring to the persecution of Christians under Nero in A.D. 64.[12] An auspicious start to a new phase in Taylor's career, and a sign of the vitality of NT studies at the École Biblique as it moves into its second century.

Two Directors

Until very recently the Director of the École Biblique was chosen from among the professors. When the term of Raymond J. Tournay, O.P. (1972-82) came to an end, it was decided to look outside the École for a Director. New blood could only be beneficial, and his competence would reinforce the faculty. Since the two subsequently elected both wrote on NT subjects, it is appropriate to round out this survey by mentioning their contributions even though they were only temporarily attached to the École Biblique.

In April 1982 Francois Refoulé, O.P., was elected Director. Previously had been Literary Director of Éditions du Cerf in Paris, and had written extensively on themes of biblical spirituality. His insightful Marx et saint Paul: Libérer l'homme (Cerf, 1973) was particularly noteworthy. During his first year in office he wrote " ... et ainsi tout Israël sera sauvé" Romains 11, 25-32 (LD 117; Cerf, 1984), in which he argued that "tout Israel" in Rom 11:26a does not refer to the whole of the Jewish people, but to the "remnant" mentioned in Rom 9:27. In other words, the Jews as a people are given no guarantee of salvation; the only way to the Father is through faith in Jesus Christ.

This material became the basis of a course the following year (1983-84). The year after he lectured on the Law in Romans, from which flowed articles on Rom 10:4 and 9:30-33.[13] At this point he was summoned back to Paris to resume his post as Literary Director at Cerf; his successor had not proved satisfactory. This was unfortunate, not only for the École, but also for NT studies, because he might have written a commentary on Romans for the Études Bibliques to replace that of Lagrange, which is now over sixty years old.

Refoulé's successor as Director of the École Biblique was Jean-Luc Vesco, O.P. (1984-90), who had just completed two terms as Provincial of Toulouse, a province which has given a number of distinguished professors to the École. Although an OT specialist, he had written the very popular En Méditerranée avec l'apôtre Paul (Cerf, 1972). While at the École he analysed the understanding of the Psalter developed in the second century A.D.

---

12 "'The Love of Many will grow Cold': Matthew 24:9-13 and the Neronian Persecution," RB 96 (1989).

13 "Romains x, 4. Encore une fois," RB 91 (1984) 321-350; "Note sur Romains, ix, 30-33," RB 92 (1985) 161-186.

Epistle of Barnabas,[14] annotated <u>Le Nouveau Testament. Une Parole qui fait vivre</u> (Paris: Livre de Poche, 1988), and published a study of Luke's theology, <u>Jérusalem et son Prophète</u> (Paris, 1988).

---

[14]   "La lecture du Psautier selon l'Épître de Barnabé," RB 93 (1986) 5-37.

Chapter 8

A LAST WORD

Even though history is concerned with "the unique, the unrepeatable, and the unpredictable,"[1] there would be something unsatisfactory about ending the story of NT research at the École Biblique without some general reflections. A survey that merely noted what had been observed would be nothing more than an inventory.

Each of the lives considered proclaimes its own message. Do they coalesce into a collective meaning which would give the École Biblique a specific identity, at least in its relationship to the study of the NT? This is perhaps the central question, and it can be given a classical form, which in this case might appear to be a paradox; is the École Biblique a school?

The distinctive features of schools differ. The school of Alexandria was identified by its allegorical method of interpreting the Scriptures. The history of religions school distinguished itself by its approach to the NT; it insisted that Christianity can be understood properly only if it is studied as one phenomenon among the other religious phenomena of the Greco-Roman world. The Tübingen school drew its identity from its basic thesis, a theory of intense conflict between Jewish and Gentile Christianity, a conflict which was resolved only in the middle of the second century. The Chicago school's distinctive characteristic was its overriding concern for the social implications of the gospel.

By these criteria the École Biblique is not a school. It has neither a distinctive methodology nor a unique approach to the NT; it shares those common to all who treat the Bible seriously enough to appreciate its difficulties. Nor does it propagate a particular thesis. It will be clear from what has been said of the positions of various professors that they cannot be associated with a particular point of view. In this respect if the École Biblique has a party line it can only be defined negatively. It has consistently looked at and dismissed trends, e.g. structuralism, which subsequently turned out to be fads without permanent value. While the École Biblique has always shared a pastoral concern, this has not affected its publications in such a way as to make it a specific characteristic.

---

[1] S. Neill, <u>The Interpretation of the New Testament 1861-1961,</u> London: OUP, 1966, 280.

There were, however, schools much older than those just mentioned. NT scholars speak of the school of Matthew and of the Johannine school. They were preceded by the Academy of Plato, the Lyceum of Aristotle, the Garden of Epicurus, and the Stoa. As analysed by R. Alan Culpepper these manifest the following common denominators: "1) they were groups of disciples which usually emphasized *philia* and *koinonia* [friendship and fellowship]; 2) they gathered round and traced their origins to a founder whom they regarded as an exemplary wise, or good man; 3) they valued the teachings of their founder and the traditions about him; 4) members of the schools were disciples or students of the founder; 5) teaching, learning, studying, and writing were common activities; 6) most schools observed communal meals, often in memory of their founders; 7) they had rules or practices regarding admission, retention of membership, and advancement within the membership; 8) they often maintained some degree of distance or withdrawal from the rest of society; and 9) they developed organizational means of insuring their perpetuity. Since most of the schools studied above share in all of these characteristics, this list of characteristics can be used as a definition of what constituted an ancient 'school.'"[2]

There is little difficulty in applying this definition to the École Biblique. Moreover, it has the added advantage of highlighting the antiquity of the tradition in which religion is not the enemy of scholarship but its vitalizing matrix. The definition fits only because the research of the École Biblique is produced by members of a religious order, which is characterized by a *koinonia* much more profound than that envisaged by the ancients.

This community also embraces the students who have always been few in number. This is due to two factors, which enhance the distinctiveness of the École Biblique. It does not offer primary degrees (B.A. or M.A.). Students must be well-trained and specialized in order to be accepted. Classes, in consequence, are few; the emphasis is on personal research into the original texts designed to make the student an independent scholar.

Lagrange, of course, was not the founder of the Dominican Order to which the majority of the professors of the École Biblique belong. But if he is compared with others who set up analogous institutes, it becomes clear that he was much more than the one assigned under obedience to establish a biblical school in Jerusalem. He gave it a method and a program, but these were available elsewhere. More importantly, he gave it a style and an ethos, which were distinctive; it combined freedom and obedience, unquestioning acceptance and radical criticism. His students, even when they became his collaborators or rose to eminence elsewhere in the world, considered themselves his disciples, and revered him as an exemplary wise and good man.

---

2   The Johannine School: An Evaluation of the Johannine School Hypothesis based on an Investigation of the Nature of Ancient Schools (SBLDS 26), Missoula: Scholars Press, 1975, 258-259.

This trait was particularly marked in Benoit, who regarded Lagrange as the perfect scholar-religious, and who communicated this attitude to his own students. They were and are proud to stand in the tradition of Lagrange, and find in him a role model, not only in terms of originality and productivity, but in terms of the patient persistence which enabled him to facilitate significant change and growth in one of the most authoritarian and monolithic institutions in the world, the Roman Catholic Church.

It is in this sense that the École Biblique can be seen to maintain some degree of distance from society. Its scholarship is primarily directed to the education of the church; its thrust is fundamentally pastoral. Its publications, though not popular, are widely accessible. Yet it does not ignore the academic world. Colleagues of all nationalities and persuasions are frequent guests at the École Biblique, and its professors regularly attend and participate actively in national and international NT meetings. The quality of their training, the scope of their reading, and the standard of their research publications are equal to the best in academe. They do not, however, permit their agenda to be set by academe either as regards the topics they work on or the conclusions they reach.

Their colleagues would certainly consider Boismard, Dreyfus and Murphy-O'Connor to be slightly out of step with the majority. Their respective interests in source criticism, the self-knowledge of Jesus, and the centrality of community in Pauline thought -- to mention only the most obvious -- separate them from the mainstream of contemporary scholarship. But these are topics of absorbing interest to ordinary members of the church, who are their most important constituency. All believers are interested in what really happened at the beginnings of Christianity, in the person of Christ, and in the framework which makes discipleship possible. This is clear from the invitations to lecture which they receive from all over the world.

A certain iconoclasm is also typical of the NT professors of the École Biblique. They tend to regard a consensus on any point with deep suspicion. They fear the sclerosis of academic dogmas, which are no more than working hypotheses canonized by lethargy. They are sceptics in the best sense, for they recognize the fragility of the human grasp on truth. It cannot be held permanently. The quest for the meaning of revelation is never over. They have shared it for a hundred years, and commit themselves to it for the future, "living the truth in love" (Eph 4:15).

BIBLIOGRAPHIES

1890-1990

Arranged and typed by Regina A. BOISCLAIR

These bibliographies are in chronological order by first edition.
They are limited to the authors' New Testament publications.

MARIE-JOSEPH LAGRANGE, O.P.

Books

1. *La méthode historique, surtout à propos de l'Ancien Testament* . (ÉB).
   Paris: Lecoffre, 1903.
   = *Historical Criticism of the Old Testament* . London, 1906.
2. *Éclaircissement sur la Méthode historique, à propos d'un livre du R. P. Delattre, S. J.* (Pro manuscripto).
   Paris: Lecoffre, 1905.
3. *Le Messianisme chez le Juifs 150 avant Jésus-Christ à 200 après Jésus-Christ* . (ÉB).
   Paris: Gabalda, 1909.
4. *Quelques remarques sur l' "Orpheus" de M. S. Reinach* .
   Paris: Gabalda, 1910.
   = *Notes on the "Orpheus" of M. Sal. Reinnach* .
   Oxford, 1910.
5. *Évangile selon saint Marc* . (ÉB).
   Paris: Lecoffre, 1911.
6. *Saint Paul: Épître aux Romains* . (ÉB).
   Paris: Gabalda, 1916.
7. *Saint Paul: Épître aux Galates* . (ÉB).
   Paris: Gabalda, 1918.
8. *Évangile selon saint Luc* . (ÉB).
   Paris: Gabalda, 1921.
9. *Évangile selon saint Marc* , Abridged edition. (ÉB).
   Paris: Gabalda, 1922.
   The Gospel According to St. Mark.
   London: Burns Oates, 1930.
10. *Évangile selon saint Matthieu* . (ÉB).
    Paris: Gabalda,1923.
11. *La vie de Jésus d'après Renan* .
    Paris: Gabalda,1923.
    = *Christ and Renan. A Commentary on Ernest Renan's* The Life of Jesus .
    London: Sheed and Ward,1928.
12. *L'Évangile selon saint Jean* . (ÉB).
    Paris: Gabalda, 1925.
13. *Synopsis evangelica graece* . With the collaboration of Père C. Lavergne.
    Barcelona: Éditions "Alpha", 1926.
    = *Synopse des quatre Évangiles en français d'après la Synopse grecque du R. P. Lagrange* ., by R. P. Lavergne, O.P.

Paris: Gabalda, 1927.
= *Sinopsi Evangelica* . Greek texts of M. J. Lagrange OP.
Catalan version with notes of L.L. Carreras and J. M.
LLovera.
Barcelona: Éditions "Alpha", 1927.
= *Sinossi dei quattro Vangeli secondo la Sinossi Greca el P.
M.-J. Lagrange.*
Brescia: Morcelliana, 1931.
= *A Catholic Harmony of the Four Gospels, Being an Adaptation of the "Synopsis Evangelica" of P. Lagrange*,
by Rev. John Barton.
London: Burns Oates and Washbourne, 1930.
14. *L'Évangile de Jésus-Christ* . (ÉB).
Paris: Gabalda, 1928.
= *The Gospel of Jesus Christ* .
London: Burns Oates and Washbourne, 1938.
15. *Le Judaïsme avant Jésus-Christ* . (ÉB).
Paris: Gabalda, 1931.
16. *La morale de l'Évangile. Réflexions sur* Les morales de l'Évangile *de
M. A. Bayet* .
Paris: Grasset, 1931.
17. *Monsieur Loisy et le modernisme. A propos des "Mémoires" d' A. Loisy.*
Paris: Cerf, 1932.
18. *Introduction à l'étude du Nouveau Testament : I. Histoire ancienne du
canon du Nouveau Testament* . (ÉB).
Paris: Gabalda, 1933.
19. *Introduction à l'étude du Nouveau Testament : II. Critique textuelle . La
critique rationnelle* , with R. P. Lyonnet, S.J. (ÉB).
Paris: Gabalda, 1935.
20. *Introduction à l'étude du Nouveau Testament : IV. Critique historique .
Les mystères: l'Orphisme* . (ÉB).
Paris: Gabalda, 1937.

Articles

21. "Les sources du troisième Évangile."
RB 4 (1895): 5-22.
22. "Le récit de l'enfance de Jésus dans saint Luc."
RB 4 (1895): 160-185.
23. "Origène, la critique textuelle et la tradition topographique."
Part 1. *RB* 4 (1895): 501-524;
Part 2. *RB* 5 (1896): 87-92.
24. "Une pensée de saint Thomas sur l'inspiration scripturaire."
RB 4 (1895): 563-571.
25. "Les sources du troisième Évangile."
RB 5 (1896): 5-38.
26. "L'inspiration des Livres Saints."
RB 5 (1896):199-220
27. "L'inspiration et les exigences de la critique."
RB 5 (1896): 496-518.

28. "Étienne."
    Dictionnaire de la Bible , ed. by F. Vigouroux. Vol. II, Paris, Letouzey et Ané, 1899, col. 2033-2035.
29. "La Dormition de la Sainte Vierge et la maison de Jean Marc."
    RB 8 (1899): 589-600.
30. "L'interprétation de la Sainte Écriture par l'Église."
    RB 9 (1900): 135-142.
31. "Projet d'un commentaire complet de l'Écriture Sainte."
    RB 9 (1900): 414-423.
32. "Notes sur le Messianisme au temps de Jésus."
    RB 14 (1905): 481-514.
33. "L'avènement du Fils de l'homme."
    RB 15 (1906): Part I, 382-411; Part II, 561-574.
34. "Le décret *Lamentabili sane exitu* et la critique historique."
    RB 16 (1907): 542-554.
35. "Le règne de Dieu dans le judaïsme."
    RB 17 (1908): 350-367.
36. "La Paternité de Dieu dans l'Ancien Testament."
    RB 17 (1908): 481-500.
37. "Nouveau fragment non canonique relatif à l'Évangile."
    RB 17 (1908): 538-553.
38. "La parabole en dehors de l'Évangile."
    RB 18 (1909): Part I, 198-212; Part II, 342-367.
39. "Les religions orientales et les origines du christianisme."
    Le Correspondant 104 (July 25, 1910): 209-241.
40. "Le but des paraboles d'apres l'Évangile selon saint Marc."
    RB 19 (1910): 5-35.
41. "Où en est la question du recensement de Quirinius?"
    RB 20 (1911): 60-84.
42. "Le catalogue des vices dans l'Épître aux Romains (I, 23-31)."
    RB 20 (1911): 534-549.
43. "Jésus a-t-il été oint plusieurs fois et par plusieurs femmes?"
    RB 21 (1912): 504-532.
44. "A propos d'une critique par le R. P. Rinieri du Commentaire de saint Marc."
    RB 21 (1912): 633-637.
45. "Une nouvelle édition du Nouveau Testament" (von Soden).
    RB 22 (1913): 481-524.
46. "La conception surnaturelle du Christ d'après saint Luc."
    RB 23 (1914): Part I, 60-71; Part II, 188-208.
47. "La justification d'après Paul."
    RB 23 (1914): 481-503.
48. "Langue, style, argumentation dans l'Épître aux Romains."
    RB 24 (1915): 216-235.
49. "Le commentaire de Luther sur l'Épître aux Romains."
    Part I, *RB* 24 (1915): 456-484; Part II, *RB* 25 (1916):90-120.
50. "La Vulgate latine de l'Épître aux Romains et le texte grec."
    RB 25 (1916): 225-239.
51. "La Vulgate latine de l'Épître aux Galates et le texte grec."
    RB 26 (1917): 424-450.

52. "La revision de la Vulgate par saint Jérôme."
    RB 27 (1918): 254-257.
53. "Les mystères d'Éleusis et le Christianisme."
    RB 28 (1919): 157-217.
54. "Attis et le Christianisme."
    RB 28 (1919): 419-480.
55. "Critique biblique. Réponse à l'article de la *Civiltà cattolica* : 'Venticin-
    que anni dopo l'enciclica *Providentissimus* '."
    RB 28 (1919): 593-600.
56. "A propos des destinataires de l'épître aux Galates."
    RApo 30 (1920): 393-398.
57. "L'exégèse biblique en Allemagne durant la guerre."
    RB 29 (1920): 285-300.
58. "L'ancienne version syriaque des Évangiles."
    Part I, *RB* 29 (1920): 321-352; Part II, *RB* 30 (1921): 11-44.
59. "Une des parole attribuées à Jésus."
    RB 30 (1921): 233-237.
60. "L'Évangile selon les Hébreux."
    Part I: *RB* 31 (1922): 161-181; Part II: *RB* 31 (1922): 321-349.
61. "Le prétendu messianisme de Virgile."
    RB 31 (1922): 552-572.
62. "Le Logos d'Héraclite."
    RB 32 (1923): 96-107.
63. "Vers le Logos de saint Jean."
    RB 32 (1923): Part I, 161-184; Part II, 321-371.
64. "Où en est la dissection littéraire du Quatrième Évangile?
    RB (33) 1924: 321-342.
65. "L'hermétisme."
    Part I, *RB* 33 (1924): 481-497; Part II, *RB* 34 (1925): 82-104
    Part III, *RB* 34 (1925): 368-396; Part IV, *RB* 34 (1925): 547-574;
    Part V, *RB* 35 (1926): 240-264.
66. "L'origine de la version syro-palestinienne des Évangiles."
    RB 34 (1925): 481-504.
67. "L'auteur du canon de Muratori."
    RB 35 (1926): 83-88.
68. "Les prologues prétendus Marcionites."
    RB 35 (1926): 161-173.
69. "La conception qui domine le IVe Évangile (échanges de vues avec le R.
    P. Olivieri)."
    RB 35 (1926): 382-397.
70. "La gnose mandéene et la tradition évangélique."
    Part I, *RB* 36 (1927): 321-349; Part II, *RB* 36 (1927): 481-515; Part
    III, *RB* 37 (1928): 5-3
71. "Un nouveau papyrus contenant un fragment des Actes."
    RB 36 (1927): 549-560.
72. "L'évangile de saint Marc n'a pas été écrit en latin."
    RB 37 (1928): 106-116.
73. "Un nouvel évangile de l'enfance édité par M. R. James."
    RB 37 (1928): 544-557.
74. "La religion des Stoïciens avant Jésus-Christ."

RThom 33 (1928): 46-68.
75. "La divinité de Jésus"
    Vit I (1928):10-28.
76. "La régénération et la filiation divine dans les mystères d'Éleusis."
    RB 38 (1929): Part I, 63-81; Part II, 201-214.
77. "Un nouveau papyrus évangélique (Pap. Michigan)."
    RB 38 (1929): 161-177.
78. "Le groupe dit Césaréen des manuscrits des Évangiles."
    RB 38 (1929): 481-512.
79. "Jean-Baptiste et Jésus d'après le texte slave de la Guerre des Juifs de
    Josèphe."
    RB 39 (1930): 29-46.
80. "La Présentation de Jésus au Temple."
    VSpir 26 (1931):129-135.
81. "L'amour de Dieu, loi suprême de la morale de l'Évangile."
    VSpirSup 26 (1931):1-16.
82. "Saint Paul ou Marcion."
    RB 41 (1932): 5-30.
83. "Le canon d'Hippolyte et le fragment de Muratori."
    RB 42 (1933): 161-186.
84. "Un nouveau papyrus évangélique."
    RB 42 (1933): 402-404.
85. "Projet de critique textuelle rationnelle du Nouveau Testament."
    RB 42 (1933): 481-498.
86. "Les papyrus Chester Beatty pour les Évangiles."
    RB 43 (1934): 5-41.
87. "Le papyrus Chester Beatty des Actes des Apôtres."
    RB 43 (1934): 161-171.
88. "Les papyrus Chester Beatty pour les Épîtres de saint Paul et l'Apoca-
    lypse."
    RB 43 (1934): 481-493.
89. "Socrate et Notre-Seigneur Jésus-Christ, d'après un livre récent."
    RB 44 (1935): 5-21.
90. "L'histoire ancienne du canon du Nouveau Testament."
    RB 44 (1935): 212-219.
91. "Deux nouveaux textes relatifs à l'Évangile."
    RB 44 (1935): 321-343.
92. "La critique textuelle avant le Concile de Trente."
    RThom 29 (1935): 400-409.
93. "La Vie de Jésus par M. François Mauriac."
    RB 45 (1936): 321-345.
94. "Les légendes pythagoriennes et l'Évangile."
    Part I, *RB* 45 (1936): 481-511; Part II, *RB* 46 (1937): 5-28.
95. "La réalisme historique de l'Évangile selon S. Jean."
    RB 46 (1937): 321-341.

Selected Book Reviews

96. Jüngst, J. *Die Quellen der Apostelgeschichte* .
    RB 4 (1895): 629-630.

97. Gore, C. *Dissertations on subjects connected with the Incarnation* .
    RB 5 (1896): 452-454.
98. Resch, A. *Aussercanonische Paralleltexte zu den Evangelien* . (TU).
    RB 5 (1896): 281-282.
99. Holtzmann, H. J. *Lehrbuch der neutestamentlichen Theologie* .
    RB 6 (1897): 468-474.
100. Schürer, E. *Geschichte des jüdischen Volkes im Zeitalter Jesu Christi* .
    RB 8 (1899): 310-313.
101. Zahn, Th. *Forschungen zur Geschichte des neutestamentlichen Kanons und der altkirchlichen Literatur.* Bd VI.
    RB 9 (1900): 616-620.
102. Harnack, A. *Das Wesen des Christentums* .
    RB 10 (1901): 110-123.
103. Bousset, W. *Die Religion des Judentums im neutestamentlichen Zeitalter* .
    RB 12 (1903): 620-625.
104. Loisy, A. *L'Évangile et l' Église* .
    RB 12 (1903): 292-313.
105. Wrede, W. *Das Messiasgeheimnis in den Evangelien* .
    RB 12 (1903); 625-628.
106. Bugge, C. A. *Die Haupt-Parabeln Jesu* .
    RB 13 (1904): 108-117.
107. Gunkel, H. *Zum religionsgeschichtlichen Verständnis des Neuen Testaments* .
    RB 13 (1904): 271-273.
108. Loisy, A. *Études évangéliques* .
    RB 13 (1904): 108-117.
109. Volz, P. *Jüdische Eschatologie von Daniel bis Akiba* .
    RB 13 (1904): 600-604.
110. Weiss, J. *Die Predigt Jesu vom Reiche Gottes* .
    RB 13 (1904): 106-108.
111. Oxford Society of Historical Theology. *The New Testament in the Apostolic Fathers* .
    RB 14 (1905): 615-617.
112. Loisy, A. *Morceaux d'exégèse* .
    RB 15 (1906): 474-479.
113. Pesch, C. *De Inspiratione Sacrae Scripturae.*
    RB 15 (1906): 303-314.
114. Lods, A. *La croyance à la vie future et le culte des morts dans l'antiquité israélite* .
    RB 16 (1907): 422-433.
115. Schmidt, N. *The prophet of Nazareth* .
    RB 16 (1907): 296-300.
116. Holtzmann, H. J. *Das messianische Bewußtsein Jesu* .
    RB 17 (1908): 280-293.
117. Loisy, A. *Les Évangiles synoptiques* .
    RB 17 (1908): 608-620.
118. Sanday, W. *The Life of Christ in recent research* .
    RB 17 (1908): 280-293.
119. Tillmann, F. *Der Menschensohn* .

RB 17 (1908): 280-293.

120. Clemen, C. *Religionsgeschichtliche Erklärung des Neuen Testaments* .
RB 18 (1909): 280-284.

121. Feine, P. *Theologie des Neuen Testaments* .
RB 19 (1910): 583-585.

122. Lebreton, J. *Les origines du dogme de la Trinité* .
RB 19 (1910): 585-593.

123. Lepin, M. *La valeur historique du quatrième Évangile* .
RB 19 (1910): 269-276.

124. Reinach, S. *Orpheus. Histoire générale des religions* .
RB 19 (1910): 129-141.

125. Sanday, W. *Christologies ancient and modern* .
RB 19 (1910): 579-583.

126. Stanton, V. H. *The Gospels as historical documents* . *Vol II. The Synoptic Gospels* .
RB 19 1(910): 266-269.

127. Goguel, M. *L'Évangile de Marc et ses rapports avec ceux de Matthieu et de Luc* .
RB 20 (1911):132-135.

128. Heer, J. M. *Die Stammbäume Jesu nach Matthäus und Lukas.*
RB 20 (1911): 447-451.

129. Loisy, A. *Jésus et la tradition évangélique* .
RB 20 (1911): 294-299.

130. Schade, T. L. *Die Inspirationslehre des heiligen Hieronymus* .
RB 20 (1911): 602-607.

131. Vogt, P. *Der Stammbaum Christi bei den heiligen Evangelisten Matthäus und Lukas* .
RB 20 (1911): 443-447.

132. Bricout, J. *Où en est l'histoire des religions ?*
RB 21 (1912): 455-460.

133. Pasquier, H. *La solution du problème synoptique* .
RB 21 (1912): 280-284.

134. Schmidtke, A. *Neue Fragmente und Untersuchungen zu den Judenchristlichen Evangelien* .
RB 21 (1912): 587-596.

135. Vogels, H. J. *Die Altsyrischen Evangelien in ihrem Verhältnis zu Tatians Diatessaron* .
RB 21 (1912): 284-294.

136. Norden, E. *Agnostos Theos* .
RB 23 (1914): 442-448.

137. Schweitzer, A. *Geschichte der paulinische Forschung von der Reformation bis auf die Gegenwart* .
RB 23 (1914): 288-292.

138. Grandmaison, L. de. *Jésus-Christ* (DA).
RB 24 (1915): 576-581.

139. Loisy, A. *L'Épître aux Galates* .
RB 25 (1916): 250-259.

140. Vosté, J. M. *Commentarius in Epistolas ad Thessalonicences* .
RB 26 (1917): 574-577.

141. Juster, J. *Les Juifs dans l'empire romain* .

RB 27 (1918): 258-267.
142. Mc Neile, A. H. *The Gospel According to S. Matthew* .
    RB 27 (1918): 584-587.
143. Burkitt, F. C. *Jewish and Christian apocalypses* .
    RB 28 (1919): 290-293.
144. Harnack, A von. *Die Entstehung des Neuen Testaments und die wich-tigsten Folgen der neuen Schöpfung* .
    RB 28 (1919): 255-261.
145. Windisch, H. *Der Hebräerbrief* .
    RB 28 (1919): 261-266.
146. Bacon., B. W. *The Fourth Gospel in Research and Debate* .
    RB 29 (1920): 138-144.
147. Loisy, A. *Les mystères païens et le mystère chrétien* .
    RB 29 (1920): 420-446.
148. Macler, F. *Le texte arménien de l'Évangile d'après Matthieu et Marc* .
    RB 29 (1920): 452-456.
149. Harnack, A. von. *Marcion: Das Evangelium vom fremden Gott* .
    RB 30 (1921): 602-611.
150. Bultmann, R. *Die Geschichte der synoptischen Tradition* .
    RB 31 (1922): 286-292.
151. Reitzenstein, R. *Das iranische Erlösungsmysterium* .
    RB 31 (1922): 282-286.
152. Bertram, G. *Die Leidensgeschichte Jesu und der Christuskult* .
    RB 32 (1923): 442-445.
153. Dalman, G. *Jesus-Jeschua* .
    RB 33 (1924): 271-273.
154. Goguel, M. *Introduction au Nouveau Testament* . *Vol II. Le Quatrième Évangile* .
    RB 33 (1924): 605-611.
155. Quentine, H. *Mémoire sur l'établissement du texte de la Vulgate.*
    RB 33 (1924): 114-123.
156. Sanday, W. *Novum Testamentum sancti Irenaei episcopi Lugdunensis* .
    RB 33 (1924): 260-263.
157. Vogels, H. J. *Beiträge zur Geschichte des Diatessaron im Abendland* .
    RB 33 (1924): 624-626.
158. Vogels, H. J. *Handbuch der neutestamentlichen Textkritik* .
    RB 33 (1924): 263--267.
159. Kraft, B. *Die Evangelienzitate des heiligen Irenäus* .
    RB 34 (1925): 449-454.
160. Scott, W. *Hermetica: The ancient Greek and Latin writings which con-tain religious or philosophic teachings ascribed to Hermes Trisme-gistus* . Vol. I and II.
    RB 34 (1925): Part I, 432-436; Part II, 593-597.
161. Simon, H. *Praelectiones biblicae ad usum scholarum* . *Vol. I, Intro-ductio et Evangelia* .
    RB 34 (1925): 132-139.
162. Streeter, B. H. *The four Gospels* .
    RB 34 (1925): 454-458.
163. Pernot, H. *Pages choisies des Évangiles traduites de l'original et com-mentées à l'usage du public lettré* .

RB 35 (1926): 296-300.

164. Bruyne, D. De. *Le plus anciens prologues des Évangiles.*
     RB 38 (1929): 115-121.

165. Schmid, J. *Der Epheserbrief des Apostels Paulus. Seine Adresse, Sprache und literarischen Beziehungen* .
     RB 38 (1929): 290-293.

166. Vogels, H. J. *Die Evangelien der Vulgata untersucht auf ihre lateinische und griechische Vorlage* .
     RB 38 (1929): 261-264.

167. Harnack, A von. *Die ältesten Evangelien-Prologe und die Bildung das neuen Testaments* .
     RB 39 (1930): 619-621.

168. Joüon, P. *L'Évangile de Notre-Seigneur Jésus-Christ (traduction et commentaire du texte original grec, compte tenu du substrat sémitique)* .
     RB 39 (1930): 463-466.

169. Odeberg, H. *The Fourth Gospel* .
     RB 39 (1930): 455-458.

170. Stahl, R. *Les Mandéens et les origines chrétiennes* .
     RB 40 (1931): 147-151.

171. Goguel, M. *Jésus et les origines du christianisme. La vie de Jésus* .
     RB 41 (1932): 598-614.

172. Adam, K. *Le Christ notre frère* .
     RB 42 (1933): 127-130.

173. Goguel, M. *La foi en la résurrection de Jésus dans le christianisme primitif* .
     RB 42 (1933): 569-583.

175. Guignebert, M. *Questions évangéliques* . *Jésus* .
     RB 42 (1933): 435-440,

176. Schweitzer, A. *Die Mystik des Apostels Paulus* .
     RB 42 (1933): 114-123.

177. Blumenthal, M. *Formen und Motive in den apocryphen Apostelgeschichten* .
     RB 43 (1934): 285-288.

178. Labriolle, P de. *La réaction païenne. Étude sur la polémique antichrétienne du Ier au VIe siècle* .
     RB 44 (1935): 606-609.

179. Rideau, É. *En marge de la question synoptique* .
     RB 44 (1935): 279-283.

180. Goodenough, E. R. *By Light, Light* .
     RB 45 (1936): 265-269.

PIERRE BENOIT, O.P.

Books

1. *Somme théologique de Saint Thomas d'Aquin. La prophétie. 2a-2ae, questions 171-178* .French translation by P. Synave and P. Benoit.
   Paris: Jeunes-Desclée,1947.
   > = *Prophecy and Inspiration. A Commentary on the Summa Theologica, II-IIae , Questions 171-178* , by P. Synave and P. Benoit.
   > New York, Rome, Paris, Tournai: Désclée, 1961.
2. *Les épîtres de saint Paul aux Philippiens, à Philémon, aux Colossiens, aux Ephésiens* . (La Sainte Bible de Jérusalem.)
   Paris: Cerf, 1949. 2d Ed. Rev., 1953. 3d Ed. Rev. 1959.
3. *L'évangile selon St. Matthieu* . (La Sainte Bible de Jérusalem.)
   Paris: Cerf, 1950; 2d Ed. Rev., 1953;. 3d Ed. Rev., 1961; 4th Ed. Rev., 1972.
4. *Le problème de Jésus et la pensée de Jean Guitton* .
   Paris: Gabalda, 1957.
5. *Les grottes de Murabba^c ât* (Discoveries in the Judaean Desert , 2) with J. T. Milik and Roland de Vaux and with contributions by Mrs. G. M. Crowfoot, E. Crowfoot and A. Grohmann, 209-280. Part I, *Texte* Part II, *Planches* .
   Oxford: Clarendon Press, 1961.
6. *Exégèse et théologie* . Vol. 1-2 .(Cogitatio fidei, 1-2). Paris: Cerf, 1961.
   Vol. 3. (Cogitatio fidei, 30) Paris: Cerf, 1968. Vol. 4. Paris: Cerf, 1982.
   > = *Esegesi e teologia* . Vol. 1 (Bibl. Cultura Rel. 2/74) Rome: Paoline, 1964, Vol. 2 (La Parola di Dio, 4.) Rome: Paoline, 1971.
   > = *Exegese und Theologie* . Gesammelte Aufsätze. *Kommentare und Beiträge zum Alten und Neuen Testament* .
   > Düsseldorf: Patmos-Verlag, 1965.
   > = *Jesus and the Gospel. A Translation of Selected Articles from Exégèse et Théologie Vol. 1-2* .
   > London : Darton, Longman and Todd, Vol. 1, 1973. Vol. 2, 1974.
   > = *Exègesis y teologìa. Vol 1 , Cuestiones de introducción general*
   > Madrid: Studium Ediciones, 1979.
7. *Inspiration and the Bible* .
   London, Melbourne, New York: Sheed & Ward, 1965.
   > = *Aspects of Biblical Inspiration* .
   > Chicago: The Priory Press, 1965.

  = *Rivelazione e ispirazione secondo la Bibbia, in San Tom-maso e nelle discussioni moderne.* (Bibl. Minima Cultura Rel. 12).
  Brescia: Paideia, 1966.

8. *Synopse des quatre évangiles en français, avec parallèles des Apocryphes et des Pères,* by P. Benoit and M.-E. Boismard. Vol I, *Textes* . Paris: Cerf, 1965. 2d Ed. Rev. and Corrected by P. Sandevoir, Paris: Cerf, 1972. 3rd Ed. Rev. with an added concordance by M.-E. Boismard and A. Lamouille. Paris: Cerf, 1981.

  = *Sinopsis de los cuatro evangelios con paralelos de los apocrifos y de los Padres* , by P. Benoit, M.-E. Boismard and J. L Malillos. Vol. I, *Textos.*
  Bilbao: Desclée De Brouwer, 1975.

9. *Passion et résurrection du Seigneur* . (Lire la Bible, 6).
  Paris: Cerf, 1966.

  = *Passione e resurrezione del Signore. Il mistero pasquale nei quattro evangeli* . (La Parola di Dio).
  Torino: Gribaudi, 1967.

  = *Passion and Resurrection of Jesus Christ.*
  New York: Herder and Herder, 1969. London: Darton, Longman and Todd, 1969.

  = *Paixão e Ressurreição do Senhor* . (Estudos Biblicos)
  São Paulo: Edições Paulinas, 1975.

10. *L'église et Israël.* (Flèches, 7).
  Paris: Apostolat des Editions, 1968.

11. *Christmas . A Pictorial Pilgrimage* , by P. Benoit, K. Leuve and E. Hagolani.
  Nashville/New York: Abingdon, 1969.

12. *Easter. A Pictorial Pilgrimage* , by P. Benoit, K. Leube and E. Hagolani.
  Nashville/New York: Abingdon, 1969.

13. *Le Père Lagrange au service de la Bible. Souvenirs personnels.* Paris: Cerf, 1967.

  = *El Padre Lagrange al servicio de la Biblia. Recuerdos personales*
  Madrid: Desclée, 1970.

  = *Père Lagrange . Personal Reflections and Memories.*
  New York/Mahwah: Paulist, 1985.

Articles

14. "Le codex paulinien Chester Beatty."
  RB 46 (1937): 58-82.

15. "L'horizon paulinien de l'épître aux Ephésiens.
  RB 46 (1937): Part One: 342-361; Part Two: 506-525.

  = *Exégèse et Théologie* , Vol 2, 53-96. Paris: Cerf, 1961.

16. "La loi et la croix d'après saint Paul (Rom VII,7-VIII,4)."
  RB 47 (1938): 481-509.

  = *Exégèse et Théologie* , Vol. 2, 9-40. Paris: Cerf, 1961.
  = *Esegesi e teologia* , Vol 1, 355-395. Roma: Paoline, 1964.

= *Exegese und Theologie* , 221-245. Düsseldorf: Patmos , 1965.

= *Jesus and the Gospel* , Vol. 2, 11-39. New York: Herder and Herder , 1971/ London: Darton, Longman and Todd, 1974.

17. "Le récit de la cène dans Lc XXII, 15-20. Étude de critique textuelle et littéraire."

RB 48 (1939): 357-393.

= *Exégèse et Théologie* . Vol. 1, 163-203. Paris: Cerf, 1961.

18. "Le procès de Jésus."

Vie Intel.-Rev. Jeunes . Part I, (February, 1940): 200-213; Part II, (March, 1940): 371-378; Part III, (April, 1940): 54-64.

= *Exégèse et Théologie* , Vol. 1, 265-289. Paris: Cerf, 1961.

= *Esegesi e teologia* , Vol 1, 217-254. Roma: Paoline, 1964.

= *Exegese und Theologie* , 113-125. Düsseldorf: Patmos , 1965.

= *Jesus and the Gospel* , Vol. 1,123-146. New York: Herder and Herder, 1971/ London: Darton, Longman and Todd, 1973.

19. "Jésus devant le sanhédrin."

Biblica et Orientalia; Rev. Patri Iacobo-M. Vosté Dicata Ob XII Lustra Aetatis , 143-165. Roma: Pont. Athenaeum "Angelicum", 1943.

= *Exégèse et Théologie* , Vol. 1, 290-311. Paris: Cerf, 1961.

= *Exegese und Theologie* , 133-148. Düsseldorf: Patmos, 1965.

= *Jesus and the Gospel* , Vol. 1,147-166. New York: Herder and Herder , 1971/ London: Darton, Longman and Todd, 1973.

20. "Sénèque et saint Paul."

RB 53 (1946): 7-35.

= *Exégèse et Théologie* , Vol. 2, 383-414. Paris: Cerf, 1961.

= *Esegesi e teologia* , Vol 1, 685-752. Roma: Paoline, 1964.

= *Exegese und Theologie* , 297-335. Düsseldorf: Patmos, 1965.

21. "Réflections sur la *Formgeschichtliche Methode* ."

RB 53 (1946):481-512.

= *Exégèse et Théologie* , Vol. 1, 290-311. Paris: Cerf, 1961.

= *Esegesi e teologia* , Vol 1, 11-62. Roma: Paoline, 1964.

= *Exegese und Theologie* , 23-52. Düsseldorf: Patmos , 1965.

= *Jesus and the Gospel* , Vol. 1,11-46. New York: Herder and Herder, 1971/ London: Darton, Longman and Todd, 1973.

= *Exègesis y teologìa*. Vol 1, *Cuestiones de introducción general* , 211-252. Madrid: Studium Ediciones, 1979.

22. "Luc XXII.19b-20."

JTS 46 (1948): 145-147.

23. "L'ascension."

RB 58 (1949): 161-203.

= *Exégèse et Théologie* , Vol. 1, 363-411. Paris: Cerf, 1961.

= *Esegesi e teologia* , Vol 1, 285-352. Roma: Paoline, 1964.
= *Exegese und Theologie* , 182-220. Düsseldorf: Patmos , 1965.
= *Jesus and the Gospel* , Vol. 1, 209-253. New York: Herder and Herder , 1971/ London: Darton, Longman and Todd, 1973.

24. "Remarques sur les 'sommaires' des Actes II, IV et V."
Aux sources de la tradition chrétienne; Mélanges offerts à M. Maurice Goguel , 1-10.
Paris: Delachaux & Niestlé, 1950.
= *Exégèse et Théologie* , Vol. 2, 181-192. Paris: Cerf, 1961.
= *Jesus and the Gospel* , Vol. 2, 95-103. New York: Herder and Herder, 1971/ London: Darton, Longman and Todd, 1973.

25. "La septante est-elle inspirée?"
Vom Wort des Lebens; Festschrift für Max Meinertz , 41-49.
Münster: Aschendorffsche Verlagsbuchhandlung, 1951.
= *Exégèse et Théologie* , Vol. 1, 41-49. Paris: Cerf, 1961.
= *Exegese und Theologie* , 15-22. Düsseldorf: Patmos , 1965.
= *Jesus and the Gospel* , Vol. 1, 1-10. New York: Herder and Herder, 1971/ London: Darton, Longman and Todd, 1973.
= *Exègesis y teologìa.* Vol 1, *Cuestiones de introducción general* , 155-166. Madrid: Studium Ediciones, 1979.

26. "'Nous gémissons, attendant la délivrance de notre corps.' (Rom. VIII, 23)."
Recherches de Science Religieuse 39 (*Mélanges Jules Lebreton*), (1951): 267-280.
= *Exégèse et Théologie* , Vol. 2, 41-52. Paris: Cerf, 1961.
= *Jesus and the Gospel* , Vol. 2, 40-50. New York: Herder and Herder, 1971/ London: Darton, Longman and Todd, 1973.

27. "Fragment d'une prière contre les esprits impures?"
RB 58 (1951): 549-565.

28. "Nouvelles 'brattées' trouvées en Palestine"
RB 59 (1952); 252-258.

29. "Prétoire, lithostroton et Gabbatha."
RB 60 (1952): 531-550.
= *Exégèse et Théologie* , Vol. 1, 312-339. Paris: Cerf, 1961.
= *Exegese und Theologie*, 149-166. Düsseldorf: Patmos , 1965.
= *Jesus and the Gospel* . Vol. 1, 167-188. New York: Herder and Herder, 1971/ London: Darton, Longman and Todd, 1973.

30. "Les origines du symbole des apôtres dans le Nouveau Testament."
Lumière et Vie 2 (1952):39-60.
= *Exégèse et Théologie* , Vol. 2, 193-211. Paris: Cerf, 1961.
= *Esegesi e teologia* , Vol 1, 461-488. Roma: Paoline, 1964.

     = *Jesus and the Gospel* , Vol. 2, 104-120. New York: Herder
      and Herder, 1971 / London: Darton, Longman and
      Todd, 1973.
31." La mort de Judas."
   Synoptische Studien; Alfred Wikenhauser , 1-19.
   München: Karl Zink Verlag,1953.
     = *Exégèse et Théologie* , Vol. 1, 340-359. Paris: Cerf, 1961.
     = *Esegesi e teologia* , Vol. 1, 255-284. Roma: Paoline, 1964.
     = *Exegese und Theologie* , 167-176. Düsseldorf: Patmos,
      1965.
     = *Jesus and the Gospel* . Vol. 1, 189-208. New York: Herder
      and Herder, 1971/ London: Darton, Longman and
      Todd, 1973
32. "La divinité de Jésus."
   Lumière et Vie 9 (1953):43-74.
     = *Son and Saviour; the Divinity of Jesus Christ in the Scrip-*
      tures, 50-85.
     London: Geoffrey Chapman, 1960.
     = *Exégèse et Théologie* , Vol. 1, 117-142. Paris: Cerf, 1961.
     = *Esegesi e teologia* , Vol. 1, 103-138. Roma: Paoline, 1964.
     = *Exegese und Theologie* , 53-72. Düsseldorf: Patmos, 1965.
     = *Jesus and the Gospel* . Vol. 1, 47-70. New York: Herder
      and Herder, 1971/ London: Darton, Longman and
      Todd, 1973.
33. "Inspiration," *Initiation Biblique* , ed. by A. Robert and A. Tricot, 6-44.
   Paris: Desclée, 1954.
     = "Inspiration" *A Guide to the Bible*, I: 9-64. (New York,
      Desclée 1960.
34. "La primauté de saint Pierre selon le Nouveau Testament."
   Istina 2 (1955): 305-334.
     = *Exégèse et Théologie* ,Vol. 2, 250-284. Paris: Cerf, 1961.
     = *Esegesi e teologia* , Vol. 1, 511-560. Roma: Paoline, 1964.
     = *Jesus and the Gospel* , Vol. 2,121-153. New York: Herder
      and Herder, 1971/ London: Darton, Longman and
      Todd, 1973.
35. "La foi."
   Lumière et Vie 22 1(955): 45-64.
     = *Exégèse et Théologie* , Vol. 1, 143-159. Paris: Cerf, 1961.
36. "Corps, tête et plérôme dans les épîtres de la captivité."
   RB 64 (1956): 5-44.
     = *Exégèse et Théologie* . Vol. 2, 107-153. Paris: Cerf, 1961.
     = *Esegesi e teologia* . Vol. 1, 397-460. Roma: Paoline, 1964.
     = *Exegese und Theologie* , 246-279. Düsseldorf: Patmos,
      1965.
     = *Jesus and the Gospel* . Vol. 2, 51-94. New York: Herder
      and Herder , 1971/ London: Darton, Longman and
      Todd, 1973.
37. "The Holy Eucharist."
   Part I, *Scripture* 8 (1956): 97-108; Part II, *Scripture* 9 (1957): 1-
   14.

= *Exégèse et Théologie* . Vol. 1, 210-239. Paris: Cerf, 1961.
38. "Note complémentaire sur l'inspiration."
   RB 64 (1956): 416-422.
39. "L'enfance de Jean-Baptiste selon Luc 1."
   NTS 3 (1956-57): 169-194.
   = *Exégèse et Théologie* , Vol. 3, 165-196. Paris: Cerf, 1968.
   = *Esegesi e teologia* , Vol. 1, 253-300.Roma: Paoline, 1964.
40. "Les analogies de l'inspiration."
   Sacra Pagina. Miscellanea biblica congressus internationalis de re biblica, ed. by J. Coppens, A. Descamps, E. Massaux, Vol. 1 (1959): 86-99. (BETL, 13) Paris-Gembloux, 1959.
   = *Exégèse et Théologie* , Vol. 3, 17-30. Paris: Cerf, 1968.
   = *Esegesi e teologia* , Vol. 2, 33-54.Roma: Paoline, 1964.
   = *Exègesis y teologìa* , Vol 1, *Cuestiones de introducción general* , 63-78. Madrid: Studium Ediciones, 1979.
41. "La deuxième visite de saint Paul à Jérusalem."
   Biblica 40 (1959): 778-792.
   = *Exégèse et Théologie* , Vol. 3, 285-299. Paris: Cerf, 1968.
   = *Esegesi e teologia* , Vol. 2, 435-456. Roma: Paoline, 1964.
42. "La plénitude de sens des Livres Saints."
   RB 68 (1960): 161-196.
   = *Exégèse et Théologie* , Vol. 3, 31-68.Paris: Cerf, 1968.
   = *Esegesi e teologia* , Vol. 2, 53-108. Roma: Paoline, 1964.
   = *Exègesis y teologìa,* Vol 1, *Cuestiones de introducción general* , 109-154. Madrid: Studium Ediciones, 1979.
43. " Marie-Madeleine et les disciples au tombeau selon Joh 20:1-18."
   Judentum Urchristentum Kirche; Festschrift Für Joachim Jeremias , 141-152. (BZNW, 26).
   Berlin: Verlag Alfred Töpelmann, 1960.
   = *Exégèse et Théologie* , Vol. 3, 270-282.Paris: Cerf, 1968.
   = *Esegesi e teologia* , Vol. 2, 413-434. Roma: Paoline, 1964.
44. "Qumrân et le Nouveau Testament."
   NTS 6 (1960-1961): 276-296.
   = *Exégèse et Théologie* , Vol. 3, 361-386.Paris: Cerf, 1968.
   = *Esegesi e teologia* , Vol. 2, 545-582. Roma: Paoline, 1964.
   = "Qumran and the New Testament"
      Contemporary New Testament Studies , ed. by M. Rosalie Ryan, 61-88. Collegeville: The Liturgical Press, 1965.
   = *Paul and Qumran; Studies in New Testament Exegesis* , ed. by Jerome Murphy -O'Connor, 1-30. London: Geoffrey Chapman, 1968.
45. "Les origines de l'épiscopat dans le Nouveau Testament."
   L'évêque dans l'église du Christ , 13-57. (Texte et études Théologiques).
   Paris: Desclée de Brouwer, 1963.
   = *Exégèse et Théologie* , Vol. 2, 232-246. Paris: Cerf, 1968.
   = *Esegesi e teologia* , Vol. 1, 489-510. Roma: Paoline, 1964.

46. "Les outrages à Jésus Prophète (Mc xiv 65 par.)."
Neotestamentica et Patristica; Eine Freundesgabe, Herrn Professor Dr. Oscar Cullman , 92-110.
Leiden: Brill, 1962.
= *Exégèse et Théologie* , Vol. 3, 251-269. Paris: Cerf, 1968.
47. "Les épis arrachés (Mt 12, 1-8 et par.)."
Liber Annuus 13 (1962-1963)): 76-92.
= *Exégèse et Théologie* , Vol. 3, 228-250. Paris: Cerf, 1968.
= *Esegesi e teologia* , Vol. 2, 349-372. Roma: Paoline, 1964.
48. "Paulinisme et Johannisme."
NTS 9 (1962-1963):193-207.
= *Exégèse et Théologie* . Vol. 3, 300-317. Paris: Cerf, 1968.
= *Esegesi e teologia* . Vol. 2, 457-482. Roma: Paoline, 1964.
49. "L'unité de l'église selon l'épître aux Ephésiens."
Studiorum Paulinorum Congressus Internationalis Catholicus,1
Analecta Biblica 17 (1961): 57-77.
= *Exégèse et Théologie* , Vol. 3, 335-357. Paris: Cerf, 1968.
= *Esegesi e teologia* , Vol. 2, 509-544. Roma: Paoline, 1964.
50. " 'Et toi-même, un glaive te transpercera l' âme!' (Luc 2,35)."
CBQ 25 (1963): 251-261.
= *Exégèse et Théologie* . Vol. 3, 216-227. Paris: Cerf, 1968.
= *Esegesi e teologia* . Vol. 2, 329-348. Roma: Paoline, 1964.
51. "Inspiration Biblique"
Catholicism, hier, aujourd'hui, demain, ed. by G. Jacquemet, 5:1539-1549.
Paris: Letouzey & Ané, 1963.
52. "Inerrance Biblique."
Catholicisme hier, aujourd'hui, demain, ed. by G. Jacquemet, 5: 1710-1721.
Paris: Letouzey & Ané, 1963.
53 "Révélation et l'inspiration selon la Bible chez Thomas et dans les discussions modernes."
RB 70 (1963): 321-370.
= *Exégèse et Théologie* , Vol. 3, 90-142. Paris: Cerf, 1968.
= *Esegesi e teologia* , Vol. 2, 143-220. Roma: Paoline, 1964.
= *Exègesis y teologìa.* Vol 1, *Cuestiones de introducción general* , 1-62. Madrid: Studium Ediciones, 1979.
54. "Rapports littéraires entre les épîtres aux Colossiens et aux Ephésiens."
Neutestamentliche Aufsätze; Festschrift für Prof. Josef Schmid , ed. by J. Blinzler, O. Kuss, F. Mußner, 11-22.
Regensburg: Friedrich Pustet, 1963.
= *Exégèse et Théologie* , Vol. 3, 318-334. Paris: Cerf, 1968.
= *Esegesi e teologia* , Vol. 2, 483-508. Roma: Paoline, 1964.
55. "L'inspiration des septante d'après le Pères."
L'homme devant Dieu ; mélanges offerts au Père H. de Lubac, 1 (1963): 169-187.
Paris: Aubier, 1963.
= *Exégèse et Théologie,* Vol. 3, 69-89. Paris: Cerf, 1968.
= *Esegesi e teologia* , Vol. 2, 109-142. Roma: Paoline, 1964.

= *Exègesis y teologìa.* Vol 1, *Cuestiones de introducción ge-neral* , 167-192. Madrid: Studium Ediciones, 1979.
56. "L'annonciation."
    Assemblées du Seigneur 6 (1965): 40-57.
    = *Exégèse et Théologie* , Vol. 3, 69-89. Paris: Cerf, 1968.
    = *Esegesi e teologia* , Vol. 2, 109-142. Roma: Paoline, 1964.
57. "L'inspiration et révélation."
    Concilium 10 (1965): 13-26.
58. "La chiesa e Israele."
    La chiesa e le religioni non cristiane. Collana "Ecclesiam Suam", 3, 129-166.
    Napoli: Edizioni Domenicane Italiane, 1966.
    = *Exégèse et Théologie* , Vol. 3, 422-441. Paris: Cerf, 1968.
    = *Esegesi e teologia* , Vol. 2, 635-654. Roma: Paoline, 1964.
59. "Paul (Épîtres attribuées à saint). 1. Colossiens (épître aux)."
    In *Dictionnaire de la Bible: Supplément VII.* Paris: Letouzey & Ané, 1966, cols. 157-170.
60. "Paul (Épîtres attribuées à saint). 3. Ephésiens (épitre aux)."
    In *Dictionnaire de la Bible: Supplément VII.* Paris: Letouzey & Ané, 1966, cols. 195-211.
61. "Philémon (Épître à). "
    In *Dictionnaire de la Bible: Supplément VII.* Paris: Letouzey & Ané, 1966, cols. 1204-1211.
62. "Conspectus biblici de ecclesia et mundo."
    Angelicum 43 (1966): 311-320.
    ="The Biblical Outlook on the Church in the World."
    Interest 3:3 (1969):43-48.
63. "Inspiration de la tradition et inspiration de l'Écriture."
    Mélanges offerts a M.-D. Chenu , 111-126.
    Paris: Librairie Philosophique J. Vrin, 1967.
64. "Exégèse et théologie biblique."
    Exégèse et Théologie , Vol. 3, 1-13. Paris: Cerf, 1968.
    = *Esegesi e teologia* , Vol. 2, 7-32. Roma: Paoline, 1964.
    = *Maria in Sacra Scriptura* 2 (1967):17-33.
65. "Découvertes archéologiques autour de la Piscine de Béthesda."
    Jerusalem Through the Ages. The Twenty-fifth Archaeological Con-vention , 48-57, Plates 8-9.
    Jerusalem: Israel Exploration Society, 1968.
66. "La vérité dans la sainte Écriture."
    Exégèse et Théologie , Vol. 3, 143-164. Paris: Cerf, 1968.
    = *Esegesi e teologia* .,Vol. 2, 221-242. Roma: Paoline, 1964.
    = *Giornale di teologia* 21 (1968): 147-179.
    = *Exègesis y teologìa.* Vol. 1, *Cuestiones de introducción ge-neral* , 83-98.Madrid: Studium Ediciones, 1979.
    = *Acta Congressus Internationalis de Theologia Concilii Vaticani II,* 513-523.
    Romae:Typis Polyglottis Vaticanis, 1968.
67. "La value spécifique d'Israël dans l'histoire du salut."
    Exégèse et Théologie , Vol. 3, 400-421. Paris: Cerf, 1968.
    = *Esegesi e teologia* , Vol. 2, 604-634. Roma: Paoline, 1964.

68. "Le problème de la résurrection du Christ."
    Table Ronde 250 (November, 1968):131-143.
69. "L'église corps du Christ."
    Populus Dei. II. Ecclesia. Studi in onore del Card. Alfredo Otta-
    viani , 971-1028.
    Roma: Communio, 1970.
    = *Exégèse et Théologie* , Vol. 4, 205-262. Paris: Cerf, 1982.
70. "'Non erat eis locus in diversorio.' (Luc 2,7)."
    Mélanges Bibliques en hommage au Béda Rigaux , 173-186.
    Paris: Duculot, 1970.
    = *Exégèse et Théologie* , Vol. 4, 95-112. Paris: Cerf, 1982.
71. "Préexistence et incarnation."
    RB 77 (1970): 5-29.
    = *Exégèse et Théologie* . Vol. 4, 11-62. Paris: Cerf, 1982.
72. "Résurrection à la fin des temps ou dès la mort?"
    Concilium 60 (1970): 91-100.
    = *Exégèse et Théologie* , Vol. 4, 113-125. Paris: Cerf, 1982.
73. "Introductions Catholiques," by R. de Vaux, P. Benoit and M.-E. Bois-
    mard.
    Catholiques, Juifs, Orthodoxes, Protestants lisent la Bible; Intro-
    duction à la Bible.
    Paris: Cerf, 1970.
74. "L'Antonia d'Hérode le Grand et le Forum oriental d'Aelia Capitolina."
    Harvard Theological Review 64 (1971):135-167.
    = *Exégèse et Théologie* , Vol. 4, 311-346. Paris: Cerf, 1982.
75. "The Archaeological Reconstruction of the Antonia Fortress."
    Qadmoniot 5 (1972):127-129. [in Hebrew].
    = *Australian Journal of Biblical Archeology* 1/6 (1973): 16-
    22.
    = *Jerusalem Revealed; Archaeology in the Holy City ,1968-*
    1974, 87-89.
    Jerusalem: Israel Exploration Society, 1975.
76. "Note sur les fragments grecs de la grotte 7 de Qumrân."
    RB 79 (1972):321-324, plate 17 A.
77. "L'Annonciation. Lc 1, 26-38. 4e Dimanche de l'Avent."
    Assemblées du Seigneur 2/8 (1972):39-50.
78. "Nouvelle note sur les fragments grecs de la grotte 7 de Qumrân."
    RB 80 (1973): 5-12, plate 1.
79. "Saint Thomas et l'inspiration des Ecritures."
    Tommaso d'Aquino nel suo VII centenario ,115-131.
    Congresso Internazionale Roma - Napoli, 17-24 aprile, 1974.
80. "L'emplacement de Bethléem au temps de Jésus."
    Dossiers de l'Archéologie 10 (Mai-Juin, 1975): 58-63.
81. "L'hymne christologique de Col. 1,15-20. Jugement critique sur l'état
    des recherches."
    Christianity, Judaism and Other Greco Roman Cults; Studies for
    Morton Smith at Sixty, ed. by Jacob Neusner. Part One, *New Testa-*
    ment, 226-263. (Studies in Judaism and Late Antiquity, 12).
    Leiden: Brill, 1975.
    = *Exégèse et Théologie* , Vol. 4, 159-204. Paris: Cerf, 1982.

82. "Jésus et le serviteur de Dieu."
    Jésus aux origines de la christologie , ed. by J. Dupont, 111-140.
    (BETL, 40).
    Leuven: Leuven University Press, 1975.
83. "Où en est la question du 'troisième mur'?"
    Studia Hierosolymitana in onore del P. Bellarmino Bagatti . Vol. 1,
    Studi Archeologici , 111-126.
    Jerusalem: Franciscan Printing Press, 1976.
84. "L'évolution du langage apocalyptique dans le corpus paulinien."
    Apocalypses et Théologie de l'espérance , 299-335. (Lectio Divina,
    95)
    Paris, Cerf, 1977.
85. "Conclusion par mode de synthèse."
    Die Israelfrage nach Röm 9-11 , 217-243. (Monographische Reihe
    von "Benedictina", 3) Rom: Abtei St. Paul vor den Mauern, 1977.
86. "La prière dans les religions gréco-romaines et dans le christianisme
    primitif."
    Tantur: Ecumenical Institute for Advanced Theological Studies.
    Yearbook / Annales / Jahrbuch 1978-1979: 19-43.
87. "Quirinius (Recensement de.)"
    In *Dictionnaire de la Bible: Supplément IX* . Paris: Letouzey & Ané,
    1979, cols. 693-720.
89. "Genèse et évolution de la pensée paulinienne."
    Paul de Tarse, Apôtre de notre temps , ed. by Lorenzo De Lorenzi,
    75- 100.
    (Série monographique de "Benedictina" Section paulinienne, 1).
    Rome: Abbaye de S. Paul h.l.m.,1979.
90. "The Jerusalem Bible."
    Review and Expositor 76 (1979): 341-349.
91 "Christian Marriage according to Saint Paul."
    Clergy Review 65 (1980): 309-321.
        = *Exégèse et Théologie* . Vol. 4, 263-290. Paris: Cerf, 1982.
92. "Angélologie et démonologie paulinienes. Réflexions sur la nomencla-
    ture des puissances célestes et sur l'origine du mal angélique chez
    S. Paul."
    Foi et Culture à la lumière de la Bible., 217-233. (Commission Bib-
    lique Pontificale).
    Torino: Ed. Elle Di Cri, 1981.
        ="Pauline Angelology and Demonology. Reflections on the
        Designations of the Heavenly Powers and on the
        Origin of Angelic Evil according to Paul." *Religious*
        Studies Bulletin (3) 1983: 1-18.
93. " *'Agioi* en Colossiens 1:12: Hommes ou Anges?"
    Paul and Paulinism; Essays in honour of C. K. Barrett , ed. by M.
    D Hooker and S. G. Wilson, 83-101.
    London: SPCK,1982.
94. "L'exercice de charismes.
    Charisma und Agape (I Ko 12-14) , ed. by Lorenzo De Lorenzi,
    280-285. (Monographische Reihe von "Benedictina", 7).
    Rom: Abtei St. Paul vor den Mauern, 1985.

95. "Le prétoire de Pilate à l'époque byzantine."
    RB 91 (1984):161-177.
96. "The Plèrôma in the Epistles to the Colossians and the Ephesians."
    Svensk Exegetisk Årsbok 49 (1984):136-158.
97 "Colossiens 2:2-3."
    The New Testament Age; Essays in honor of Bo Reicke Vol. 1: 41-51.
    Macon, GA: Mercer University Press, 1984.
98. "L'aspect physique et cosmique du salut dans les écrits pauliniens."
    Bible et Christologie, 253-269. (Commission Biblique Pontificale).
    Paris: Cerf,1984.
99. "Activités archéologiques de lÉcole Biblique et Archéologique Française à Jérusalem depuis 1890."
    RB 94 (1987): 397-424.

Selected Book Reviews

100. Kietaig, D. *Die Bekehrung des Paulus* .
     RB 42 (1933): 427-429.
101. Roberts, C.H. *An Unpublished Gragment of the Fourth Gospel* .
     RB 45 (1936): 269-273.
102. Marmardji, A.-S. *Diaterssahon de Tatien* .
     RB 46 (1937): 124-128.
103. Allo, E.-B. *Saint Paul. Seconde Épître aux Corinthiens* .
     RB 46 (1937): 571-577.
104. Vannutelli, P. *Synoptica* .
     RB 47 (1938): 111-115.
105. Wikenhauser, A. *Die Kirche als der mystische Leib Christi nach dem Apostel Paulus* .
     RB 47 (1938):115-119.
106. Lagrange, M.-J. *Les Mystères: l'Orphisme* .
     RB 47 (1938): 426-432.
107. Hahn, W. T. *Das Mitsterben und Mitauferstehen mit Christus bei Paulus.*
     RB 47 (1938): 432-435.
108. Pohlmann, H. *Die Metanoia als Zentralbegriff der Chrislichen Frömmigkeit* .
     RB 47 (1938): 590-593.
109 Neilen, J. M. *Gebet und Gottesdienst im Neuen Testament* .
     RB 47 (1938): 594-596.
110. Finkelstein, L. *The Pharisees* .
     RB 48 (1939): 280-285.
111. Percy, E. *Untersuchungen über den Ursprung der johanneischen Theoogie*
     RB 49 (1940): 259-264.
112. Chaine, J. *Les Épîtres Catholiques* .
     Vivre et Penser, I = *RB* 50 (1941): 134-140.
113. Knox, W. L. *St. Paul and the Church of the Gentiles.*
     Vivre et Penser, I = *RB* 50 (1941): 140-147.

= "Les Message de Paul aux Gentils Selon W. L. Knox." *Exégèse et Théologie,* Vol. I. (Paris: Cerf, 1961), 97-106.

114. Peters, C. *Das Diatessaron Tatians* .
     RB 53 (1946): 277-280.

115. Friedrichsen, G. W. S. *The Gothic Version of the Gospels* .
     RB 53 (1946): 280-286.

116. Schweizer, E. *Ego Eimi.*
     RB 53 (1946): 576-578.

117. Kundsin, K. *Charakter und Ursprung der johanneischen Reden* .
     RB 53 (1946): 578-582.

118. Zuntz, G. *The Ancestry of the Harklean New Testament* .
     RB 54 (1947): 127-131.

119. Percy. E. *Der Leib Christi in den paulinischen Homologoumena* .
     RB 54 (1947): 150-152.
     ="Le Corps du Christ Seon E. Percy, L. Tondelli et T. Soiron." *Exégèse et Théologie*, Vol. II. (Paris: Cerf, 1961) 154-162.

120. Sahlin, H. *Der Messias und das Gottesvolk.*
     RB 54 (1947) 287-291.

121. Festugière, A.J. *La Révélation d'Hermès Trismégiste* .
     RB 54 (1947): 291-295; 62 (1955): 108-113.

122. Lestringant, P. *Essai sur l'unité de la Révélation Biblique* .
     RB 54 (1947): 295-299.

123. Goguel, M. *La naissance du Christianism* ; Guignebert, C. *Le Christ* .
     RB 54 (1947): 606-612.

124. Cullman, O. *Christus und die Zeit* .
     RB 55 (1948):104-108.

125. Leenhart, F. J. *Le Baptême chrétien* .
     RB 55 (1948): 130-131.
     ="Le Baptème chrétien selon F. J. Leenhardt et selon M. Barth." *Exégèse et Théologie*, Vol. II. (Paris: Cerf, 1961) 224-231.

126. Michaelis, W. *Einleitung in das Neue Testament* .
     RB 55 (1948): 279-282.

127. Schmidt, L. *Die Judenfrage im Lichte der Kapitel 9-11 des Römerbriefes.*
     RB 55 1948): 310-312.
     ="La question juive selon Rom IX-XI d'après K.L. Schmidt." *Exégèse et Théologie*, Vol. II. (Paris: Cerf, 1961) 337-339.

128. Spicq, C. *Saint Paul. Les Épîtres Pastorales* .
     RB 55 (1948): 448-452.

129. Kilpatrick, G. D. *The Origins of the Gospel according to Matthew.*
     RB 55 (1948): 590-594.

130. Jeremias, J. *Die Gleichnisse Jesu* .
     RB 55 (1948): 594-599

131. M. Leone Tondelli, *La pensée de S. Paul* .
     RB 55(1948): 618-619.

="Le Corps du Christ selon E. Percy, L. Tondelli et T. Soi-
ron." *Exégèse et Théologie*, Vol. II. (Paris: Cerf,
1961) 154-162.

132. Goguel, M. *L'Église primitive* .
RB 56 (1949): 139-143.

133. Cullmann, O. *Le baptême des enfants et la doctrine biblique du bap-
tême.*"
RB 56 (1949): 312-320.
="Le baptême des enfants et la doctrine biblique du baptême
selon O. Cullmann." *Exégèse et Théologie*, Vol. II.
(Paris: Cerf, 1961) 212-223.

134. Jeremias, J. *Unbekannte Jesusworte* .
RB 56 (1949): 443-446.

135. Isaac, J. *Jésus et Israël* .
RB 56 (1949): 610-613.
="Jésus et Israel d'après Jules Isaac." *Exégèse et Théologie*,
Vol. II. (Paris: Cerf, 1961), 321-327.

136. Sahlin, H. *Studien zum dritten Kapitel des Lukasevangelium* .
RB 57 (1950): 134-137.

137. Schoeps, H. J. *Theologie und Geschichte des Judenchristentums* and
Aus frühchristlicher Zeit.
RB 57 (1950) 604-611.

138. Kittel, G. *Theologisches Wörterbuch zum Neuen Testament* .
RB 58 (1951): 94-99.

139. Bieder, W. *Die Vorstellung von der Höllenfahrt Jesu Christi.*
RB 58 (1951): 99-102.
="La Descente aux enfers selon W. Bieder." *Exégèse et
Théologie*, Vol. I. (Paris: Cerf, 1961) 412-416.

140. Jeremias, J. *Die Abendmahlsworte Jesu.*
RB 58 (1951): 132-134.
="Note sur une étude de J. Jeremias." *Exégèse et Théologie*,
Vol. I. (Paris: Cerf, 1961) 240-243.

141. R. Bultmann, *Theologie des Neuen Testaments* .
RB 58 (1951): 252-257.
="La Pensée de R. Bultmann." *Exégèse et Théologie*, Vol. I.
(Paris: Cerf, 1961) 62-90.

142. Florit, E. *Ispirazione Biblica* .
RB 58 (1951): 609-610.
="L'Inspiration Biblique selon Mgr Florit." *Exégèse et Théo-
logie*, Vol. I. (Paris: Cerf, 1961)13-14.

143. Michaelis, W. *Versöhnung des Alls* .
RB 59 (1952): 100-103.
="La Réconciliation universelle selon W. Michaelis" *Exégèse et Théologie*, Vol. I. (Paris: Cerf, 1961) 172-
177.

144. Descamps, A. *Les Justes et la Justice dans les évangiles et le christianisme primitif* .
RB 59 (1952): 259-264.

145. *Das Neue Testament Deutsch* .
RB 59 (1952): 419-425.

146. Cerfaux, L. *Le Christ dans la Théologie de saint Paul*
     RB 59 (1952): 591-597.
147. Taylor, V. *The Gospel According to Mark* .
     RB 60 (1953): 295-299.
148. Blinzler, J. *Der Prozess Jesu* . and Démann, P. *Les Juifs dans la caté-
     chèse chrétienne.*
     RB 60 (1953):452-454.
               ="Le Procès de Jésus selon J. Blinzler et P. Démann." *Ex-
               égèse et Théologie*, Vol. I. (Paris: Cerf, 1961) 312-
               315.
149. Cullmann, O. *Saint Pierre, Disciple-Apôtre-Martyr; Histoire et Théo-
     logie.*
     RB 60 (1953): 565-579.
               ="Saint Pierre d'après O. Cullmann." *Exégèse et Théologie*,
               Vol. II. (Paris: Cerf, 1961) 285-308.
150. Barth, M. *Die Taufe ein Sakrament?*
     RB 60 (1953): 620-623.
               ="Le Baptême Chrétien selon F. J. Leenhardt et selon M.
               Barth." *Exégèse et Théologie*, Vol. II. (Paris: Cerf,
               1961) 224-231.
151. Dupont, J. *Syn Christo. L'union avec le Christ suivant saint Paul* .
     RB 61 (1954): 120-124.
152. Démann, P. *La Catéchèse Chrétienne et le Peuple de la Bible*
     RB 61 (1954): 136-142.
               ="La catéchèse Chrétienne et le peuple de la Bible d'après P.
               Démann." *Exégèse et Théologie*, Vol. II. (Paris: Cerf,
               1961), 328-336.
153. Bonnard, P. *L'Épître de saint Paul aux Galates* and Masson, C. *L'Épî-
     tre de saint Paul aux Ephésiens*
     RB 61 (1954): 237-242.
154. Spicq, C. *L'Épître aux Hébreux* .
     RB 61 (1954): 242-247.
155. Schürmann, H. *Der Paschamahlbericht Lk 22 (7-14),15-18.*
     RB 61 (1954): 284-287.
               ="Note: Les Études de H. Schürmann sur Lc XXII" *Exégèse
               et Théologie*, Vol. I. (Paris: Cerf, 1961) 204-209.
156. Lohse, E. *Die Ordination im Spätjudentum und im Neuen Testament.*
     RB 61(1954): 298-299.
               ="L'Ordination dans le Judaïsme et dans le Nouveau Testa-
               ment selon E. Lohse." *Exégèse et Théologie*, Vol. II.
               (Paris: Cerf, 1961) 247-249.
157. *Für und wider die Theologie Bultmanns. Denkschrift der Ev. Theol.
     Fakultät der Universität Tübingen* .
     RB 61 (1954): 436-438.
158. Seynaeve, J. *Cardinal Newman's Doctrine on Holy Scripture.*
     RB 61 (1954): 603-605.
               ="La doctrine de Newman sur la Sainte Écriture" *Exégèse et
               Théologie*, Vol. I. (Paris: Cerf, 1961) 15-19.
159. Cullmann, O. *La Tradition. Problème exégétique, historique et théo-
     logique* .

RB 62 (1955): 258-264.
="La tradition selon O. Cullmann" *Exégèse et Théologie*,
Vol. II. (Paris: Cerf, 1961) 309-317.

160. Vincent, L. H. and Steve, A. M. *Jérusalem de L'Ancien Testament* .
RB 62 (1955): 264-268; 64 (1957): 269-272.

161. Dupont, J. *Les Béatitudes* .
RB 62 (1955): 420-424.

162. Munck, J. *Paulus und die Heilsgeschichte* .
RB 62 (1955): 590-595.

163. Brown, R. E. *The* Sensus plenior *of Sacred Scripture* .
RB 63 (1956): 285-287.
="Le *Sensus Plenior* de l'Écriture." *Exégèse et Théologie*,
Vol. I. (Paris: Cerf, 1961), 19-21.

164. Malevez, L. *Le message chrétien et le mythe. La théologie de Rudolf*
Bultmann.
RB 64 (1956):299-301.
="La Pensée de R. Bultmann critiquée par le P. Malevez."
Exégèse et Théologie, Vol. I. (Paris: Cerf, 1961) 91-
93.

165. Guitton, J. *Le Problème de Jésus et les fondements du témoignage*
chrétien.
RB 64 (1956): 433-442.
="Le Problème de Jésus et la Pensée de Jean Guitton." *Ex-*
égèse et Théologie, Vol. I. (Paris: Cerf, 1961), 97-
114.

166. Mussner, Franz. *Christus das All und die Kirche. Studien zur Theolo-*
gie des Epheserbriefes
RB 64 (1956): 464-465.
="Le Christ, L'Univers et L'Église selon F. Mussner." *Ex-*
égèse et Théologie, Vol. II. (Paris: Cerf, 1961),163-
164.

167. Leenhardt, F.J. *Le Sacrement de la Sainte Cène.*
RB 64 (1956):578-583.
="Note sur deux études de F. J. Leenhardt" *Exégèse et Théo-*
logie, Vol. I. (Paris: Cerf, 1961) 244-254.

168. Rigaux, B. *Saint Paul. Les épîtres aux Thessaloniciens* .
RB 64 (1957): 407-412.

169. Robinson, J. A. T. *The Body. A Study in Pauline Theology*
RB 64 (1957): 581-585.
="Le Corps dans la Théologie de S. Paul selon J. A. T. Robinson." *Exégèse et Théologie*, Vol. II. (Paris: Cerf,
1961) 165-171.

170. Cullmann, O. *Die Christologie des Neuen Testaments.*
RB 65 (1958): 268-275.

171. Laurentin, R. *Structure et Théologie de Luc I-II*
RB 65 (1958): 427-432.

172. Jaubert, Annie. *La Date de la Cène . Calendrier biblique et liturgie*
chrétienne .
RB 65 (1958): 590-594.

= "La date de la cène." *Exégèse et Théologie*, Vol. I (Paris: Cerf, 1961) 255-261.

173. Robin, C. *Qumran Studies*.
  RB 66 (1959):118-121.

174. Spicq, C., *Agapè dans le Nouveau Testament, I* .
  RB 66 (1959): 262-265.

175. Solages, B de, *Synopse grecque des Évangiles* .
  RB 67 (1960): 93-102.

176. Judant, D. *Les deux Israel*.
  RB 68 (1961): 458-462

177. Winter, P. *On the Trial of Jesus* .
  RB 68 (1961): 593-599.

178. Boismard, M.-E. *Quatre hymnes baptismales dans la premièrre épître de Pierre*.
  RB 70 (1963): 133-135.

179. Gerhardsson, B. *Memory and Manuscript* .
  RB 70 (1963) 269-273.

180. Léon-Dufour, Xavier. *Les évangiles et l'histore de Jésus*.
  RB 71 (1964): 594-598.
    ="Les Évangiles et l''histoire de Jésus selon Xavier Léon-Dufour." *Exégèse et Théologie*, Vol. III. (Paris: Cerf, 1968) 159-164.

181 Baum. G. *The Jews and the Gospel. A Re-examination of the New Testament*.
  RB 71 (1964): 80-92.
    ="Les Juifs et l'évangile d'apres Gregory Baum" *Exégèse et Théologie*, Vol. III. (Paris: Cerf, 1968) 387-399.

182. Davies, W. D. *The Setting of the Sermon on the Mount*.
  RB 72 (1965): 595-601.

183 Cerfaux, L. *Les chrétiens dans la théologie paulinienne*.
  RB 73 (1966): 591-597.

184. Hurd, J. C. *The Origin of I Corinthians*.
  RB 74 (1967): 264-267.

185. Kenyon, K. *Jerusalem. Excavating 3000 Years of History*.
  RB 76 (1969): 260-272.

186. Lyonnet, S. *Les étapes del'histoire du salut*.
  RB 80 (1973): 432-436.

187. Burtchaell, J. *Catholic Theories of Biblical Inspiration Since 1810*.
  RB 81 (1974): 121-124.

188. Coüasnon, C. *The Church of the Holy Sepulchre in Jerusalem*.
  RB 81 (1974): 260-266.

189. Davies, W. D. *The Gospel and the Land. Early Christianity and Jewish Territorial Doctrine*.
  RB 83 (1976): 590-596.

190. *Atlas of Jerusalem* .
  RB 84 (1977): 438-445.

191. Corbo, V. et. al., *Cafarnao*.
  RB 84 (1977): 438-445.

192. Robinson, J. A. T. *Redating the New Testament*.
  RB 86 (1979): 281-287.

193. Avigad, N. *La ville haute de Jérusalem* (in Hebrew).
    RB 88 (1981): 250-256.
194. Mussner, F. *Traktat über die Juden.*
    RB 89 (1982): 588-595.
195. Trever, J. C. *The Dead Sea Scrolls. A Personal Account.*
    RB 90 (1983): 435-438.
196. Legrand, L. *L'annonce à Marie.*
    RB 90 (1983): 435-438.
197. Corbo, V. *Il Santo Sepolcro di Gerusalemme.*
    RB 91 (1984): 281-287.

MARIE-EMILE BOISMARD, O.P.

Books

1. *L'Apocalypse.* (La Sainte Bible traduite en français sous la direction de l'École biblique de Jérusalem).
    Paris: Cerf,1950.
2. *Le Prologue de saint Jean.*
    (Lectio Divina,11).
    Paris: Cerf,1953.
        = *St. John's Prologue.*
            London: Blackfriars, 1957.
        = *El pròlogo de S. Juan.* (Actualidad biblica, 8).
            Madrid: Relié, 1967.
3. *Du Baptême à Cana (Jean 1,19-2,11).*
    (Lectio Divina, 18).
    Paris: Cerf, 1956.
4. *Quatre hymnes baptismales dans la première épître de Pierre.*
    (Lectio Divina, 30).
    Paris: Cerf, Cerf1961.
5. *Synopse des quatre évangiles en français avec parallèles des apocryphes et des Pères.* Vol. I, *Textes,* with P. Benoit.
    Paris: Cerf, 1965.
        =*Sinopsis de los Cuato Evangelios* . Vol. I, *Testos* .
            Bilbao: Desclée de Brouwer, 1975.
6. *Synopse des quatre évangiles en français.* Vol. II, *Commentaire,* with P. Benoit, A. Lamouille and P. Sandevoir.
    Paris: Cerf,1972.
        = *Sinopsis de los Cuatro Evangelios* Vol. II
            Bilbao; Desclée de Brouwer, 1977.
7. *L'évangile de Jean. Commentaire* ,with A. Lamouille and G. Rochais.
    (Synopse des quatre évangiles en français, 3) Paris: Cerf, 1977.
8. *La vie des évangiles. Initiation à la critique des textes,* with A. Lamouille.
    Paris: Cerf, 1980.
        = *Aus der Werkstatt der Evangelisten. Einführung in die Literarkritik.*
            München: Kösel, 1980.
        = *La vida de los Evangelios. Iniciacion à la critica de textos..*
            Bilbao: Desclée de Brouwer, 1981.
9. *Le texte Occidental des Actes des apôtres. Reconstitution et réhabilitation.* Vol. 1, *Introduction et textes,* with A. Lamouille.
    (Synthèse, 17).
    Paris: Editions Recherche sur les Civilisation, 1984. (= 1985)

10. *Le texte Occidental des Actes des apôtres. Reconstitution et réhabilitation.* Vol. 2, *Apparat critique. Index des caractéristiques stylistiques. Index des citations patristiques,* with A. Lamouille. (Synthèse, 17).
     Paris: : Éditions Recherche sur les Civilisation, 1984. (= 1985).
11. *Synopsis Graeca Quattuor Evangeliorum,* with A. Lamouille.
     Leuven-Paris: Peeters, 1986.
12. *Moïse ou Jésus. Essai de christologie johannique.* (BETL, 86).
     Leuven: University Press/ Peeters 1988.

Articles

13. "Le chapitre XXI de saint Jean. Essai de critique littéraire."
     RB 54 (1947): 473-501.
14. "A propos de Jean V, 39. Essai de critique textuelle."
     RB 55 (1948): 5-34.
15. "Clément de Rome et l'évangile de Jean."
     RB 55 (1948):376-387.
16. "La connaissance dans L'Alliance Nouvelle, d'après la première lettre de saint Jean."
     RB 56 (1949): 365-391.
17. "'L'Apocalypse', ou 'Les Apocalypses' de s. Jean."
     RB 56 (1949): 55007--541.
18. "Critique textuelle et citations patristiques."
     RB 57 (1950): 388-408.
19. "L'évangile à quatre dimensions. Introduction à la lecture de saint Jean."
     LVie 1 (1951):94-114.
20. "Lectio brevior, potior."
     RB 58 (1951): 161-168.
21. "Dans le sein du Père, (Jo.,I, 18)."
     RB 59 (1952): 23-39.
22. "Notes sur l'Apocalypse."
     RB 59 (1952):161-181.
23. "Note sur l'interprétation du texte: Multi sunt vocati … (Mt 22,14 par.)"
     RThom 52 (1952): 569-585.
24. "La Bible parole de Dieu et révélation."
     LVie 6 (1952): 13-26.
25. "Constitué Fils de Dieu (Rom 1,4)."
     RB 60 (1953): 5-17.
26. "Problèmes de critique textuelle concernant le quatrième évangile."
     RB 60 (1953): 347-371
27. "Je ferai avec vous une alliance nouvelle, (1 Joh.)."
     LVie 8 (1953): 94-109.
28. "La divinité du Christ d'après Paul."
     LVie 9 (1953): 75-100.
29. "Le retour du Christ."
     LVie 11 (1953): 53-76.
30. "Jésus, Sauveur d'après saint Jean."
     LVie 15 (1954):103-122.
     ="Jesus the Saviour According to Saint John."

In *Word and Mystery. Biblical Essays on the Person and Mission of Christ*, ed. by L. J. O'Donovan, 69-85. Glen Rock,1968.

="Jesús, el Salvador según. San Juan"

In *Palabra y Misterio. Ensayos biblicos sobre la persona y mision de Cristo,* ed. by L.J. O'Donovan. (Palabra Inspirada, 13). Santander, 1971.

31. "Rapprochements littéraires entre l'évangile de Luc et l'Apocalypse."
Synoptische Studien FS A. Wikenhauser, 53-63.
Freiburg: Herder, 1954.

32. "La révélation de l'Esprit Saint."
RThom 55 (1955): 5-21.

33. " La loi et l'esprit."
LVie 21 (1955): 345-362.

34. "La foi selon S. Paul.
LVie 22 (1955): 489-514.

35. "La literatura de Qumran y los escritos de S. Juan."
Cultura Biblica 12 (1955): 250-264.

36. "Une liturgie baptismale dans la Prima Petri."
Part I *RB* 63 (1956): 182-208 and Part II *RB* 64 (1967): 161-183.

37. "Je renonce à Satan, à ses pompes, à ses oeuvres."
LVie 26 (1956): 105-110.

38. "Baptême et renouveau."
LVie 27 (1956): 103-118.

39. "La première semaine du ministère de Jésus selon S. Jean."
VSpir 94 (1956): 593-603.

40. "Le papyrus Bodmer II."
RB 64 (1957): 363-398.

41. "L'Eucharistie selon S. Paul."
LVie 31 (1957): 93-106.

42. "De son ventre couleront des fleuves d'eau (Jo., VII, 38)."
RB 65 (1958): 523-546.

43. "Importance de la critique textuelle pour établir l'origine araméenne du quatrième évangile."
In *L'évangile de Jean. Études et problèmes* , edited by F. M. Braun, 41-57. (Recherches biblique, 3). Bruge: Desclée, 1958.

44. "Le Christ-Agneau, rédempteur des hommes."
LVie 36 (1958): 91-104.

45. "Dieu notre Père. Exode, marche vers Dieu."
In *Grands thèmes bibliques* , ed. by J. Giblet, Part I, 67-75; Part II, 159-165. Paris: Feu Nouveau, 1958.

46. "Les citations targumiques dans le quatrième évangile."
RB 66 (1959): 374-378.

47. "Le caractère adventice de Jo., XII, 45-50."
In *Sacra Pagina. Miscellanea biblica congressus internationalis de re biblica,* ed. by J. Coppens, A. Descamps, E. Massaux, Vol. 2, 189-192. (BETL, 13). Paris-Gembloux: Duculot 1959.

48. "L'Apocalypse."
In *Introduction à la Bible.* Vol 2, *Nouveau Testament,* ed. by A. Robert and A. Feuillet, 710-742. Tournai-Paris: Desclée, 1959.

49. "Conversion et vie nouvelle dans S. Paul."
    LVie 47 (1960): 71-94.
50. "L'évolution du thème eschatologique dans les traditions johanniques."
    RB 68 (1961): 507-524.
51. "L'ami de l'époux (Jo. III,29)."
    In *A la rencontre de Dieu. Mémorial A. Gelin*, 289-295. Le Puy: Mappus, 1961.
52. "Saint Luc et la rédaction du quatrième évangile (Jn, IV, 46-54)."
    RB 69 (1962): 185-211.
53. "Le lépreux et le serviteur du centurion."
    Assemblées du Seigneur 17 (1962): 29-44.
54. "La royauté du Christ dans le quatrième évangile."
    LVie 57 (1962): 43-63.
55. "Les traditions johanniques concernant le Baptiste."
    RB 70 (1963): 5-42.
56. "Le lavement des pieds (Jn, XIII, 1-17).
    RB 71 (1964): 5-24.
57. "Guérison du fils d'un fonctionnaire royal (Jn 4, 46b-53)."
    Assemblées du Seigneur 75 (1965): 26-37.
58. "L'évangile des Ébionites et le problème synoptique (Mc I,2-6 et. par.)."
    RB 73 (1966): 321-352.
59. " Pierre (Première épître de)."
    In *Dictionnaire de la Bible: Supplément VII*, Paris: Letouzey & Ané, 1966, cols. 1415-1455.
60. " La royauté universelle du Christ (Jn 18, 33-37)."
    Assemblées du Seigneur 88 (1966): 33-45.
61. "Satan selon l'Ancien et Nouveau Testament."
    LVie 78 (1966): 61-76.
62. "Immortalité ou résurrection?"
    Bulletin de l'Union Catholique des Scientifiques français 115 (1970): 2-8.
63. "Introductions Catholiques, " with R. de Vaux and P. Benoit.
    Catholiques, Juifs, Orthodoxes, Protestants lisent la Bible; Introduction à la Bible. Vol. III, *Le Nouveau Testament.* (Théologie sans frontières,17). Paris: Cerf, 1970.
64. "Le réalisme des récits évangéliques."
    LVie 107 (1972): 31-41.
    = *La Resurrezione* . (Studi biblici, 27). Brescia, 1974.
65. "The First Epistle of John and the Writings of Qumran."
    John and Qumran, ed. by J.H. Charlesworth, 156-165. London: Chapman 1972.
66. "Aenon, près de Salem (Jean, III, 23)."
    RB 80 (1973): 218-229.
67. "Influences matthéennes sur l'ultime rédaction de l'évangile de Marc."
    L'évangile selon Marc. Traditon et rédaction, ed. by M. Sabbe, 93-101. (BETL, 34). Leuven: University Press, 1974. 2d ed. ,1988.
68. "Jésus, le Prophète par excellence, d'après Jean 10, 24-39."
    Neues Testament und Kirche. FS R. Schnackenburg , ed. by J. Gnilka, 160-171. Freiburg: Herder, 1974.
69. "Notre victoire sur la mort d'après la Bible."

Concilium (Paris) 105 (1975): 95-103.

70. "Un procédé rédactionnel dans le quatrième évangile: la *Wiederauf-nahme* ."
    In *L'évangile de Jean. Sources, rédaction, théologie* , ed. by M. de Jonge, 235-241. (BETL, 44). Gembloux-Leuven: Duculot 1977. 2d ed. 1987.

71. "L'Apocalypse de Jean,"with E. Cothenet.
    In *La tradition johannique* (Introduction à la Bible, ed. by A. George and P. Grelot, Vol. 3, Introduction critique au Nouveau Testament, 4.) 13-55. Paris: Desclée 1977.

72. "The Two-source Theory at an Impasse."
    NTS 26 (1979-80): 1-17.

73. "Deux exemples d'évolution régressive (Jn 17,3; 1 Jn 5,19)."
    LVie 149 (1980): 65-74.

74. "Le martyre d'Étienne. Actes 6,8 - 8,2."
    RSR 69 (1981): 181-194.

75. "The Text of Acts. A Problem of Literary Criticism."
    New Testament Textual Criticism FS B.M. Metzger , ed. by E.J. Epp and G. D. Fee, 147-157. Oxford: Clarendon, 1981

76. "La guérison du lépreux (Mc 1,40-45 et par.)."
    Escritos de Biblia y Oriente , ed. by R. Aguirre and R. Garcia-Lopez, 283-291. (Bibliotheca Salmanticensis, Estudios, 38). Salamanca-Jerusalem: Universidad Pontificia Instituto Español Bíblico Y Arqueológico, 1981.

77. "Rapports entre foi et miracles dans l'évangile de Jean."
    ETL 58 (1982): 357-364.

78. "L'hypothèse synoptique de Griesbach."
    Le siècle des lumières et la Bible , ed. by Y. Belaval and D. Bourel, 129-137. (Bible de tous les temps, 7). Paris: Beauchesne, 1986.

79. "Le texte Occidental des Actes des Apôtres. A propos de Actes 27,1-13," with A. Lamouille.
    ETL 63 (1987): 48-58.

80. "Critique textuelle et problèmes d'histoire des origines chrétiennes."
    In *Recherches sur l'historie de la Bible latine* , ed. by R. Gryson and P.-M. Bogaert, 123-136. (Cahiers de la Revue théologique de Louvain, 19). Louvain-la-Neuve: Publication de la Faculté de Théologie, 1987.

81. "Une tradition para-synoptique attestée par les Pères anciens."
    The New Testament in Early Christianity , ed. by J.-M. Sevrin. (BETL, 86). Leuven, 1988.

Selected Book Reviews

82. Dupont, Dom Jacques. *Gnosis, la connaissance religieuse dans les épîtres de saint Paul* .
    RB 57 (1950): 271-274.

83. Ruckstuhl, E. *Die literarische Einheit des Johannesevangeliums* .
    RB 59 (1952): 425-427.

84. Cullmann, O. *Les sacrements dans l'évangile johannique, la vie de Jésus et le culte de l'Église primitive* .

RB 60 (1953): 117-119.
85. Dibelius, Martin. *Botschaft und Geschichte* , I Bd.
    RB 61 (1954): 587-592.
86. Barrett, C.K. *The Gospel according to St. John* .
    RB 63 (1956): 267-272.
87. Schmid, Josef. *Studien zur Geschichte des griechischen Apokalypse-Textes* .
    RB 63 (1956): 583-586.
88. Leenhardt, Franz-J. *L'Épître de saint Paul aux Romains* .
    RB 65 (1958): 432-436.
89. Eltester, F.W. *Eikon im Neuen Testament* .
    RB 66 (1959): 420-424.
90. Kragerud, A. *Der Lieblingsjünger im Johannesevangelium* .
    RB 67 (1960): 405-410.
91. Braun, F.-M. *Jean le Théologien et son évangile dans l'Église ancienne.*
    RB 67 (1960): 592-597.
92. Philonenko, M. *Les interpolations chrétiennes des Testaments des Douze Patriarches et les manuscrits de Qoumrân* .
    RB 68 (1961): 419-423.
93. Guilding, A. *The Fourth Gospel and Jewish Worship* .
    RB 68 (1961): 599-602.
94. Schultz, S. *Komposition und Herkunft der johanneischen Reden* .
    RB 69 (1962): 421-424.
95. Martin, V. and J.W.B. Barns. *Papyrus Bodmer II* .
    RB 70 (1963): 120-133.
96. *La venue du Messie. Messianisme et eschatologie* .
    RB 70 (1963) 273-276.
97. Braun, F.-M. *Jean le Théologien* , Vol. II.
    RB 72 (1965): 108-116.
98. Schnackenburg, R. *Das Johannesevangelium.*
    RB 74 (1967): 581-585; *RB* 85 (1978): 631-633.
99. Brown, R.E. *The Gospel According to John (i-xii)* .
    RB 74 (1967): 581-585.
100. de Solanges, B. *La composition des Evangiles de Luc et de Matthieu et leurs sources* .
    RB 80 (1973): 588-593.
101. Aland, K., éd. *Die alten Übersetzungen des Neuen Testaments, die Kirchenväterzitate und Lektionare* .
    RB 82 (1975): 616-620.
102. de Jonge, M. *L'évangile de Jean* .
    RB 85 (1978): 633-634.
103. Cullmann, O. *Der Johanneische Kreis* .
    RB 85 (1978): 634.
104. Richter, G. *Studien zum Johannesevangelium* .
    RB 86 (1979): 148-149.
105. Potterie, I. de la. *La vérité dans saint Jean* .
    RB 86 (1979): 609-613.
106. Smalley, S.S. *John, Evangelist and Interpreter* .
    RB 88 (1981): 469-470.
107. Brown, R.E. *The Community of the Beloved Disciple* .

RB 88 (1981): 470-471.
108. de Solanges, B. *Jean et les Synoptiques* .
      RB 90 (1983): 423-424.
109. Nestle-Aland, *Novum Testamentum Graece* .
      RB 90 (1983): 439-441.
110. Dreyfus, F. *Jésus savait-il qu'il était Dieu?*
      RB 91 (1984): 591-601.
111. Rolland, Ph. *Les premiers évangiles* .
      RB 95 (1988) 97-101.

JEROME MURPHY-O'CONNOR, O.P.

Books

1. *Paul on Preaching.*
    London/New York: Sheed and Ward, 1964.
    = *La prédication selon saint Paul.*
        Paris: Gabalda, 1966.
    = *Neubelebung der Predigt. Die Predigt bei Paulus, dem Verkünder.*
        Luzern / München: Rex-Verlag, 1968.
2. *Paul and Qumran,* Ed. by Jerome Murphy-O'Connor.
    London: Chapman, 1968.
3. *L'existence chrétienne selon saint Paul.*
    Paris: Cerf, 1974.
    = *A Vida de Homem Novo.*
        Sao Paulo: Ediçoes Paulinas, 1975.
4. *Becoming Human Together: The Pastoral Anthropology of St. Paul.*
    Wilmington: Glazier, 1977. rev. and exp. ed., 1982.
5. *The First Epistle to the Corinthians.* (NewTestament Message, 10)
    Wilmington: Glazier, 1979.
        = *Primeira Epístola aos Coríntios.*
        Sao Paulo: Ediçoes Paulinas, 1981.
6. *Saint Paul's Corinth.* (Good News Studies, 6)
    Wilmington: Glazier, 1983.
        = *Corinthe au temps de saint Paul d'après les textes et l'archéologie.*
        Paris: Cerf, 1986.
7. *The Holy Land. An Archaeological Guide from Earliest Times to 1700 .*
    London: Oxford University Press, 1980; Rev. and expanded, 1986.
    Das Heilige Land. Ein archäologischer Führer.
        München: Piper, 1981.
    Guide archéologique de la Terre Sainte.
        Paris: Denoël, 1982.
8. *The Theology of Second Corinthians .*
    Cambridge: Cambridge University Press, 1990.

Articles

9. "La verité chez saint Paul et à Qumran."
    RB 72 (1965): 29-76.
10. "Who wrote Ephesians?"
    Bible Today 3 (1965): 1201-1209.
11. "Paul: Philippiens (Épître aux)."

In *Dictionnaire de la Bible: Supplément VII.* Paris: Letouzey & Ané, 1966, cols. 1211-1233.

12. "Péché et communauté dans le Nouveau Testament."
   RB (1967):161-193.
      = " Sin and Community in the New Testament."
         In *Sin and Repentance,* ed. by D. O'Callaghan, 18-50.
         Dublin: Gill, 1967.
            = *Theological Digest* 16 (1968): 120-125.
            = *Theologie der Gegenwart* 11 (1968): 75-81.

13. "Colossians." and "Philemon."
   In *A New Catholic Commentary on Holy Scripture.* 2d ed.
   London: Nelson, 1969.

14. "The Presence of God through Christ and in the World."
   Concilium 10 (1969): 54-59.
      = *A Companion to Paul,* ed. by M. Taylor, 1-12.
         Staten Island: Alba, 1975.

15. "The Christian and Society in St. Paul."
   New Blackfriars 50 (1969):174-182.

16. "Letter and Spirit: St. Paul."
   New Blackfriars 50 (1969): 453-460.

17. "Colossians." and "Philippians."
   In *Scripture Discussion Commentary , XI.* London/Sydney: Sheed and Ward, 1971.

18. "Community and Apostolate: Reflections on I Timothy 2:1-7."
   Bible Today 12 (1973): 1260-1266.

19. "What is Redaction-Criticism?"
   Scripture in Church 5 (1974-75):78-92.
      = *Sowing the Word. Biblical Liturgical Essays,*
         ed. by P Rogers, 96-107. Dublin: Dominican Publications, 1983.

20. "The Structure of Matthew XIV-XVII"
   RB 82 (1975): 360-384.

21. "Christological Anthropology in Philippians 2:6-11."
   RB 83 (1976): 25-50.
      = *Selecciones de Teología* 17 (1978): 295-305.

22. "Eucharist and Community in First Corinthians." Parts 1, 2.
   Worship 50 (1976): 370-285, 51 (1977): 56-69.
      = *Living Bread, Saving Cup. Readings on the Eucharist,*
         ed. by K. Seasoltz, 1-30. Collegeville: Liturgical Press, 1982.

23. "The Non-Pauline Character of I Corinthians 11: 2-16?"
   JBL 95 (1976): 615-621.

24. "1 Corinthians 5:3-5"
   RB 84 (1977): 349-361.

25. "Works Without Faith in I Corinthians 7:14."
   RB 84 (1977): 349-361.

26. "Corinthian Slogans in I Corinthians 6:12-20"
   CBQ 40 (1978): 391-396.

27. "Paul and Qumran"
   Le monde de la Bible. No. 4. (1978):60-61.

28. "1 Corinthians 8:6 - Cosmology or Soteriology?"
    RB 85 (1978): 253-267.
29."Freedom or the Ghetto (1 Corinthians 8:1-13; 10:23-11:1)."
    RB 85 (1978): 543-574.
            = *Freedom and Love. The Guide for Christian Life (1 Corin-*
                thians 8-10; Romans 14-15), 7-55. Rome: St. Paul's
                Abbey, 1981.
30. "Food and Spiritual Gifts in 1 Corinthians 8:8."
    CBQ 41 (1979): 292-298.
31. "Sex and Logic in 1 Corinthians 11:2-16."
    CBQ 42 (1980): 482-500.
32. "Tradition and Redaction in 1 Corinthians 15:3-7."
    CBQ 43 (1981): 582-589.
33. "What Paul Knew of Jesus."
    Scripture Bulletin 12 (1981): 35-40.
34. "The Divorced Woman in 1 Corinthians 7:10-11."
    JBL 100 (1981): 601-606.
35. "'Baptized for the Dead' (1 Corinthians 15:29) - A Corinthian Slogan?"
    RB 88 (1981): 532-543.
36. "Pauline Missions Before the Jerusalem Conference."
    RB 89 (1982): 71-91.
37. "Corinthian Bronze."
    RB 90 (1983):80-93.
38. "Redactional Angels in 1 Timothy 3:16."
    RB 91 (1984): 178-187.
39. "The Corinth that Saint Paul Saw."
    BA 47 (1984): 147-159.
40. "A Feminist Re-reads the New Testament."
    Doctrine and Life 34 (1984): 398-404, 495-499.
41. "On the Road and on the Sea with St. Paul."
    Bible Review 1 (Summer 1985): 38-47.
42. "Paul and Macedonia: The Connection between 2 Corinthians 2:13 and
    2:14."
    Journal for the Study of the New Testament 25 (1985): 99-103.
43. "Interpolations in 1 Corinthians."
    CBQ 48 (1986): 81-94.
44. " 'Being at home in the body we are in exile from the Lord,' (2 Corin-
    thians 5:6b)."
    RB 93 (1986): 214-221.
45. "*Pneumatikoi* and Judaizers in 2 Corinthians 2:14-4:6."
    Australian Biblical Review 34 (1986): 42-58.
46. "Relating 2 Corinthians 6:14-7:1 to its Context."
    New Testament Studies 33 (1987):272-275.
47. "A Ministry Beyond the Letter (2 Corinthians 3:1-6)."
    In *Paolo Ministro del Nuovo Testamento (2 Co 2,14-4,6),* Ed. by
    L. De Lorenzi, 104-157. Roma: Benedictina Editrice, 1987.
48. "What Really Happened at the Transfiguration?"
    Bible Review 3 no.3 (1987): 8-21.
49. "Pneumatikoi in 2 Corinthians."
    Proceedings of the Irish Biblical Association 11 (1988): 59-68.

50. "Philo and 2 Corinthians 6:14-7:1."
    RB 95 (1988): 55-69.
51. "1 Corinthians 11: 2-16 Once Again."
    CBQ 50 (1988): 265-274.
52. "Faith and Resurrection in 2 Corinthians 4:13-14."
    RB 95 (1988): 543-550.
53. "The First Letter to the Corinthians"
    The New Jerome Biblical Commentary, ed. by R. E. Brown, J. A. Fitzmyer and R. E. Murphy. Englewood Cliffs: Prentice Hall, 1989.
54. "The Second Letter to the Corinthians"
    The New Jerome Biblical Commentary, ed. by R. E. Brown, J. A. Fitzmyer and R. E. Murphy. Englewood Cliffs, NJ: Prentice Hall, 1989.

Selected Book Reviews

55. Martin, R. P. *Carmen Christi. Philippians 2:5-11 in Recent Interpretation.*
    RB 75 (1968): 113-116.
56. Gärtner, B. *The Temple and Community in Qumran and in the New Testament.*
    RB 75 (1968): 443-445.
57. Gnilka, J. *Der Philipperbrief.*
    RB 76 (1969): 276-278.
58. Schenke,L. *Auferstehungsverkündigung und leeres Grab.*
    RB 76 (1969): 431-434.
59. Walker, R. *Die Heilsgeschichte im ersten Evangelium* and Hare, D. *The Theme of Jewish Persecution of Christians in the Gospel According to St. Matthew.*
    RB 76 (1969): 597-601.
60. Spicq, C. *Les épîtres pastorales.*
    RB 77 (1970): 419-421.
61. Fortna, R.T. *The Gospel of Signs.*
    RB 77 (1970): 603-606.
62. Bligh, J. *Galatians*
    RB 78 (1971): 93-96.
63. Linnemann, E. *Studien zur Passionsgeschichte.*
    RB 79 (1972): 121-125.
64. Boismard, M.-E. and Arnaud Lamouille. *Synopse des quatre évangiles, Tome II.*
    RB 79 (1972): 431-435.
65. Klinzing, G . *Die Umdeutung des Kultus in der Qumran Gemeinde und im Neune Testament.*
    RB 79 (1972): 435-440.
66. Broer, I. *Die Urgemeinde und das Grab Jesu.*
    RB 81 (1974): 266-269.
67. Hubbard, B. *The Matthean Redaction of a Primitive Apostolic Commissioning* , and Lange, J. *Das Erscheinen des Auferstandenen im Evangelium nach Matthäus.*
    RB 83 (1976): 97-102.

68. Mussner, F. *Theologie der Freiheit nach Paulus.*
    RB 83 (1976): 618-623.
69. Soares Prabhu, G. M. *The Formula Quotations in the Infancy Narrative of Matthew.*
    RB 84 (1977): 292-297.
70. Sanders, E. P. *Paul and Palestinian Judaism.*
    RB 85 (1978): 122-126.
71. Rivkin, E. *The Hidden Revolution.*
    RB 87 (1980): 430-433.
72. Thiering, B. *Redating the Teacher of Righteousness.*
    RB 87 (1980): 425-430.
73. Betz, H. D. *Galatians*
    RB 89 (1982): 257-261.
74. Lüdemann, G. *Paulus der Heidenapostel. II. Antipaulinisimus im frühen Christentum.*
    RB 92 (1985): 601-605.
75. Boismard, M.-E. and A. Lamouille. *Texte occidental des Actes des Apôtres.*
    RB 93 (1986): 598-601.
76. Furnish,V. P. *2 Corinthians.*
    RB 94 (1987): 264-267.

FRANÇOIS-PAUL DREYFUS, O.P.

Books

1. *Jésus savait-il qu'il était Dieu ?*
   Paris: Cerf, 1984.
   = *Gesú Sepeva d'Essere Dio ?* Torino: Paoline, 1985.
   = *Sabia Jesus Que Era Dios ?* Coyoacán: Universidad Ibero-
   americana, 1987.
   = *Jesus Sabia que Era Deus ?* São Paulo: Loyola, 1987
   = *Did Jesus Know He Was God ?* Chicago: Franciscan Herald
   Press, 1989.

Articles

2. "La doctrine du reste d'Israël chez le prophète Isaïe"
   RSPT 39 (1955): 361-386.
3. "La primauté de Pierre à la lumiere de l'Ancien Testament."
   Istania 2 (1955): 335-346.
4. "Le thème de l'héritage dans l'Ancien Testament."
   RSPT 42 (1958): 3-49.
5. "L'argument scriptuare de Jésus en faveur de la résurrection des morts
   (Marc , XII , 26-27)."
   RB 66 (1959): 213-224.
6. "Maintenant la foi, l'espérance et la charité demeurent toutes les trois (I
   Cor 13,13). " (Analecta Biblica, 17).
   *Studiorum Paulinorum Congressus Internationalis Catholicus,
   1961*, 403-412. Romae: Pontificio Instituto Biblico,1963.
7. "L'inspiration de la Septante. Quelques difficultés à surmonter."
   RSPT 49 (1965): 210-220.
8. "L'Évangile (Lc 10,23-37) 'Qui est mon prochain?' "
   Assemblées du Seigneur 66 (1965): 32-49.
9. "La valeur existentielle de l'Ancien Testament"
   Concilium 30 (1965): 35-43.
10. "Exégèse en Sorbonne, exégèse en église."
    RB 83 (1976): 321-359.
11. "L'actualisation à l'intérieur de la Bible"
    RB 83 (1976): 161-202.
12. "Le passé et le présent d'Israël . (Rom. 9, 1-5;11,1-24)."
    Die Israelfrage nach Röm, 9-11, 131-192. (Monographische Reihe
    von "Benedictina", 3). Rom, Abtei St Paul vor den Mauern, 1977.
13. "L'actualisation de l'Écriture. I. Du texte à la vie; II. L'action de l'Esprit;
    III. La place de la tradition."
    RB 86 (1979): Part I: 5-58; Part II: 161-193. Part III: 321-384.

14. "Pour la louange de sa gloire (Ep 1,12.14). L'origine vétéro-testamentaire de la formule."
Paul der Tarse, Apôtre de notre temps , ed. by Lorenzo De Lorenzi, 233-248. (Série monographique de "Benedictina"; Section paulinienne,1). Rome: Abbaye de S. Paul h.l.m., 1979.
15. " L'Araméen voulait tuer mon père": L'actualisation de Dt 26,4 dans la tradition juive et la tradition chrétienne."
De la Tôrah au Messie; Melages Henri Cazelles , ed. by Maurice Carrez, Joseph Doré and Pierre Grelot, 147-161. Paris: Desclée, 1981.
16. "'The Scales are even' (Tanhuman, Ki Tissa, 34)." [in hebrew].
Tarbiz 52 (1982): 139-142.
17. "La condescendance divine (*synkatabasis*) comme principe herméneutique de l'Ancien Testament dans la tradtion juive et dans la tradition chrétienne."
(Supplements to Vetus Testamentum, 36). *Congress Volume Salamanca, 1983,* (1985): 96-107.
=" Divine Condescendence (*Synkatabasis*) as a Hermeneutic principle of the Old Testament in Jewish and Christian Tradition."
Immanuel 19 (1984): 74-86.
17. " Reste d'Israël."
In *Dictionnaire de la Bible. Supplément X.* Paris: Letouzey & Ané, 1985, col 321-351.

BENEDICT T. VIVIANO, O.P.

Books

1. *Study as Worship. Aboth and the New Testament.* (SJLA, 26).
   Leiden: Brill, 1978.
2. *Illustrated Dictionary and Concordance of the Bible* . New Testament
   edited by Benedict T. Viviano and G. Wigoder.
   New York/London: Macmillan, 1986.
3. *The Kingdom of God in History.* (Good News Studies, 27).
   Wilmington: Glazier, 1988.

Articles

4. "St. Paul and the Ministry of Women."
   Spirituality Today , 30 (1978): 37-44.
5. "The Letter to the Ephesians: A Vision for the Church."
   The Bible Today , 23 (1979): 2019-2026.
6. "Where was the Gospel according to Matthew Written?"
   CBQ 41 (1979): 533-546.
7. "The Kingdom of God in Albert and Thomas."
   The Thomist , 44 (1980): 502-522.
8. "Schillebeeckx' *Jesus* and *Christ* – Contributions to Christian Life."
   Spirituality Today , 34 (1982): 129-143.
9. "Matthew, Master of Ecumenical Infighting."
   Currents , 10 (1983): 325-332.
10. "The Missionary Program of John's Gospel."
    The Bible Today , 22 (1984): 387-393.
11. "L'Église en perpétuelle dialectique entre Jacques et Étienne."
    Proche-Orient Chrétien , 36 (1986) 3-5.
12. "The Kingdom of God in Qumran Literature."
    The Kingdom of God in 20th Century Interpretation . Ed. by Wen-
    dell Willis, 97-107. Peobody, MA: Hendrickson, 1987.
13. "Render unto Caesar: Power and Politics in the Light of the Gospel."
    Bible Today 26 (1988): 272-276.
14. "Invitation." *Dominican Ashram* (December,1988): 172-175.
15. "Commentary on Matthew."
    New Jerome Bible Commentary . Ed. by R. E. Brown, J. A. Fitz-
    myer. and R. E. Murphy Englewood Cliffs, NJ: Prentice-Hall, 1989.
16. "The High Priest's Servant's Ear: Mark 14:47."
    RB 96 (1989) 71-80.
17. "The Rabbi at the Transfiguration: A Note on Mark 9:5."
    New Testament Studies (forthcoming).

Selected Book Reviews

18. Käsemann, Ernst. *Commentary on Romans* .
    The Thomist 45 (1981): 642-647.
19. Schaberg, Jane. *The Father, the Son and the Holy Spirit: The Triadic Phrase in Matthew 18:19b* .
    CBQ 46 (1984): 177-179.
20. Brown, Raymond E. *The Churches the Apostles Left Behind* .
    RB 92 (1985): 310-312.
21. Puig i Tàrrech, Armand. *La Parabole des Dix Vierges (Mt. 25:1-13)* .
    RB 94 (1987): 425-428.
22. Neufeld, K. H., *Adolf von Harnack: Theologie als Suche nach der Kirche, Tertium genus ecclesiae"* and *Adolf Harnacks Konflikt mit der Kirche* .
    RB 94 (1987): 473-475.
23. Reumann, John, et. al.*" Righteouness" in the New Testament: "Justification" in U. S. Lutheran-Roman Catholic Dialogue* .
    RB 95 (1988): 631-633.

JUSTIN TAYLOR, S.M.

Books

1. *Alive in the Spirit* .
   Auckland, New Zealand: Catholic Publications Center, 1984.
2. *As it Was Written: an Introduction to the Bible.*
   New York/Mahwah: Paulist Press, 1987.

Articles

3. "The Johannine Discourses and the Speech of Jesus: Five Views."
   Scripture Bulletin 14 (1984): 33-41.
4. "Reading the Bible Today."
   Prudentia 16 (1985): 71-79.
5. "A New Gospel Synopsis."
   Scripture Bulletin 18 (1987): 20-22.
6. "'The Love of Many Will Grow Cold: Matthew 24:9-13 and the Neronian
   Persecution."
   RB 96 (1989) (forthcoming).
7. "The Portrait of the Jerusalem Church in the Acts of the Apostles, 2:42-
   47 and 4:32-35."
   In *Proceedings of the Second International Colloquium on the Study
   of Marist History and Spirtuality.* Rome, 28-31 March, 1989.

Selected Book Reviews

8. Aejmelaeus, L. *Die Rezeption der Paulusbriefe in der Miletrede (Apg
   20:18-35)* and Cassidy, R. J. *Politics in the Acts of the Apostles.*
   RB (forthcoming).

ABBREVIATIONS

AusBR	Australian Biblical Review.
BA	Biblical Archaeologist.
BLE	Bulletin de Litterature Ecclesiastique.
BTB	Biblical Theology Bulletin.
CBQ	Catholic Biblical Quarterly.
DBS	Dictionnaire de la Bible, Supplément.
DRev	Downside Review.
ETL	Ephemerides Theologicae Lovanienses.
HTR	Harvard Theological Review.
JBL	Journal of Biblical Literature.
JRH	Journal of Religious History.
JSNT	Journal for the Study of the New Testament.
JTS	Journal of Theological Studies.
LD	Lectio Divina.
LVie	Lumière et Vie.
MTZ	Münchener Theologische Zeitschrift.
NRT	Nouvelle Revue Theologique.
NTS	New Testament Studies.
PIBA	Proceedings of the Irish Biblical Association.
RApo	Revue Apologetique.
RB	Revue Biblique.
RevQ	Revue de Qumran.
RHE	Revue d'Histoire Ecclesiastique.
RHPR	Revue d'Histoire et de Philosophie Religieuses.
RHR	Revue d'Histoire de Religions.
RSPT	Revue des Sciences Philosophiques et Théologiques.
RSR	Recherches de Science Religieuse.
RThom	Revue Thomiste.
SEA	Svensk Exegetisk Arsbok.
SPC	Studiorum Paulinorum Congressus Internationalis Catholicus 1961.
SR	Studies in Religion / Sciences Religieuses.
TRev	Theologische Revue.
TS	Theological Studies.
TZ	Theologische Zeitschrift.
VInt	Vie Intellectuelle.
VSpir	Vie Spirituelle.
VSpirSup	Supplément à la Vie Spirituelle.
ZNW	Zeitschrift für die Neutestamentliche Wissenschaft.

Zum vorliegenden Buch

Eine detailreiche und spannende Darstellung der wissenschaftlichen Arbeit, die in den ersten 100 Jahren des Bestehens der *École Biblique et Archéologique Française à Jérusalem* von deren Professoren im Bereich der Exegese des Neuen Testaments geleistet wurde: M.-J. Lagrange, P. Benoit, M.-E. Boismard, J. Murphy-O'Connor, F.-P. Dreyfus, B. T. Viviano, J. Taylor. Zugleich eine Geschichte der katholischen Exegese des Neuen Testaments in diesem Jahrhundert intensiver exegetischer Auseinandersetzung.

ISBN 3-7278-0682-6 (Universitätsverlag)
ISBN 3-525-53914-2 (Vandenhoeck & Ruprecht)

DATE DUE

HIGHSMITH   # 45220